JAEPL, Vol. 28, 2023

JAEPL

The Assembly for Expanded Perspectives on Learning (AEPL), an official assembly of the National Council of Teachers of English, is open to all those interested in extending the frontiers of teaching and learning beyond the traditional disciplines and methodologies.

The purposes of AEPL are to provide a common ground for theorists, researchers, and practitioners to explore innovative ideas; to participate in relevant programs and projects; to integrate these efforts with others in related disciplines; to keep abreast of activities along these lines of inquiry; and to promote scholarship on and publication of these activities.

The *Journal of the Assembly for Expanded Perspectives on Learning, JAEPL*, also provides a forum to encourage research, theory, and classroom practices involving expanded concepts of language. It contributes to a sense of community in which scholars and educators from pre-school through the university exchange points of view and boundary-pushing approaches to teaching and learning. *JAEPL* is especially interested in helping those teachers who experiment with new strategies for learning to share their practices and confirm their validity through publication in professional journals.

Topics of interest include but are not limited to:

- Aesthetic, emotional & moral intelligences
- Learning archetypes
- Kinesthetic knowledge & body wisdom
- Ethic of care in education
- Creativity & innovation
- Pedagogies of healing
- Holistic learning
- Humanistic & transpersonal psychology
- Environmentalism and post-humanism
- (Meta)Cognition
- Imaging & visual thinking
- Intuition & felt sense theory
- Meditation & pedagogical uses of silence
- Narration as knowledge
- Reflective teaching
- Spirituality
- New applications of writing & rhetoric
- Memory & transference
- Multimodality
- Social justice

Membership in AEPL is $45. Contact Jonathan Marine, AEPL, Membership Chair, email: jmarine@gmu.edu. Membership includes current year's issue of *JAEPL*.

Send submissions, address changes, and single hardcopy requests to Wendy Ryden, Editor, *JAEPL*, email: wendy.ryden@liu.edu. Address letters to the editors and all other editorial correspondence to Wendy Ryden (wendy.ryden@liu.edu).

AEPL website: www.aepl.org
Back issues of *JAEPL*: http://trace.tennessee.edu/jaepl/
Blog: https://aeplblog.wordpress.com/
Visit Facebook at **Assembly for Expanded Perspectives on Learning**
Production of *JAEPL* is managed by Parlor Press, www.parlorpress.com.

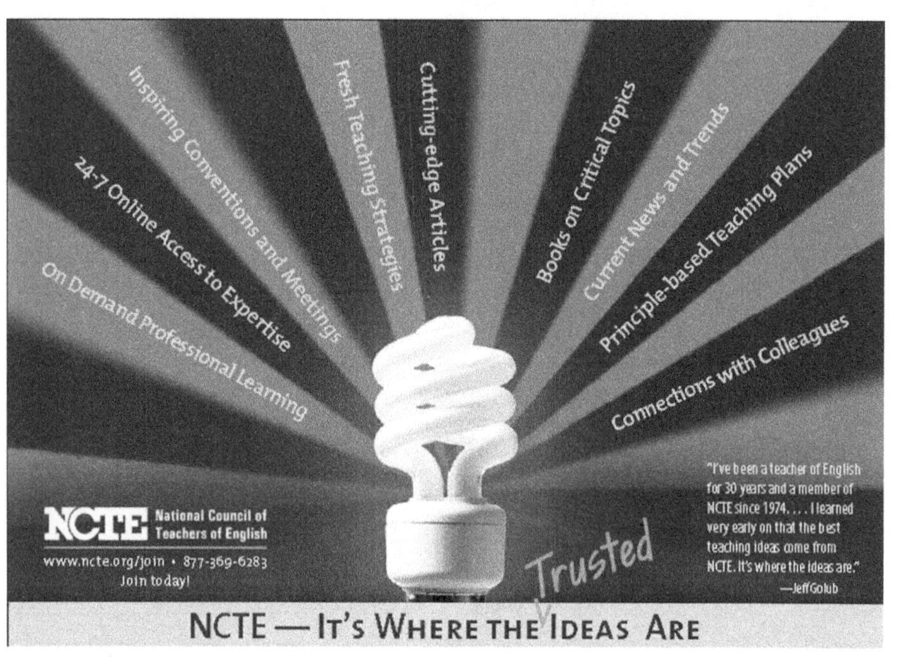

Inspiring Conventions and Meetings
Fresh Teaching Strategies
Cutting-edge Articles
Books on Critical Topics
Current News and Trends
Principle-based Teaching Plans
24-7 Online Access to Expertise
On Demand Professional Learning
Connections with Colleagues
NCTE
National Council of
Teachers of English
www.ncte.org/join • 877-369-6283
Join today!
"I've been a teacher of English
for 30 years and a member of
NCTE since 1974. . . . I learned
very early on that the best
teaching ideas come from
NCTE. It's where the ideas are."
—Jeff Golub
Trusted
NCTE — IT'S WHERE THE IDEAS ARE

Contents

Moffett's Corner

Communicating Science Special Issue

Connecting

Books

Our Perspectives Continue to Expand: *JAEPL* Does Science

Wendy Ryden

I am teaching a new course this semester, a freshman seminar I call Caring for Nature: Developing Environmental Literacy. From the description: "We will learn how to develop an affinity for nature as well as gain practical knowledge about how to foster healthy ecosystems in which biodiverse, non-human life can thrive." Teaching this course will involve knowledge of scientific conclusions and conflicts, but I am an English teacher, not a scientist. What's going on?

I'm not a scientist, but I'm aware of the work of scientists who have communicated information to nonspecialists like me so that we can make informed decisions about, for example, how to work to make a healthy landscape that creates and supports biodiversity. These folks try to improve our scientific literacy, not so that we can become scientists, but so that we might be educated citizens who are able to think, make our best decisions, and act responsibly in our world—not to mention experience the great enjoyment that such knowledge holds, as well as to help shoulder the burden of dangerous, unhappy truths science sometimes shows us.

I suppose as editor of a journal devoted to expanded perspectives on learning, it's difficult for me to be surprised by forays into new terrain, and, honestly, I feel no contradiction in my own focus on the natural world itself as a text we can "write" (with) and "read." It's clear to me that understanding the more-than-human world is an essential literacy for the 21st century, and we need to find ways to educate ourselves and integrate this kind of environmental instruction into all our classes. As Laura Madden points out regarding climate catastrophe, "it's important to cover climate across subjects, because science alone doesn't hold all the solutions"; we need all hands on, including artists, writers, and more (qtd. in Kamenetz). Some states have begun initiatives to include climate education in K-12 curriculum—with the predictable backlash that has accompanied teaching those subjects and ideas some find too upsetting to learn. Such resistance is all the more reason to begin what I'm calling an ELAC movement: Environmental Literacy Across the Curriculum. To work towards environmental justice, many of us will need to learn new things and ways of thinking—and be brave. What a terrific opportunity to become more—and better—than what/who we are. Scientists will continue to discover what is happening to the earth and the life it supports, but all of us will need to learn and teach others about our obligations and about how we will care for our very damaged home and the beings that dwell here.

At the same time, we must also be leary of and not oblivious to the limitations of Western science steeped in anthropocentrism and other systemic oppressions such as colonialism/capitalism, in which indigenous and other knowledges are ignored or discredited out of arrogance and for the sake of greed and profit. Wide-ranging conversations among different peoples and throughout different disciplines may be the most difficult and most necessary work we need to do to avoid what indigenous scientist Jessica Hernandez identifies as "helicopter research" (83), a science approach where knowledge is extracted by a privileged few within narrowly defined parameters, irrespective of consideration for extended consequences or the greater ecological webs in which living and nonliving are embedded. This summer's Hollywood blockbuster *Oppenheimer* is a reminder of the lethality of that narrow science that takes for granted its privilege to destroy the earth without consulting it, all in pursuit of one kind of knowledge and application. Such violence and necrophilia cannot be allowed to stand, through siloed silence and elitism, as what constitutes science.

This special issue, "Communicating Science," as our guest editor Julia Kiernan explains, is about forging connections among disciplines and through contexts in order that we reconsider science communication as a multifaceted enterprise exceeding disciplinary emphasis on intra-professional communication alone. A STEM focused special issue might feel a bit outside the bailiwick of our typical "expanded perspectives." That we have usual suspects is a sure sign it is time to stretch *JAEPL*'s concerns in accordance with what life has given us: we must attend to the state of the world, and we must equip ourselves with the understanding necessary to do so. The contributors to this year's issue are doing their part to help us by expanding our perspectives of what science communication might look like—its ethical and practical dimensions—and why we all need to pay attention. I am thrilled to be able to offer these selections to the readership.

In addition to these wonderful essays and Connecting pieces, regular readers will note some other changes in this issue's content that I'm very happy to include. We have the inaugural "Moffett's Corner," which will be edited by Stephen Lafer and Jonathan Marine, two devotees of the great James Moffett, fiercely committed to keeping the work of the late scholar and educator alive for present and future teachers. And also a different twist on our usual book reviews section: a sharing of recipe-writing from the *JAEPL* community inspired by recent work of Lynn Z. Bloom, *Recipe* (Bloomsbury 2022). As you will see, this is an issue filled with nourishment!

Works Cited

Hernandez, Jessica. *Fresh Banana Leaves: Healing Indigenous Landscapes through Indigenous Science*. North Atlantic Books, 2022.

Kamenetz, Anya. "New Jersey is Teaching Kids about Climate. Opponents Call It 'Indoctrination.'" *Grist*, 7 June 2023. https://grist.org/politics/culture-wars-come-for-climate-education-new-jersey/

MOFFETT'S CORNER

Why Moffet Matters Now

Stephen Lafer and Jonathan Marine

James Porter Moffett (1929–1996) was a ground-breaking teacher, author, and theorist of language learning who had a profound impact on the fields of English Education, Language Arts, Composition, and Educational Psychology in the mid to late 20th century and was the first member of the Assembly for Expanded Perspectives on Learning (AEPL). In the inaugural Moffett's Corner, Steve Lafer and Jonathan Marine discuss how they came together, why they wanted to start this column, and what they hope to accomplish.

STEVE LAFER: Out of the blue, Jonathan Marine reached out to ask me if I was willing to be interviewed about my thoughts and experiences with James Moffett. Jonathan identified himself as an academic working with others to study and, as he puts it, sponsor the "uptake" of Moffett's ideas in order to, ultimately, influence language instruction in the classroom. Jonathan was encouraged to reach out to me by Tom Gage, Professor Emeritus at Cal Poly Humboldt, who was my advisor while I was a member of the first class in his Master's in the Teaching of Writing program at (then) Humboldt State University. Tom was a colleague and close friend of James Moffett, and in his courses (and in our many conversations over the years) James Moffett was the central animating force which guided our conversations and beliefs about teaching, learning, and pedagogy. Though I graduated long ago and am now retired myself, Tom's and Moffett's voices continue to resonate loudly in my head.

In fact, when Jonathan wrote, I was still citing Moffett in my writing, and he was still a central figure in my thinking. However, having retired from my position in the College of Education at the University of Nevada after 28 years, I was a disappointed academic and, worse, becoming more cynical as time wore on. And I remain skeptical that students can be exposed to the types of educational experiences that might help them develop the skills, knowledge, and dispositions I believe characterize thoughtful and truly literate human beings capable of contributing positively to create and maintain a sane and humane society. I corresponded with James Moffett throughout the latter days of his life and knew him to be profoundly disappointed, too.

So when Jonathan reached out to me asking for an interview, I gladly agreed. And during our two-hour-long (at least) conversation, I was overjoyed to discover a new generation of scholars, thinkers, and teachers dedicated to reviving the same interest in Moffett that had been the central quest of much of my life's work. The wonderful editor of this journal, Wendy Ryden, has graciously agreed to our request for a small space in *JAEPL* to instigate thinking and spark discussion of James Moffett's work and how it can be used to influence the way in which students are educated, around the world. And our focus will be on Moffett's educational philosophy, the theory that emanated from it, and pedagogy he described and worked so hard to implement in his lifetime. Further still, we hope for this space to be an ongoing site of encounter with the many new and exciting initiatives at work by Moffett scholars the world round.

We introduce the Moffett's Corner with the conversation that follows, an article that is a dialectic I-to-you-about-it interaction by two people thinking about similar things and doing their best to "get it right" along the way, constantly redefining "it," confusing matters for one another in a way that inspires ever deeper levels of thought, a discourse of the kind that is essential to Moffett's influential *Universe of Discourse* (1968), where the human mind is used to make sense of what was and is in order to contemplate what should and could be and make decisions that can lead to the sane and humane world that should come of a society governed by and for the people.

JONATHAN MARINE: My own discovery of Moffett came through the same lineage as Steve's; another of Tom Gage's students in the Master's in the Teaching of Writing program, Paul Rogers, was teaching a Composition Theory class which I decided to take on a whim. We read "Kinds and Orders of Discourse," the 2nd chapter in *Teaching the Universe of Discourse*, and it was like having my innermost thoughts as a teacher articulated for me in plain language. All my beliefs about effective teaching—that students should write about what they know and care about, learn from interacting with one another, and that literacy was an integral part of how they conceived of their existences—were encapsulated in Moffett's theories, and once I finished the book I wanted more! I was lucky to get tapped into a deep network of Moffett figures, including Tom Gage, Sheridan Blau, and Don Gallehr, and quickly realized not only how important Moffett's work was and the potential value it posed to the field, but also the opaqueness of his oeuvre and the difficulty in navigating, or even locating, his many works and the works about him.

For me, at the risk of sounding hagiographic, Moffett is the most important thinker of the twentieth century when it comes to language learning, literacy, writing, and educational assessment and policy. He provided a Platonic aggregation of what we learned about learning in the twentieth century which surfaced the role of the cognitive and mindful in language learning and pushed the field of Language Arts and English Education fifty years forward. In the second half of his career, he increasingly turned his attention toward the role of educational policy and assessment while broadening his conception of education to encompass the ultimate civilizing mandate he felt lay at the core of democracy and society: the right for each person to follow *their own* path, make *their own* meaning and pursue what *they* find meaningful as a part of their own efforts to achieve a fully realized existence.

Yet, the fact is that Moffett's nontraditional career, which bucked academe in favor of supporting teachers directly through independent consultancies and working with organizations like NCTE, the NWP, and AEPL (among others), has made the uptake and pushing forward of his work all the harder. All of his books are now out of print, and in a very real way, he's all but forgotten by all but the old guard (many of whom knew and worked with him). For all of these reasons, it is a critical time to reconsider and reconceptualize what the field of Moffett studies is, should, or could be.

My view is that we can best support this effort through big tent thinking; through attending to the entire ecosystem of thought which undergirds his work. As always, it begins and ends with teachers. Moffett's entire career was dedicated to serving teachers of English and Language arts by pushing forward a student-centered view of education where students could learn from one another and, in doing so, perpetually discover the limitations of their understanding. But how do we get to the teachers?

First of all, through making his work available. The fact that all of his books are out of print is the single largest hurdle we face in getting the word out about James Moffett's role in the historical development of our field and the many potential contemporary applications of his ideas. Dwindling used copies inch up in price on eBay and Amazon as fewer and fewer are available. For that reason, we recently worked with the WAC Clearinghouse to republish five of Moffett's canonical works (https://wac.colostate.edu/books/landmarks/moffett/), including *Teaching the Universe of Discourse, Student-Centered Language Arts,* and *Coming on Center.* We've also started a Moffett Reading Group, hosted by the National Writing project, (for more info, download the NWP's WriteNowStudio app, which can be found here: https://studio.nwp.org/). Lastly, we're working to digitize the Moffett archive at UC Santa Barbara in order to make his personal correspondences, drafts, and unpublished works available to scholars and researchers.

And that's the other part of the puzzle: new scholarship. On top of making *his* work available, we also need others to take up and push forward his ideas through the publication of fresh scholarship which either empirically tests his ideas or attempts to translate them into functional classroom practice. The day that graduate courses in teacher education are assigning articles which cite Moffett (or, better yet, his own work) is the day that we will have regained the crucial ground lost since his untimely passing in 1996.

I am trying to offer a multi-level conception of how to elevate Moffett studies both for scholars and teachers. But it is the teachers who ultimately matter because they, as Moffett knew, will be the ones to lead the charge in changing education in our country for the better. It is a primal belief in the timeless principles and edicts which Moffett's work provides along with the immense sense of privilege I feel to have had the chance to work with many who knew and worked with James Moffett—like Steve—which fills me with the motivation requisite to pushing his ideas forward for this generation, the next, and beyond. As Moffett said, "paradoxically, the way to bring everyone together is to let them go their own ways—together, in the same communal learning network." That's gawddamn right.

STEVE LAFER: That word, "hagiographic," (which, I admit, I had to look up) and which means, in essence, a pronouncement of saintliness, scared me, as it did Jonathan, who recognized the risk involved in using it to describe the strength of his understanding in the value of James Moffett's work. My affinity to Moffett's theory, its effect on my thinking and on my work as a teacher and professor of teacher education, is something I have questioned the longer I have held on to it. I used Moffett's work, in whole or part, in every course I taught over a thirty-year career as an English teacher, in almost every paper I wrote, and in a good many of the conversations in which I participated. Even if I did not mention his name explicitly, I was applying Moffett's theory implicitly. And this enduring influence has remained with me for so long because Moffett got so much right concerning the fundamentals of language learning, literacy, and writing.

Moffett did in many ways move, as Jonathan says, the field forward, but the effect was not long lasting, in good part because, as Jonathan also notes, he bucked academe. And one of the reasons that Moffett now needs resurrection is that, as the fact that his works are no longer in print shows, his name has faded from attachment to many of the lasting changes he fomented. Further still, I believe that much of the real change in education and language learning that Moffett inspired has either been heavily muted in its application and effect or undermined by subsequent changes in a field that has now rejected or moved past the insights that Moffett offered. What Jonathan calls "gawd-damn right", to my mind, is not. Moffett's work, outside the box, was paradigm shifting, but only outside that box. So, the "box" must be affected this time around, in order to allow for the theory and best practices derived from Moffett's work to have institutional effects that in turn lead to changes in the way that people are educated in our society. And the first order of business is to begin a discussion of truly sensible goals for education.

To incite that conversation, I offer my sense of the framework in which they need to exist so that they lead to valid and worthwhile outcomes for education in democratic societies. The basic properties of democratic society are the rights of citizens to participate in the decision-making processes about rules for society that, at once, serve the needs and the desire of each and all at the same time, as best as can possibly be done—which reflects the same paradox which Jonathan notes concerning the need to bring everyone together to decide on how to best make it possible for everyone to go his or her own way. I would add, in so far as where one goes interferes as little as possible with where anyone else can go, as little as possible in closing opportunities for individual exploration, invention, creation, and application of where individuality might take one.

Yet, for a society to truly sponsor individual freedom it must also educate citizens in how to decide on what is right and good for the one as well as for all. Moffett's belief, especially near the end of his life, was that curriculum and methods should be shaped to help student citizens develop the capacity to serve their native curiosity and to explore and invent and create and apply; to use their minds to make the conditions of life ever better for themselves and, in the context of the good of society, better for all. It is my deepest hope that we can find a new and realistic way to achieve the fantastic vision that Moffett believed possible, and that he could not achieve on his own during his own life time, by finding a sufficiently large number of others with which to do so together.

JONATHAN MARINE: It actually wasn't me (or, at least, it wasn't *only* me) who argued that Moffett pulled the profession of the teaching of English "fifty years forward"—it was John Hartley, editor of the *McGill Journal of Education* (Moffett, "Eighties" 102). And many other notable scholars since that time, such as John Warnock (2000), Sheridan Blau (2011), and Russell Durst (2015), have quoted, paraphrased, or cited that same idea in order to continue to discuss the incredibly unique legacy of James Moffett. And while I agree with you (and lament) that in some ways that impact has been impermanent, it bears reminding that Moffett confronted a field in the form of the language arts of the mid-twentieth century that valued most of all grammatical correctness and obedience to the teacher. Students all sat in neat rows facing the teacher, raising their hand to talk, being drilled continuously on the finer points of participles and gerunds, punished verbally (or worse) whenever they made an error. That we now recognize, however muted, the extraordinary import in language learning of social interaction with peers, of trying out new ideas without fear of punishment, and the vital role language learning plays in our conceptions of identity, understanding, and collective belonging speaks to the tectonic shift which Moffett's ideas about cognitive development and growth had, and continued to have, on our field and education at large.

So, we find ourselves at a crossroads; Moffett's ideas and influence remain like the haze of spectral illumination which dense fog brings about a star; you can sense it's there, but only faintly. Hopefully, through this continued conversation, we may find others interested in discussing, reviving, and applying Moffett's ideas and, in doing so, uphold the ultimately civilizing edict at the core of all his thought and work: the dire need for all of us to understand one another well enough to get along in a world where it is far too easy to fall into what Moffett termed "agnosia"—the rejection of alternative perspectives, which in many ways has been the founding and guiding principle of AEPL itself.

References

Blau, Sheridan. "Theory for practice: James Moffett's Seminal Contribution to Composition." In P. Lambert Stock (Ed.), *Composition's Roots in English Education*, Portsmouth, NH: Boynton, (2012): 81-104.

Durst, Russel K. "The Stormy Times of James Moffett." *English Education,* vol. 47, no. 2, 2015, pp. 111-130.

Moffett, James. *Teaching the Universe of Discourse.* Houghton Mifflin, 1968.

—. "Language Learning in the Eighties." *McGill Journal of Education.* vol. 14, no. 1, (1979): 102-14.

—. *Storm in the Mountains: A Case Study of Censorship, Conflict, and Consciousness.* Southern Illinois University Press, 1988.

Warnock, J. James Moffett. In M. G. Moran & M. Ballif (Eds.), *Twentieth Century Rhetorics and Rhetoricians: Critical Studies and Sources.* Westport, CT: Greenwood Press, (2000): 258-265.

COMMUNICATING SCIENCE SPECIAL ISSUE

Rethinking Science Communication: The Need for Dialogic, Transdisciplinary Collaboration

Julia E. Kiernan

Many moons ago, I was an undergraduate student *and* a dual major—pursuing degrees in both the sciences and the humanities. At the time, I knew my chosen path was uncommon, but I didn't actually realize the extent to which my learning deviated from peers (who had chosen either sciences or humanities). Upon reaching graduate school I shifted my educational focus exclusively to the humanities and didn't really look back; until my professional career began: I joined an interdisciplinary liberal arts department (in a STEM institution) and began teaching humanities courses to almost exclusively science students. It was not until this moment that I came to understand how my undergraduate experience, which was varied, diverse, and distinctly interdisciplinary, put me at an advantage not just academically, but as a social being who existed in a world outside the university. Moreover, as I began teaching science communication courses, inviting students to try on different communicative strategies—traditional text-based, as well as new genres and new media—I realized that to be an effective science communicator one needed to communicate not simply in multiple spaces, but to listen carefully, thoughtfully, and intentionally in these spaces. It is this listening that I think is at the heart of this special issue. And not just listening within the classroom (although this is incredibility important!), but outside the classroom—on the street, the bus, social media, and all the places in between.

Thus, this special issue emerged in response to what I saw as a lack of attention to science communication in STEM-focused institutions, and not just science communication, but dialogic and transdisciplinary-informed science communication. For many of us who teach English, writing, and other language-specific courses in higher education settings, there is often a reluctance among colleagues to engage with STEM-focused topics and themes in non-STEM courses—resulting in coursework that is rigidly discrete. This resistance is understandable given the often marginalized position of language education in STEM institutions; however, this approach, which is marked by disciplinarity, is a disservice to science students who will leave our classrooms and enter professions where they are required, but often ill-equipped, to engage with myriad public audiences.

Understanding the various implications of this disconnect requires us to rethink post-secondary approaches to teaching science communication. We can teach students the importance of communicating with both peers *and* non-peers; this is needed to excel within not just the classroom, but outside of it as well. Such attention to science communication and public outreach must happen not just in Writing-in-the-Disciplines (WID) courses but across the entire educational experience via the implementation of focused and thorough Writing-Across-the-Curriculum (WAC) initiatives. The authors in this special issue describe a number of pedagogical and programmatic interventions that can respond to this gap in student ability, which include attention to collaboration across disciplines as well as skillsets that enable students to communicate effectively across shifting public discourse communities.

As these essays show, there is a clear need for faculty who teach science communication in writing and other language-oriented courses to invite students to consider the transdisciplinary nature of these communicative interactions. Situating science communication within a single discipline is short-sighted; however, we must also understand why science communication must be more than interdisciplinary. And, while interdisciplinary learning is certainly important within academic spaces that teach the tenets of science communication, it cannot be the end point. Transdisciplinary approaches are integral because they exist beyond the classroom, bridging academic and public life by valuing and engaging with the outside world—a world that is full of values and perspectives that often deviate from those within the classroom. Underprepared science students moving into professional spaces exacerbate the disconnects between scientists and citizens, which results in vast chasms of misunderstanding and skepticism. The current pandemic is evidence of this divide. Now, in 2023, I am regularly struck by the dystopian nature of public attitudes that rebuff science: swaths of people who wholeheartedly believe that the Covid-19 pandemic is not real, that vaccines are filled with tracking devices (or crushed up human embryos), or that drinking bleach and other disinfectants is a form of treatment. Yet, to many citizens, compliance with science is itself a dystopian stance. As examined in a number of the essays herein, such division is evident across various facets of science; this is particularly noteworthy in environmental and climate science, where (unlike the current pandemic) scientists have been attempting to communicate to the public for decades rather than years. These realities are frightening and, one may argue, a clear indication that contemporary science communication education is not effective. At the same time, the opposite could also be argued; some modes of science communication have been incredibly effective. Take, for instance, the ways that large (trusted) international corporations'—ExxonMobil, Volkswagen, Johnson & Johnson, etc.—have worked with company scientists to manipulate scientific information for economic gains that result in social calamity—climate pledges, diesel dupes, and cancer epidemics. There is clearly an ethical dimension inherent in any teaching of science communication, yet when we train students in disciplinary silos learners are often unaware of the socioscientific nature of their future professions. This is an educational failure. As teachers, administrators, and program directors, we need to embrace an approach that values the synergistic nature of socioscientific pedagogies; their ability to "facilitat[e] scientific reasoning and sociocultural development" (Zeidler 20).

In these ways, this special issue's attention to broadening pedagogical and methodological approaches to science communication aims to expand perspectives on the ways scientific language functions differently across shifting situations. It takes this stance so that, as practitioners, we are prepared to expand students' repertoire of science communication and, in turn, students are prepared to proactively engage with a growing public that has and continues to lose trust in science. As indicated in many of the included essays, we can no longer relegate science communication to only science courses (or only first-year-composition courses); we need to come together across disciplines to solve this dangerous communicative dilemma. Solving requires not simply understanding, but meeting these issues head on and designing strategies that are usable and replicable across shifting contexts and audiences. This special issue is one attempt to embolden this sea change and includes approaches that are familiar—narrative and narratology, blended learning, student agency, etc.—but also those that are not as widely adopted across the curriculum. Many contributors come from English and writing studies, but others come from spaces throughout the university—libraries, interdisciplinary institutes, medical schools, and science programs. In these ways, interdisciplinarity takes shape, but the focus of these essays is expanding these conversations into transdisciplinary spaces. The approaches described herein situate science communication as a holistic endeavor, one that is shaped by many disciplines and voices. In these ways, this special issue invites readers to imagine new ways of promoting science communication across the curriculum and extend our discussions beyond traditional disciplinary and interdisciplinary learning spaces.

In addition to the full-length articles that address the aforementioned issues, this special issue includes two *Connecting Essays*, which are offered as complements to each other. The first positions WAC as a pedagogical solution to building scientific literacy; the second echoes this positioning, extending this argument to academic responsibility. What is interesting about each is not simply the shared attention to harnessing scientific knowledge, science literacy, and citizen-science, but also the ways that both sets of collaborators are clear in their articulation of why such pedagogical moves matter to scientific disciplines, yes, but also society at large. Both groups of collaborators, like the other contributors, note that these efforts must be collaborative and transdisciplinary—arguing that humanities and science programs need to work together to rectify this knowledge gap. However, even though both pieces offer clear pathways forward, Gerstle et al. providing a series of interventions and Carrion et al. offering a replicable programmatic approach, my apprehension is that without buy-in from those who teach science—without the support of science programs and administrators—we cannot change the current status quo.

The teaching of science communication is a transdisciplinary task and cannot be driven (or expected to be driven) by a single college, department, or school. Teaching students to be scientifically literate must be realized as important across all facets of education and, as Carrion et al. explain, be sustained and sustainable. Of course, as Gertsle et al. describe, the primary barrier to this intervention is time. And, because undergraduate science education has not traditionally valued science communication—communication being a humanities construct, not framed by hard science—this area of science education continues to be neglected. This negligence, as outlined in my opening vignette and subsequent examples, is—to quote Gerstle et al.—"dangerous." Dangerous for students and dangerous for citizens. It is dangerous to separate the science from the social, positioning both as discrete entities, because this is not how broader society lives. As citizens our lives are embroiled in *socio*scientific experiences. Accordingly, what the many examples of science communication gone awry offered throughout this special issue point to is a needed rethinking and reimagining of post-secondary education's approach to teaching scientific education. As both *Connecting Essays* illustrate, our current siloed, disciplinary approach to teaching science students is—as Carrion et al. explain—isolating *and* dangerous. Instead, we need to structure our teaching of science communication via a transdisciplinary lens that is not simply collaborative, but also socially responsible.

Fortuitously, this special issue offers replicable solutions to this gap. Yet, as educators and administrators we need to swallow hard, ignore the moans of complaint amongst (some of) our colleagues, and carve out time and space for a new type of science education: one that is framed not simply by scientific knowledge, but also science literacy and science citizenship. As both *Connecting Essays* argue, to be effective and confident professionals, science students need to engage in layered and scaffolded approaches *across the curriculum*—learning takes time and we need to make that time. The learning of science communication must be designed as a meaningful, lasting, and responsive experience that takes place (to varying degrees) in all the required courses that science students take; this means that we need to value a synergistic, socioscientific approach that is collaborative and transdisciplinary.

Work Cited

Zeidler, Dana L. "STEM Education: A Deficit Framework for the Twenty-First Century? A Sociocultural Socioscientific Response." *Cultural Studies of Science Education*, vol. 11, 2016, pp. 11-26.

Science Storytelling beyond the Dramatic Arc: Narrativity and Little Red Schoolhouse Principles in Science Communication

Daniel Aureliano Newman

Abstract: *Narrative is widely recommended for improving science communication, yet the main approach to science storytelling is limited and limiting, advocating fixed dramatic arcs and the ideal of narrativehood, the absolute quality of being a coherent narrative. Neglected by this approach, I argue, are the finer grained linguistic patterns that give texts local narrativity, the quality of being narrative in a scalar, adjectival sense. I harmonize narrativity with the well-established principles of clear technical writing developed by Joseph Williams, then demonstrate how these principles might be used and taught through a comparative reading of several texts discussing a single topic in genres ranging from amateur blogs to specialized scientific journals. The narrativity-based approach has several advantages. It avoids the reductionism of the template-based approach, as well as its questionable dependence on narrative structures derived from the arts and entertainment. In terms of adoption by scientists and other science communicators, the approach also has the advantage of not requiring a radical overhaul of current communicative practices; it also reduces the difference between technical and public-facing writing. In short, the approach proposed here offers a workable and effective way to telling science stories with minimal simplification or distortion of scientific information.*

Introduction

Science communicators of all stripes have become increasingly interested in the promise of narrative (e.g. Joubert et al.), yet they are anything but united in their view of what narrative is exactly, let alone how it should be used. Some scientists dispute the promise of storytelling (Katz), and even those who are more receptive admit "there is much more we have to learn about how we as scientists can incorporate storytelling into our professional lives as we strive to make science more understandable, more inclusive, and ultimately, more beneficial to the world" (Suzuki et al. 9470). By contrast, a small but influential group of authors suggest, sometimes outright, that we already know all we need about storytelling. These science-story popularizers tend to downplay or dismiss concerns that narrative can oversimplify, distort, or misrepresent complex scientific information (Blanton and Ikizer; Winterbottom et al.). Storytelling may well be part of the answer to the problems facing science communication, but it is certainly not, as Rafael Luna puts it, "the simple answer" (7).

For the science-story popularizers, simplicity is the whole point, and many of their views rely on a concept known as *narrativehood*. Narrative, in their view, is a simple dramatic arc, typically a version of Freytag's Pyramid (Angler; ElShafie; Luna; Olson), Joseph Campbell's monomyth (Angler; ElShafie; Olson), or the Hegelian Dialectic

(Angler; Olson). "Every story," argues Randy Olson, "can be reduced to this simple structure" (16): it is a "template" (Olson 9) or a "formula" (Angler 105) whose use is straightforward and appeal universal. Its vaunted simplicity is exactly what worries sceptics. Retelling "the same story" (Olson 34) is a dubious strategy given that science so often describes processes and phenomena that defy our cognitive frames and representative conventions. This is not to suggest abandoning science storytelling, but its risks and limitations require more consideration from popularizers. If the challenge is to harness the power of narrative without compromising the science (Dahlstrom and Scheufele), we must expand working definitions of narrative beyond the doubtful simplicity of templates.

Here, I offer a modest step toward such a goal. It is a small, practical part of a larger project aiming to strengthen science communication with insights and methods from narrative theory (narratology), a field largely unacknowledged in discussions of science storytelling. I begin by proposing an alternative to the structural definition of narrative currently favored by science-story popularizers, in which narrative equates with *narrativehood*, a "binary predicate" (Herman 90)—a text in this context either is or is not *a* narrative. Narrativehood is in my view a counterproductively reductive target, excluding a wide range of potentially helpful narrative features. A more promising quality is *narrativity*, "a scalar predicate" that admits varying degrees of narrative (Herman 91). Whereas narrativehood refers to a text's global structure, narrativity encompasses more granular local dynamics that are crucial to making complex scientific information intelligible and interesting. In Part Two of the essay, I outline principles for identifying and boosting narrativity, based on the Little Red Schoolhouse (LRS) writing program developed by Joseph Williams. Finally, to help put these principles into teaching and communication practice, I compare narrativity in various accounts of the same biological phenomenon in texts ranging from amateur-science blogs to technical articles. The comparison illustrates how LRS principles reflect narrativity and model a flexible, nuanced, and responsible approach to science storytelling.

Narrativity beyond Story Templates

As evidenced by the acclaim of a fictional work like Rachel Cusk's complex, plotless fiction, *The Outline Trilogy*, stories need not be simple, dramatic, or globally coherent to be compelling. So let's look beyond the intuitive appeal of the dramatic arc to a more rigorous and more expansive theory of narrative. Good storytelling may not *need* theory, but a workable and responsible framework for science storytelling probably does. Theory can jolt us out of conceptual ruts and calcified practices, and indeed narratological research hints at how much we can still learn about the role and diversity of narrative practices in science.[1] In the meantime, however, we need a theory of narrative that is both practical and consistent with existing communicative practices in science.

There is no need to reinvent the communicative wheel, thankfully, because narrative is already inherent in scientific descriptions of phenomena, in models, and in data repre-

---

1. See, for example, work on narrative and science in philosophy (e.g., Rosales), literary studies (e.g., Scherr), psychology (e.g., Dahlstrom) and pedagogy (e.g., Corni et al.).

sentations. "Science has stories in it," writes Nobel chemist Roald Hoffmann (253), who finds scientific articles and lectures packed with "narrative devices…, employed both spontaneously and purposefully" (250). Attending to narrative *devices*, as opposed to narrative *structures*, sounds promising. It would also move us past the notion of story as a mere vessel for scientific content. An effective program for science storytelling should focus more on how "story elements" produce narrativity, and perhaps less on how "plot elements" give form to whole narratives (White 20). Also promising is Hoffman's recognition that scientific texts have their own narrativity, if only here and there; it counters the assumption, common among popularizers, that narrative is foreign to science, in need of importation from the Humanities (Luna 7) or Hollywood (ElShafie; Olson). Overall, when our view of story shifts away from coherent plots and fixed structures toward a mode of argumentation, the distance between narrative and scientific thinking narrows considerably.

If narrative is a logic for stringing together propositions, science storytelling should attend more to local scales of discourse. While some science-story popularizers do consider sentences and paragraphs, they generally treat these structures as microcosms of the global (Olson 73–4; Schimel 95–6), thus retaining the primary framework of narrativehood. Meanwhile many texts "are full of narratives and micro-narratives, yet many would hesitate to call the works as a whole narrative" (Abbott 14). It is indeed at "causal locations" within and between sentences that readers are most influenced by stories (Dahlstrom 857), the sentence level being "where meaning is created" (Junker 251). A shift in focus from plot elements to local narrative elements that contribute little to overall structure would, however, productively expand what counts as science storytelling.

If we treat science writing as a *weave of narrative elements*, we might productively shift our focus on storytelling from narrativehood to narrativity, from plotting to narrating.[2] This shift would not require a deep dive into narrative theory, or even a major change in writing approach. A very basic engagement with narratology should suffice to help link narrative principles to familiar stylistic approaches to effective writing. Science communication and scientific writing cannot and likely will not adopt radical overhauls of current practice. Academic fields are resistant to changes in practice, and most scientists I have worked with prefer practical over theoretical approaches to better writing. Instead of reinventing the wheel, we might exploit the tools already available to those concerned, as teachers or practitioners, with science communication.

Narrativity as Clarity

A promising way to proceed lies in the principles associated with the University of Chicago's "Little Red Schoolhouse" (LRS) writing and pedagogy program. Developed in 1980 by Joseph Williams and Gregory Colomb, LRS teaches "an approach to writing

---

2. Tellingly, a local focus is characteristic of studies measuring the impact of narrative on citation rates and other metrics of communicative success. Doing so would not require a deep dive into narrative theory. Such studies use "indicators of narrativity" at the sentence and paragraph level (Hillier et al. 3–4) or "measures of writing style" of which "narrative structure" is a key criterion (Freeling et al. 342).

that considers the particular challenges of writing about complex, expert subject matter for a variety of readerships" ("Who we are"). Crucially, the approach is framed in narrative terms, though this feature has enjoyed scant attention from narratologists; even writing scholars and teachers often treat it as incidental or metaphorical, rather than essential to the method.

Storytelling emerged as the core of Williams's writing pedagogy in direct response to the inaccessibility of scientific writing. It was while teaching clear writing to medical scientists that he "discovered…the importance of story" (Williams, qtd in Gee). The result was the LSR program and his book *Style: Toward Clarity and Grace* (1981), an early section of which is duly entitled "Telling Stories" (19). But these stories are not the dramatic plots of the science-story popularizers; such a feature, Williams suggests, is unnecessary in documents concerned primarily with "explanation" (20). Williams would seem to see narrative much as Hayden White does, "less as a form of representation than as a manner of speaking about events" (White 2). This account, which dissolves the intuitive opposition between narrative and exposition, offers a granular and malleable model of storytelling. Because it is already established, its use demands no major overhaul in approaches to science writing.

Williams's approach is simple, pairing two grammatical categories with two narratological concepts: subjects with characters and verbs with actions. Recognizable, consistent and tangible characters and tangible actions generate narrativity, so that "even prose that may seem wholly discursive and abstract," writes Williams, "usually has behind it *the two central components of a story—characters and their actions*" (20, my emphasis). Clear writing foregrounds these components, especially when the subject-characters and action-verbs are arranged into interconnected stretches of continuous discourse

> at the beginning of a series of sentences, creat[ing] for your reader a reasonably consistent point of view, a consistent topic string. When that consistent topic string consists of your cast of characters as subjects, and you immediately connect those subjects with verbs that express the crucial actions, you are a long way toward writing prose that your readers will perceive as clear, direct, and cohesive. (Williams 52–3)

This is storytelling, if not telling *a* story. Topic strings produce continuity across sentences, creating a narrative or narrative-like sequence. The link between Williams's syntactic-stylistic approach and narrative is more than metaphorical: its focus on characters and actions over stretches of continuous discourse is easy to assimilate, for example, with philosophical perspectives on causality in science and narrative (e.g. Junker 251).

The syntactic patterns targeted by LRS principles are readily visible in effective science writing for non-experts. Consider a *New York Times* article by immunologists Akiko Iwasaki and Ruslan Medzhitov, published in mid-2020 when a Covid-19 vaccine still seemed fanciful. As an attempt to educate and reassure the public about a confusing and politicized health crisis, the article is science communication at its most high stakes. It is not a story, but it has a high degree of narrativity thanks to its careful management of subject-characters and verb-actions. Witness the following passage, in which I bold subjects, capitalized their verbs (actions) and, because they occasionally differ from subjects, underline characters:

> Virtually **all viruses** that INFECT humans CONTAIN in their genomes blueprints for producing <u>proteins</u> **that** HELP <u>them</u> evade detection by the innate immune system. For example, **SARS-CoV-2** APPEARS to have a gene dedicated to silencing the innate immune system. Among <u>the viruses</u> **that** HAVE BECOME endemic in humans, **some** HAVE also FIGURED OUT ways to dodge the adaptive immune system: **H.I.V.-1** MUTATES rapidly; **herpes viruses** DEPLOY <u>proteins</u> **that** CAN TRAP and INCAPACITATE antibodies. (Iwasaki and Medzhitov 2020)

These sentences consistently favor subjects that are easily graspable as characters: while hardly anthropomorphic, viruses are discrete entities that can be conceived as agents. Such clause- and sentence-level patterns are crucial for narrativity, though not sufficient. Narrativity cannot be *too* local and requires some degree of continuity (Sturgess 8). Note, then, the topical continuity linking the sentences above, whose subject-characters are mostly viruses. Such "[c]onsistency of protagonists" is essential to both narrativity (Fludernik 158) and cohesive prose (Williams 52). The pattern Williams calls "topic strings" is effectively the creation and maintenance of character over stretches of discourse: by populating the beginning of successive sentences with "a limited set of referents," topic strings produce what "readers will take the main characters of the story" (82) to be. Of course, narrativity can accommodate more than one character (Williams 82). In the passage surrounding the sentences quoted above, Iwasaki and Mdezhitoz do not always feature viruses. Some of their sentences have less clearly agential subject-characters:

> The **immunity** created by vaccines DIFFERS…

> **Vaccines** COME in different flavors…

While not viruses, immunity and vaccines are thematically and biologically part of the same general story of infection, immunity, and vaccination. In short, the clarity and narrativity of Iwasaki and Medzhitov's article emerge from just a few related patterns at the level of clauses, sentences, and paragraphs.

The *Times* article's reach and reception are undeniably inflected by the authors' status as Harvard experts and its publication in a "liberal-elite" newspaper. But the syntactic patterns that give the article narrativity are transferable, able to serve in any number of forums and mediums, from children's books and school materials to science blogs and peer-reviewed journals, from TV news to the Covid-19 update emails I receive from my city councillor. This fact provides the basis for teaching science communicators about narrativity and how to incorporate it in science stories.

Comparing Narrativity across Science-writing Genres

As a quality of clear writing, narrativity varies predictably across science writing genres, from the entertaining to the most informational. The variation should be detectable in the choice and consistency of a text's main characters and actions. Less specialized texts likely feature a smaller cast of characters that tend toward concrete agential entities like scientists or caribou, or dynamic things like atoms or clouds. Narrativity also varies within genres, depending on authorial idiosyncrasies, editorial practices, and other contextual factors. In any case, the existence of such scalar variation suggests a comparative approach for teaching science communicators how to recognize and generate narrativity, whether across drafts of one document or simply different documents. Juxtaposing different texts with similar content helps highlight modulations in narrativity across communicative situations rather than reducing narrative to a present/absent binary. The comparisons that follow might thus inspire practical exercises and/or assignments for students aiming to improve their academic writing or become science communicators.

In its simplest form, the approach involves contrasting two versions of one sentence. It is much easier to see what gives incipient narrativity to a sentence from Iwasaki and Medzhitov's article, for example, if it is juxtaposed with a revision (my own) that rearranges its elements in ways that obscure character and action:

> Thankfully, **SARS-CoV-2** DOES NOT SEEM TO HAVE EVOLVED any such tricks yet. (Iwasaki and Medzhitov)

> Thankfully, the **evolution of such tricks** HAS NOT yet OCCURRED in the case of SARS-CoV-2.

My revision replaces the original's concrete character (a virus) with a complex abstraction (the evolution of tricks), and the kinetic, specific verb (evolve) with a static, general one (occur). My revision is not a bad sentence, but the original is clearer both on its own and in its larger textual environment, as part of a topic string spanning several sentences.

We can also compare narrativity across genres. In what follows, I model how such comparisons serve to concretize the abstract notion of narrativity and to illustrate the related LRS principles. As a case study, I chose the topic of coevolutionary arms races, first hypothesized by Darwin to explain why some pollinators have very long proboscides (tongues) and the plants they visit have very deep corolla tubes. The topic lends itself to the concerns of science storytelling: the science is complex, defying simple storification. Like anything Darwinian, it is also polarizing. Finally, it has broad appeal, as attested by its recurrent discussions in popular-science magazines (*National Geographic*), newspapers (*The Guardian*), and blogs (Laidback Gardener). The topic's manifestations across genres reveal similarities and differences in narrativity and form the basis for lessons on understanding, teaching, and practicing the art of science storytelling.

Let's begin with an accessible, high-narrativity account that also satisfies the popular notion of story as a dramatic arc. This excerpt, bearing the same typographical markers as above, is from Angel Eduardo's "The Orchid and the Moth: Why Scientists Are the True Prophets," published by the science-advocacy Center for Inquiry:

> In 1862, **Charles Darwin** RECEIVED a sample of orchids from Madagascar. Among them, **he** NOTICED, WAS **a flower with an unusually long nectary**, the orchid's nectar-producing gland. At nearly a foot in length, **this** WOULD KEEP the nectar from any known insect looking to partake. **It** GOT Darwin wondering.

Days later, **Darwin** MADE a prediction: In Madagascar, there MUST BE **moths** with tongues long enough to feed on that flower. Through his knowledge of evolution and ecology, **he** KNEW that **the orchid and this moth** MUST HAVE CO-EVOLVED—but **no one** HAD ever SEEN the moth.

Twenty years after Darwin's death, **the moth** WAS DISCOVERED.

This passage, because it has both high narrativity and narrativehood, offers an account of Darwin as problem-solver that conforms to the dramatic arc of rising tension and resolution advocated by most science-story popularizers. The structure is typical of amateur or outreach accounts of moth-orchid coevolution. Effective as it is for such purposes, it demands a tight focus on the researcher as hero, often at the expense of complex scientific explanation. A dramatic arc may be appropriate in some communicative contexts, but limiting in others.

Such situations would call for relaxing the pursuit of narrativehood and focusing instead on boosting local narrativity. Consider how Ed Yong, author of *National Geographic*'s "Not Exactly Rocket Science" blog, embeds an accessible yet finer-grained explanation in his account:

> [**Darwin**] SUGGESTED that **the two species** WERE LOCKED in an 'evolutionary arms race'. **Orchids and pollinators** gradually CO-EVOLVED over time, lengthening both tongues and spurs in response to each other. **Orchids with the longest spurs** HAVE an advantage. **Their nectar stores** ARE only just within reach of pollinators, so **they** ARE tempting but DON'T SACRIFICE too much valuable nectar. For <u>pollinators</u>, **the advantage** BELONGS to <u>those with the longest tongues</u> because **they** HAVE access to the most food.

Initially foregrounding Darwin, Yong rapidly shifts to orchids and pollinators, placing them at the head of most clauses and thus creating fairly consistent topic strings. Though he finally returns to Darwin, the scientist-as-detective narrative is more diffuse than Eduardo's, the focus shifting for relatively long stretches of discourse to micro-narratives whose characters are orchids, moths, or parts of their anatomy. This is not to say one approach is better; each has its purpose and audience, and each narrates accordingly. What parallel readings uncover is how science communicators range up and down the ladder of narrativity, by negotiating three related variables: subject-characters, verbs, and sentence topics.

Parallel readings can also bridge the perceived divide between "popular" and "professional" science writing, helping make science communication less foreign and forbidding to those accustomed to technical writing. Real differences notwithstanding, comparisons reveal stylistic and narrative commonalities between even the most accessible and the most specialized texts. Consider the rather technical explanation of coevolution in *New Phytologist*:

> According to Darwin's hypothesis, **selection on the pollinator** FAVOURS longer proboscides to achieve easy access to the nectar, while **selection on the plant** FAVOURS longer <u>corolla tubes</u>, **which** ENSURE <u>the pollinator</u>'s contact with the reproductive parts and thus MAXIMIZE pollen transfer. **This**

> **kind of selective regime** CAN LEAD to <u>reciprocal coevolution</u> **that** ESCA-LATES the length of both traits. (Paudel et al. 1402; in-text references omitted)

This is undeniably more difficult, and less narrative, than the previous texts. Darwin, plants, and pollinators all appear, but because they are excluded from subject and topic positions, it is a stretch to call them characters. Yet the passage does exhibit some narrativity, produced by the topic string foregrounding *selection* as a consistent albeit abstract subject-character. Even abstractions can become legible as characters if they recur consistently enough in strategic locations (Williams 27). Had the authors chosen a *different* abstraction for each subject the passage would be even less narrative. The accounts in *New Phytologist* and in the *National Geographic* blog thus differ in degree of narrativity.

The same is true even of highly simplified accounts. Consider Isabella Armour's folksy account on *Botany Thoughts*, an amateur plant-themed blog hosted by *Medium.com*:

> Say **a Sphinx moth** GOES UP to a Star Orchid and STICKS its long proboscis into the flower's deep nectar spur. To get all the way down to the nectar, **the moth** WILL HAVE TO PUT its face on the flower. If **the spur** IS long enough, **it** WILL FORCE the moth [to] get so close to the flower that **it** GETS COVERED in pollen. Then **the moth** GETS the food reward and GOES to the next flower to get more food.

Unsophisticated as it may seem, this passage features the same syntactic patterns targeted by LRS principles. Different as Armour's characters and actions are from those of Paudel et al., both texts similarly manage those elements in ways that facilitate reading, engagement, and comprehension.

These insights extend to writing in scientific journals, an observation that many emerging scientists find illuminating, since it helps reduce the perceived gulf between specialized and public writing. Even specialized scientific texts vary in narrativity, not only among different journals and articles but also within articles. Articles in generalist journals are more narrative than those in specialized forums, as the following passage from *Nature*, in contrast with the *New Phytologist* excerpt, suggests:

> [W]ithin a population, **the plants with the longest nectar spurs** HAVE a selective advantage because **their reproductive organs** optimally CONTACT pollinators and thus **they** ACHIEVE the greatest reproduction, whereas **pollinators with the longest tongues** HAVE a selective advantage because **they** OBTAIN the largest food reward. **Spur length** and **pollinator tongue length** then COEVOLVE by following gradually shifting adaptive peaks. (Whittall and Hodges 706; in-text references omitted)

Other high-narrativity accounts might strategically place moths and orchids themselves, as opposed to anatomical parts of them, in subject-character positions. The spectrum of narrativity carries over distinctions between scholarly, technical writing, and educational, entertaining communication. The following account by David Hone falls somewhere between accounts quoted above:

> **Some species of plants and insect** EVOLVE complex relationships where **both** CAN BENEFIT – if **the insect** IS the only one **that** CAN ACCESS the nectar

> **it** IS GUARANTEED food **others** ARE DENIED, while **the flower** further REDUCES the risk of misdelivered pollen and CAN BACK on its investments.
>
> **One way of restricting access to nectar** IS to elongate the part of <u>the flower</u> **that** HOLDS this sugary liquid, ensuring that only **the longest-tongued of insects** CAN REACH it. **Orchids** CAN TAKE this to extremes and **it** WAS <u>one such flower</u> **that** LED to the creation of a famous hypothesis by the most famous biologist.

Hone swings from the first, high-narrativity paragraph (with "plants and insects" as subject-characters) to the second, whose abstract subjects approximate the style of specialized writing. This is not a failure to maintain narrativity: the high-narrativity first paragraph equips readers to navigate the difficulties of the lower-narrativity second. In telling science stories, then, it may help to frame the key difference between specialized and popular texts not in terms of whether a text tells *a* story but, rather, in what kind of characters it features, and for what length of continuous discourse.

The comparative approach above suggests a way to teach science storytelling, with the added benefit of instilling proven principles for clear writing. Workshopping such comparisons with students is conceptually illuminating but also practically empowering, providing workable revision strategies for improving clarity and reach. Having used Williams's *Style* to teach science writing for ten years, I sensed that while many students learn to use LRS principles as rules, few acquire a working sense of the principles' underlying theory. Only recently, when I started presenting them *as* narrative principles, have I seen students grasp the theory profoundly enough to use it flexibly, as a holistic approach to style and narrative rather than a set of discrete, mechanical strategies. Comparison can also form the basis for creative exercises to reinforce LRS principles while demystifying the *storytelling* side of science storytelling. Students might be prompted, for example, to rewrite Hone's text for three different audiences, or with three different primary characters. Such exercises could also facilitate interdisciplinary collaboration between science communicators with very different training or expertise—scientists, journalists, novelists, policymakers and more. A narrative-centric approach to LRS principles appears to work as well in workshops on public outreach as in specialized writing courses. As I hope the comparisons above have suggested, a narrative approach can help science communicators understand the range of ways science stories can be told, as well as how to match the narrativity of their writing with their communicative purposes and the needs of their audience.

Conclusion

The approach suggested above is a modest step toward more thoroughgoing engagement between science communication and narrative theory. It is relatively easy to apply and requires minimal theoretical sophistication. But there is still much work to do. As part of a greater pedagogical endeavour, we might also aim to use creative writing for teaching scientific theories and models (Corni et al. 251). Alongside practical programs for putting science storytelling on firmer theoretical ground, I hope to see more analytical and theoretical research on the narrative elements inherent in scientific models and descriptions. Narratology has long mined innovative novels for concepts and models; why not do the same with scientific texts? With common ground between science and storytelling largely unexplored, narratology could be the *science of story* we need to tell compelling stories of science. In the short term, though, a narrative interpretation of LRS principles offers the beginnings of a practical program for taking science storytelling beyond the same old story.

Works Cited

Abbott, H. Porter. *Cambridge Introduction to Narrative.* 2nd ed., Cambridge University Press, 2008.

Angler, Martin. W. *Telling Science Stories: Reporting, Crafting and Editing for Journalists and Scientists.* Routledge, 2020.

Armour, Isabella. "Darwin's Orchids." *Medium.com,* 5 Feb. 2016, https://medium.com/think-with-me/darwin-s-orchids-c7557789bcc9.

Blanton, Hart, and Elif G. Ikizer. "Elegant Science Narratives and Unintended Influences: An Agenda for the Science of Science Communication." *Social Issues and Policy Review,* vol. 13, no. 1, 2019, pp. 154-81.

Corni, Federico, Hans U. Fuchs, and Giovanni Savino. "An Industrial Educational Laboratory at Ducati Foundation: Narrative Approaches to Mechanics based upon Continuum Physics." *International Journal of Science Education,* vol., 40, no. 3, 2018, pp. 243–67.

Dahlstrom, Michael F. "The Persuasive Influence of Narrative Causality: Psychological Mechanism, Strength in Overcoming Resistance, and Persistence over Time." *Media Psychology,* vol. 15, no. 3, 2012, pp. 303–26.

Dahlstrom, Michael F., and Dietram A. Scheufele. "(Escaping) the Paradox of Scientific Storytelling." *PLoS Biology,* vol. 16, no.10, 2018, p. e2006720.

Eduardo, Angel. "The Orchid and the Moth: Why Scientists are the True Prophets." *Center for Inquiry,* 8 Oct. 2020, https://centerforinquiry.org/blog/the-orchid-and-the-moth-why-scientists-are-the-true-prophets/.

ElShafie, Sara J. "Making Science Meaningful for Broad Audiences through Stories." *Integrative and Comparative Biology,* vol. 58, no. 6, 2018, pp. 1213–23.

Fludernik, Monika. *An Introduction to Narratology.* Translated by Patricia Häusler-Greenfield and Monika Fludernik, Routledge, 2009.

Freeling, Benjamin, Zoë A. Doubleday, and Sean D. Connell. "How Can We Boost the Impact of Publications? Try Better Writing." *Proceedings of the National Academy of Sciences,* vol. 116, no. 2, 2019, pp. 341–3.

Gee, Robyn. "Joseph Williams, Little Red Schoolhouse Founder, Dead at 74." *The Chicago Maroon,* 4 Mar. 2008, https://www.chicagomaroon.com/2008/3/4/joseph-williams-little-red-schoolhouse-founder-dead-at-74/.

Herman, David. *Story Logic: Problems and Possibilities of Narrative.* University of Nebraska Press, 2002.

Hillier, Ann, Ryan P. Kelly, and Terrie Klinger. "Narrative Style Influences Citation Frequency in Climate Change Science." *PloS One,* vol. 11, no. 12, 2016, e0167983.

Hoffman, Roald. "The Tensions of Scientific Storytelling." *Scientific American*, vol. 102, 2014, 250–3.

Hone, Dave. "Moth Tongues, Orchids and Darwin—The Predictive Power of Evolution." *The Guardian*, 2 Oct. 2013, https://www.theguardian.com/science/lost-worlds/2013/oct/02/moth-tongues-orchids-darwin-evolution.

Iwasaki, Akiko, and R. Medhzhitov. "Scared that Covid-19 Immunity Won't Last? Don't Be." *New York Times*, 31 July 2020, https://www.nytimes.com/2020/07/31/opinion/coronavirus-antibodies-immunity.html.

Joubert, Marina, Lloyd Davis, and Jennifer Metcalfe. "Storytelling: The Soul of Science Communication." *Journal of Science Communication*, vol. 18, no. 5, 2019, pp. 1–5.

Junker, Kirk. "Law and Science Serving One Master... Narrative." *Communicating Science: Professional Contexts: Reader 1*, edited by Eileen Scanlon, Roger Hill and Kirk Junker, Routledge, 1999, pp. 249–69.

Katz, Yarden. "Against Storytelling of Scientific Results." *Nature Methods*, vol. 10, no. 11, 2013, p. 1045.

Luna, Rafael E. *The Art of Scientific Storytelling: Transform Your Research Manuscript with a Step-by-Step Formula*. Amado, 2013.

Olson, Randy. *Houston, We Have a Narrative: Why Science Needs Story*. University of Chicago Press, 2015.

Paudel, Babu Ram, Mani Shrestha, Martin Burd, Subodh Adhikari, Yong-Shuai Sun, and Qing-Jun Li. "Coevolutionary Elaboration of Pollination-related Traits in an Alpine Ginger (*Roscoea purpurea*) and a Tabanid Fly in the Nepalese Himalayas." *New Phytologist*, vol. 211, no. 4, 2016, pp. 1402–11.

Rosales, Alirio. "Theories that Narrate the World: Ronald A. Fisher's Mass Selection and Sewall Wright's Shifting Balance." *Studies in the History and Philosophy of Science*, vol. 62, 2017, pp. 22–30.

Scherr, Alexander. *Narrating Evolution: Agency, Narrative Thinking, and the Epistemic Value of British and American Novels*. Verlag, 2107.

Schimel, Joshua. *Writing Science: How to Write Papers that Get Cited and Proposals that Get Funded*. Oxford University Press, 2012.

Sturgess, Philip J. M. (1992). *Narrativity: Theory and Practice*. Oxford University Press, 1992.

Suzuki, Wendy A., Mónica I. Feliú-Mójer, Uri Hasson, Rachel Yehuda, and Jean Mary Zarate. "Dialogues: The Science and Power of Storytelling." *Journal of Neuroscience*, vol. 38, no. 44, 2018, pp. 9468–70.

White, Hayden. *The Content of the Form: Narrative Discourse and Historical Representation*. Johns Hopkins University Press, 1987.

Whittall, Justen B., and Scott A. Hodges. "Pollinator Shifts Drive increasingly Long Nectar Spurs in Columbine Flowers." *Nature*, vol. 447, no. 7145, 2007, pp. 706–9.

"Who We Are." University of Chicago Writing Program, 2019, https://writing-program.uchicago.edu/who-we-are/.

Williams, Joseph M. *Style: Toward Clarity and Grace*. 1981. University of Chicago Press, 1990.

Winterbottom, Anna, Hilary L. Bekker, Mark Conner, and Andrew Mooney. "Does Narrative Information Bias Individual's Decision Making? A Systematic Review." *Social Science & Medicine*, vol. 67, no. 12, 2008, pp. 2079–88.
Yong, Ed. "Of Flowers and Pollinators—A Case Study of Punctuated Evolution." *National Geographic*, 10 Feb. 2009, https://www.nationalgeographic.com/science/article/of-flowers-and-pollinators-a-case-study-of-punctuated-evolution.

Public Narratives, Storytelling, and Trust: A Case Study in a STEM-Based Writing Program

Jeffery C. Gagnon

Abstract: In recent years, a growing body of scholars have argued that narrative storytelling is an effective and necessary science communication tool for the education of undergraduate STEM students. This research comes at a time when many in the public are becoming distrustful about science, scientists, and scientific communication. However, questions remain about which genre and style of narratives are most effective at building trust among STEM communicators and public audiences? My essay answers this question through a case study of narrative communication in my first-year writing classes. I analyze my attempts to teach STEM students that "public narratives," a genre of writing created community organizer Marshall Ganz, represent a necessary intervention for bridging the larger communication gaps that are widening levels of distrust among scientists and science-skeptical publics across the country. As a unique genre of writing, public narratives combine personal storytelling with audience-driven connection and persuasive writing. They are founded on three communicative elements that undergraduate STEM students need significantly more knowledge and training in as they prepare to engage the public in their areas of professional specialization; these areas include storytelling their own experiences with skepticism and distrust, the rejection of condescension, labeling and dismissiveness, and a compassionate approach to listening and understanding audiences that seem skeptical or even opposed to science.

Introduction

The students shifted uncomfortably in their seats. They were packed into a large campus auditorium, listening to a presentation on climate science by renowned professor of atmospheric science and climate science expert, Dr. Veerabhadran Ramanathan. Ramanathan, or "Ram" as he is popularly known on campus, was delivering a special guest lecture to over 500 first-year writing (FYW) students in the program I oversee. I had arranged for them to attend this presentation because they were enrolled in a lower-division writing course focused on teaching academic and public writing through the lens of climate science and climate communication.

Ramanathan's presentation focused on essential questions. What causes climate change? How do scientists know it is happening? What evidence do they have? What will the consequences be? And how soon will we experience them? Overall, the science was relatively accessible. His metaphors were clear and applicable. However, after more than twenty minutes into the presentation, students began to get restless. The facts were interesting, but something was missing.

Sensing that he was losing their attention, he shifted into storytelling mode. He told students that earlier in his career he was more focused on advancing the science of the climate crisis for other scientists than on educating students or the public about the problem. He felt little obligation to help the public understand the science. Students relaxed into their seats and nodded. Almost 70% of them were majoring in STEM fields, and they could relate to his point. Over the years, many of them had voiced similar observations in my FYW classes. Communicating any science-related topic to the public was a supposedly unnecessary skill for those pursuing future, and highly specialized, STEM careers. In other words, communication was a "soft skill" best left for the arts and humanities student.

However, Ramanathan surprised the students with what he said next. He revealed that his life's work took on greater meaning when something monumental happened in his life. The birth of his grandchildren awakened a new and deep urgency to advance his research and communicate that research to the public. He was terrified to realize that if he remained on the sidelines and out of public discourse his grandchildren might live through some of the most serious consequences of the climate crisis during their lifetimes. Leaning forward into the microphone, he explained that his grandchildren are only a few years younger than the students in the audience. He now had their attention.

After sharing this personal connection, he appealed to a shared passion for science in the room. Using pronouns like "we" and "us," he urged students to use their science interests to learn about the climate crisis and to research solutions. He told them that they will experience serious consequences in their lifetimes, but that there was time for everyone to work together to avoid the worst outcomes. He further clarified that students in all majors should work together to address climate change because solutions are needed in all aspects of society. When he finished this portion of his story, most students (including this author) felt inspired to use our respective skills and talents in pursuit of a larger social effort—we were joined together, as participants, in something greater than ourselves.

Ramanathan concluded his story and presentation by outlining some of the science and communication-related solutions that are most needed to address the climate crisis globally and locally. Importantly, he did not tell students what to do. Instead, he *invited* students to join him in the push for solutions across campus and in their local communities. His message was clear—he was willing to work for change, and he hoped they would join his efforts.[1]

When my students reflected on Ramanathan's presentation in our class discussion the following day, many agreed that Ramanathan's story about his grandchildren was the most meaningful part of the presentation. I pressed them for reasons. They explained that his story transformed him from a famous academic scientist talking about a complicated subject into a grandfather who wanted to care for his grandkids. In other words, he shifted from being a distant, objective scientist to someone to which they could relate. Surprisingly, instead of undermining his trust or credibility, his personal story invited trust, a sharing of common ground, and a new perspective on the topic. It helped stu-

---

1. See Ramanathan, "Climate Change Morphing," where he tells a similar story.

dents to recognize the urgency of the crisis in their own personal and familial terms; it even inspired some of them to take action.

Ramanathan's story illustrates a unique approach to narrative storytelling that inspires public trust in science and scientists. This approach is essential for climate science specifically, and science, or even STEM, communication more generally, especially at a time when such trust is declining (Kennedy). In Ramanathan's narrative approach to structure, I observe three specific moves that, when fused together, represent a version of what scholar and activist Marshall Ganz calls a "public narrative." According to Ganz, a public narrative is a three-part approach to public communication that includes: "a story of self," "a story of us," and "a story of now" (see Figure 1).

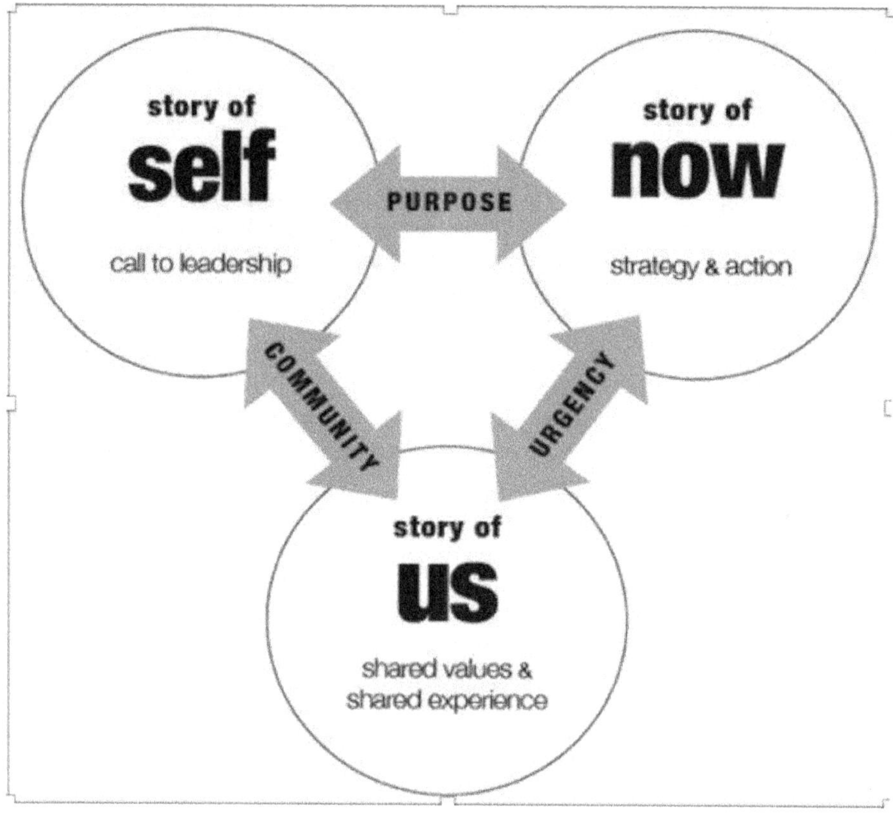

Figure 1: The Public Narrative (Ganz)

Ganz, a long-time labor activist for the United Farm Workers Movement, is both the innovator of the public narrative method and its biggest champion. He argues that public narratives allow individuals and groups to advocate for a social cause by combining the conventions of storytelling with the elements of persuasive and evidence-based writing. In other words, well-written public narratives motivate and inspire readers to join a cause or movement because the writer has connected their individual story with the shared values and experiences of intended audiences.

With its origins rooted in social and labor movements, the public narrative may at first seem out of place in a special issue devoted to developing science communication and trust among novice scientists and the public. Indeed, the genre itself has no explicit connection to science or science communication. Nor does Ganz himself specifically advocate for its usage in science classes or programs. Nevertheless, I argue that teaching STEM undergraduates how to write public narratives will prepare them to engage compassionately and effectively with non-expert audiences beyond the university. In my composition courses, I have witnessed public narratives transform students' understanding of how to communicate publicly in ways that build, rather than undermine, trusted relationships. They represent an important pedagogical tool in the toolboxes of FYW programs that are seeking to facilitate students' communication with non-expert audiences in all fields, but especially science.

My argument builds on the work of recent scholars in two related fields. First, there are those that argue that narrative storytelling is an effective and necessary science communication tool that should be taught with more regularity to undergraduate STEM students in colleges and universities (Brownell; Dahlstrom; Hayden; Kiernan; Priest). Second, some scholars argue that institutions should devote more intention and resources to integrating arts and humanities training with that of science and engineering (Kiernan; DeLuca). They maintain that writing, rhetoric, and composition scholars should take a more active role in equipping STEM students with the knowledge, skills, and practices to communicate effectively with a non-expert public. My project contributes to and expands on these perspectives by raising important questions that are still unanswered by the research. For example, is it enough to teach undergraduate science and engineering majors how to use narrative storytelling to communicate meaningfully with non-expert audiences? And what kind of storytelling approaches work best at building trust instead of dismantling it?

Marshall Ganz and the Public Narrative

When I first designed my lower-division composition course, I chose a climate change communication theme because I wanted students to think about foundations of writing and rhetoric through the lens of public communication. Approximately 65% of my students are STEM majors. The vast majority tend to be trusting of science and scientists, although they do represent a diverse range of perspectives on whether scientists are trusted communicators. Some students are open-minded about science skepticism, while others demonstrate little patience for people who are skeptical, distrustful, or even opposed to messages delivered by credentialed scientists. In course reflections and surveys, some students find writing to be necessary and essential to their own education and to public understanding of science. In contrast, others tend to assume that writing and communication skills are nonessential skills for STEM majors; these students tend to assume that responsibility for science distrust resides in a public that lacks proper scientific literacy. At times, these latter perspectives manifest into elitism, arrogance, and condescension toward those that do not share their views. This group of students struggles to relate to skeptical lay people who cannot share their love of science and their deep trust in scientific processes or even scientists themselves. Such mindsets illustrate the "us vs. them" attitude that Adam Hayden refers to in the public debates about science communication.

These contrasting and sometimes polarizing views present enormous challenges and opportunities for a FYW course. In a ten-week quarter, I want to teach students the foundations of strong academic writing and critical thinking. I structure the syllabus around three writing projects that scaffold into a final capstone project. Each project provides opportunities for students to learn and practice science writing and communication to public, non-science audiences by focusing on an issue for which there are high levels of documented public distrust of scientists. They learn the challenges of meaningfully communicating to audiences about complex science-related issues that are impacting the public good. By meaningful, I am referring to research developed by Michele Eodice, Anne Ellen Geller, and Neal Lerner in *The Meaningful Writing Project: Learning, Teaching, and Writing in Higher Education.* According to their findings, students find writing meaningful if they have some agency in choice of topic; if the context or message is relevant to their lives; if they can use it to make personal connections to their life experiences, family or family histories; and if the project has some future connection to their professional development, and/or social relationships and communities.

Science communication experts working at the intersections of science communication and undergraduate education also inspired my course theme and capstone project. In recent years, a growing number of scholars have argued that FYW programs and science communication programs should turn to narrative storytelling to prepare STEM students for communicating with non-science audiences (DeLuca; Kiernan, "Building Socioscientific Trust"). As Julia Kiernan argues, institutions should reject a rigid STEM approach to learning because "A STEAM approach…can prepare students for both outcomes as it has the capacity to complement socioscientific learning in its union of multiple perspectives and disciplines, positioning the comprehension of science topics as necessary and important to all members of society" ("Building Socioscientific Trust" 31). These approaches deliberately reject the notion that public distrust in science is rooted in science illiteracy or insufficient communication of science facts. Therefore, using research in the field of teaching climate science communication, I designed a narrative storytelling project. In my first iteration of the course and the project, students read about the causes, effects, and solutions of the climate crisis. I assign a wide variety of trusted research sources, including chapters from Veerabhadran Ramanathan's edited textbook, *Bending the Curve: Climate Change Solutions*, a textbook specifically written by University of California researchers for college student audiences. Students analyzed both the content and the writing of these sources. I introduced students to some of the research on science storytelling, and we analyzed the strategies that different storytellers would use to communicate science successfully to non-science audiences. Students then drafted their own climate stories. Some of the most powerful have stayed with me. Some wrote about having to evacuate from California wildfires. Others wrote about growing up with asthma and other health problems because they lived near an oil refinery that polluted the neighborhood with harmful toxins. Still others narrated stories of growing up in homes where climate science was rejected by family members, and how they felt confused by the paradox of loving science while rejecting climate science.

The strengths of these projects seem to reinforce the research on narrative storytelling in science communication. As Jon Christensen clarifies when it comes to communicating with public audiences, "Numbers numb, stories stick." However, while these early projects were certainly meaningful, both for the students and me, I questioned whether they were sufficient in building the kind of trust that researchers have identified as being a problem for climate skeptics. For example, some students felt drawn to telling stories that condescended to climate skeptics. Some student writers tried to narrate stories that concluded with blame and shame messages toward climate skeptics. And still others wrote narratives that focused on providing more science. These impulses are understandable. Most students trust the science, understand the urgency of the climate crisis, and are frustrated with systemic attempts to dismiss climate science and postpone taking serious actions to mitigate its effects. Nevertheless, these stories reinforce the same "us vs. them" mentality referenced earlier. They also illustrate the mistaken belief that scientific ignorance is always the problem when people doubt climate science. As Susan Fiske writes, "potential divides between scientists and the public are not merely about sheer knowledge in any simple way" (13593). It was at this point that I felt stuck. What was the best way to teach narrative storytelling and the importance of trust-building among writers and non-science audiences?

This is when I discovered Ganz's arguments about the importance of "public narratives." Ganz supports the idea that storytelling is a way to communicate effectively to audiences; however, his creation of the public narrative was designed to do more than just communicate stories. The purpose of the public narrative is to help leaders and organizations tell stories that will recruit support for transformative social movements. To fulfill such a purpose, narratives need to combine the elements of powerful storytelling with the communication of shared values.

According to Ganz, public narratives are structured in three interrelated parts. He classifies them as the story of self, the story of us, and the story of now. This unique three-part structure enables writers to communicate both a problem and a solution to that problem. Each part serves a purpose. The story of self introduces readers to the problem through the lens of the author's personal experiences. Writers communicate their experiences with the problem, the challenges or conflicts they experience, and how they have tried to overcome these challenges. In many ways, the story of self follows the common conventions of powerful narrative storytelling by encouraging writers to develop characters, plot tension, and a resolution. However, if the story of self is recognizable to most students, the story of us is not. The story of us represents a writer's attempt to shift from personal storytelling to direct communication with audiences and readers. Writers are challenged to name the common values and experiences that they share with readers, and to compose an inclusive "we" that invites them into a common struggle. Finally, the story of now offers writers a chance to communicate a solution to the problem. However, in doing so it offers an unexpected twist on the traditional proposal-driven approach to narrative storytelling. Instead of telling readers what *they* should do to solve the problem, the story of now begins with the writer's declaration of what they will do first and why they will do it. What actions need to be taken? What steps is the writer willing to follow? In beginning with this approach, the story of now transforms into a leadership invitation in which the writer invites the audience to join them in taking some future step.

What distinguishes public narratives from other genres of storytelling is that they are intentionally designed to help writers build trust with readers. They do this by identifying common ground between writer and audience. Public narratives, and the story of us, requires writers to demonstrate that they have listened to and understand the concerns that audiences may have about the climate crisis. Identifying common ground disrupts the typical argument-based approach to academic writing, which many of my students interpret as an either-or position in a debate that must be won. Student writers build trust when they meet the reader where they are, identify with the reader's ideological position, and use that shared common ground to build their story.

In the following sections, I outline and analyze my teaching strategies for assigning public narratives in my writing course focused on climate communication. As mentioned previously, I organize the class in three mini units that lead students toward the completion of their public narratives, which represent their final capstone projects in the class. In the first unit, students learn the foundations of climate science and climate communication. They write analytical reflections on their own experiences with the climate crisis and their personal engagement with climate science. In the second unit, students begin researching public audiences and varying levels of public distrust. They investigate possible public audiences for which they share common ground on these issues, and they compose analytical arguments about the best ways to communicate climate science to those audiences. In the third and final unit, students research the promises and challenges of both structural and individual climate solutions. They use this research, and their first two writing projects, to compose their public narratives.

The Story of Self

As described above, the story of self represents a writer's story of how and why they have been called to act on a certain issue, challenge, or problem. Ganz describes the story of self as "Why you were called to what you have been called to." Writers use personal storytelling elements to introduce readers to the problem that needs to be addressed. This requires the various elements of a good narrative structure, including plot, characterization, and setting. Writers introduce readers to a moment in their lives when they had to meet a challenge, overcome an obstacle, or come to some greater understanding about a topic or issue. As Ganz explains it, "The key focus is on choice points, moments in our lives when our values become real when we have to choose in the face of uncertainty" (2). Writers must become vulnerable as they reveal something about themselves, especially a struggle they have encountered. In these ways, they take on the role of a protagonist who is locked in a struggle to overcome an obstacle.

In preparing students to write climate-science driven stories of self, I begin the unit by asking students to reflect deeply on their prior knowledge of climate science itself. What do they know about the science of climate change? How well do they understand the causes of the climate crisis? The effects? Where did they learn these concepts? How trusting are they of science and scientists? How did they begin to trust the science, and the scientist, involved in this work? After doing these reflections, students read course materials designed to explain the complexities of climate science for public audiences.

These pre-writing exercises and reading assignments produce startling revelations for some students. Most students have never asked these reflective questions in an academic class. It is common for students who identify as pro-science STEM majors to be humbled by the complexities of this science. Another important recognition is that some students come to realize that age-appropriate lessons on climate science are not universal experiences for all students. Class discussions almost always reveal disparate perspectives among students when it comes to climate science. For example, some students identify as climate activists with strong trust of climate science. Other students voice confusion or even disinterest toward the research. Occasionally, some express distrust and skepticism toward it. Still others communicate how personal experiences with natural disasters have shifted their perspectives, raised their curiosities, and caused them to challenge science skepticism. For example, one student reflected on growing up in a politically conservative community and household. He was raised to be skeptical of climate change science until a series of category four and five hurricanes devastated his city. Surviving this trauma led him to question his own knowledge and to deepen his curiosity about the science behind these hurricanes. Similarly, another student shared that she had grown up questioning the severity and urgency of the climate crisis because her family identified with conservative political values. Based on family conversations, she had assumed that climate damage was a relatively minor problem that would never affect her or her family. That is, until wildfires forced her family to evacuate their home.

Reflecting on prior knowledge is essential because it provides pro-science STEM students with valuable opportunities to recall prior moments of science uncertainty. In these exercises, students face many realizations. Some realize that they do not understand climate science as much as they thought, which allows them to find common ground with those in the public who feel uncertainty about the complexities of the science. Others recall that they did not always trust climate science or scientists as strongly as they do right now. Again, this allows students to have compassion for those who are still feeling skepticism. Beginning with these foundations encourages students to compose meaningful stories of self that set the stage for trust-building with audiences. It allows them to name and frame the problem that their larger, public narrative will address.

However, composing meaningful stories of self presents significant intellectual and cognitive challenges for these STEM students. Many students are reluctant at first to even try blending narrative storytelling with science communication. Their hesitation is rooted in their limited exposure to narrative science writing combined with the assumption trap of binary thinking. Mariya Deykute refers to this binary thinking trap as the false dichotomy between creative thinking and scientific inquiry (21). Creating science-based stories of self generates an experience of cognitive dissonance among some students. They have been educated to believe that science is a process of identifying truth and fact based on an objective and unbiased analysis of data, while narrative storytelling is based on personal and political whims and biases. These oversimplified, contrasting belief systems have been internalized to such a degree that students struggle to see other perspectives: they express concern that science-based narrative storytelling is so biased that writers cannot be trusted; they have internalized the larger cultural messages that narrative communication is at odds with science and science communication and that science writers should never tell stories; they have been taught to "stick to the facts," and that if lay public audiences do not accept a particular view, it must be because they lack science literacy. I address these concerns by meeting students where they are; I acknowledge these views and validate their dissonance. I show them evidence that sometimes people who distrust climate science or climate scientists (and other forms of science) are highly educated people whose distrust stems from reasons other than knowledge deficits.

Ultimately, the unit is successful when students draft stories of self that introduce readers to the problem and frame problems of climate distrust in ways that audiences can relate to. Ganz summarizes this point, arguing,

> A good public story is drawn from the series of choice points that have structured the 'plot' of your life – the challenges you faced, choices you made, and outcomes you experienced….The story you tell of why you sought to lead allows others insight into your values, why you have chosen to act on them in this way, what they can expect from you, and what they can learn from you.

When students begin the process of writing stories driven by their experiences with climate change, or when they compose stories about how they first came to trust climate science, they begin to realize that they are doing the work of questioning the origins of their own belief systems. When did I first learn to trust climate science? How did my worldviews change or evolve throughout my childhood and adolescence? And as they share their drafts with their classmates in peer-driven revision processes, they begin thinking about what they share in common with others. They begin to think seriously about audiences that might find meaning and power in their stories.

The Story of Us

Once writers have composed a powerful story of self, the question becomes, who needs to read this climate story? How can climate stories construct a sense of trust among writer and readers so audiences are moved to some greater understanding or even new perspective on the issue? Or, how might readers be moved to take action? For Ganz the answers to these questions can be found in the most unique element of the public narrative genre: the story of us. Framed by Ganz through the inclusive us/we pronouns, the purpose of the story of us is for writers to identify and speak directly to an intended audience in their public narratives. As readers will recall, the purpose of the public narrative is to recruit intended audiences to join a cause, movement, or action (which is later communicated in the story of now). As Ganz teaches his students:

> Your challenge will be to define an 'us' upon whom you will call to join you in action motivated by shared values, values you bring alive through storytelling. However you define the "us" whom you hope to move, it must consist of *real people* with whom you can communicate, move or not move, engage or not engage, get to act or not." (my emphasis)

The story of us evokes a well-known anonymous maxim: "people do not care how much you know until they know how much you care." From what I have learned in teaching public narratives, this wisdom represents a crucial missing link in strategies for science communication.

Arguably one of the central problems for the public perception of scientists today is they do not care about the public good; scientists facing charges of elitism and condescension can respond through a well told story of us. This element of the public narrative promotes a sense of community among writers and readers. Central questions include, who are "we"? What do we stand for? What actions, principles or values defines us as an "us"? In Ganz's vision, the essential ingredient in the story of us recipe is the communication of shared values and experiences. It is best understood as an invitation of shared common ground. He explains, "One way we establish an 'us'—a shared identity—is through telling of shared stories, stories through which we can articulate the values we share, as well as the particularities that make us an 'us'" (3). Naming shared values promotes common ground among writers and readers. It also heightens the reader's sense of feeling seen, heard, and understood. In this way, the story of us plays a central role in bridging the gap between writers and audience, and it represents a unique and conflicted aspect of the genre for most students.

To begin this unit, I help students call forth a series of "us's" in their lives. In other words, we brainstorm the different groups, organizations, communities, and extended networks they belong or have belonged to. We define community broadly, beginning with extended family circles, but we also include youth groups, church groups, neighborhood groups, social, sports or recreational organizations, political groups, school-related groups and organizations, work-related groups, and academic discipline-based communities. Selecting a specific community is essential to telling the story of us. Nevertheless, students sometimes struggle to recall and name the communities to which they belong. Ganz's advice is instructive: "We are all part of multiple 'us's'—families, faiths, cultures, communities, organizations, and nations in which we participate with others. What community, organization, movement, culture, nation, or other constituency do you consider yourself to be part of, connected with? With whom do you share a common past? With whom do you share a common future?

To be effective, writers need to identify "real people" that they can communicate with, so beginning with possible audiences that students know and understand is a crucial step. Using a series of reflective questions, I ask them to narrow and eventually choose a community that will represent their intended audience or "us" for the project. For students who have rarely, if ever, invoked intended audiences in their academic writing, this aspect of the project is both challenging and exciting. They are excited to discover that writing for "real people" lends a sense of credibility and meaning to their academic writing that they have rarely encountered or been allowed to explore. For example, one student identified her college orchestra as a community that she wanted to communicate with about climate change. She understood those orchestra members to be disengaged on the issue of climate science and unaware of the carbon footprint of the orchestra's international travel schedule. She felt inspired by the challenge of communicating a meaningful message about climate science to an audience she knew well. Another student identified former members of a youth group who had been raised in conservative households; these students had been taught to question the accuracy and urgency of climate science. Using writing to connect with these former youth group members invigorated the student writer with a unique sense of meaning and possibility for their academic writing. Yet another student, who identified herself as a Latinx member of a U.S-Mexico border community, directed her public narrative toward multilingual neighbors in her home community. The opportunity to compose a meaningful message about climate change to her community was exciting because she felt as though this community was often ignored by media members, academics, and others in science communication.

Nevertheless, the potential for confusion and for misunderstanding the importance of choosing a community is high. For example, it is common for some students to select an intended audience "of people on YouTube." Another student recently brainstormed that they wanted to write to the people of Indonesia, his home country. In my experience, these choices stem from students' misguided belief that the project will be easier to write if the audience is large and general. Usually, the opposite is true. The larger and more generalized the audience, the more difficult it becomes to construct a meaningful story of us based on shared values and experiences. The more focused an audience, the easier it can be to balance the rhetorical choices necessary for an effective message. Therefore, I schedule one-on-one conferences and incentivize students to attend additional office hour coaching sessions. In these conversations, I guide students to sufficiently narrow their idea of community to a group whose demographics, values, and experiences about the climate crisis they tend to know and understand. In some cases, I also coach them to broaden their attention if their focus has become too narrow. When students have successfully worked through the challenge of community identification, they often come to several important realizations about writing and communication. First, they realize that *they* are the authorities on that community, not me (the instructor). And second, they recognize that to meet readers where they are, they will need to reflect on and listen deeply to the attitudes, beliefs, and knowledges that the chosen community possesses about the climate crisis.

The story of us teaches priniples of audience-driven communication designed to build trust among pro-science communicators and non-science audiences. One such principle is the Aristotelian rhetorical value of knowing the audience. Audience-driven communication challenges students to push past tendencies toward binary thinking and superficial labeling of communities that some students bring to the classroom. This is important for student writers that comprehend the data and the scientific consensus around the climate crisis but who struggle to communicate with audiences that are still processing the data and are unsure of how to interpret and draw conclusions about it. This is also valuable for students who are less familiar with the scientific consensus and are inclined to label their communities as either pro-science "believers" or anti-science "deniers." In class, we discuss the limitations of these positions and the nuances that writers miss when classifying audiences in these simplistic ways. Regarding this latter point, climate communication specialist Chui-Ling Tam points to the missed opportunities when communicators assume overly simplistic discourses and labeling of positional groups around this issue. She writes:

> It's simplistic to divide people into only two opposing camps of climate change: believers or deniers…between those two polarized positions are local populations living with the immediate effects of climate change on the environments they depend upon…The history and experience of individuals and communities may influence how they interpret and prioritize climate change. This diversity of lived experience and worldviews contradicts the divisions between climate change belief and denial. (Tam)

Tam's research encourages climate communicators to think locally when they target certain audiences with climate messages. She challenges readers to contextualize and consider how the lived experiences of individuals and communities might shape their attitudes, belief systems, and experiences with climate messaging. However, while Tam's insights are instructive, they are also difficult for pro-science students to grapple with. I dialogue with students about the emotional frustrations that pro-science students experience when confronting members of their communities that seem stubborn and close-minded. I ask them to reflect deeply on the limits of labeling audiences as "deniers." We review climate scientist Katharine Hayhoe's argument that, "if our goal is to label and dismiss whoever it is that we are speaking with or to, then that word [denier] will do it" (Hayhoe, "There Must Be More Productive Ways"). How does labeling close minds? How does labeling reduce opportunities for bridge building? How does labeling break trust? An essential part of the story of us is teaching students how to listen deeply and actively to the audiences they are addressing in their narratives. We practice these methods in class and use them to inspire more open-minded, curiosity-based approaches to composing stories of us.

I also introduce academic research to help students better understand the climate-science related knowledge, attitudes, and belief systems of their audiences. I assign Anthony Leiserowitz et al.'s long-term, ongoing research study, "Global Warming's Six America's." This study, first developed in 2008 and updated annually, is supported by the Yale Center for Climate Change Communication and is foundational to climate communication research. Its findings disrupt the popular media notion that there are two dominant perspectives on climate change in the United States: those that believe in climate change and those that do not. Instead, the study finds that American audiences exist on a wide spectrum of knowledge, attitudes, and beliefs about the climate crisis. They identify and classify six different groups that view the climate crisis from different perspectives.[2] I use this study to help students characterize and contextualize how much

---

2. On one side of the spectrum are the "alarmed" and the "concerned," who represent 33% and 25% of Americans, respectively, on this issue. Both groups tend to trust climate science when it comes to the causes and effects of climate change. However, they question the solutions that would work best to address the crisis. In the middle of the spectrum are the "cautious," representing 17% of Americans. The cautious face great uncertainty with climate science. They are neither sure of the causes and effects of the science, nor are they sure of the consensus of climate scientists on the issue. The

their audience understands the science and trusts the scientists doing this work. Understanding these questions sets the stage for the story of us that each will write.

Stories of us are central to the task of communicating trust among non-science audiences; yet, they are not without their risks, and there are no guarantees. Some audiences do not respond to inclusive writing or shared values, no matter how inclusive the story or how powerful the narrative. Nevertheless, although stories of us are the most challenging of the public narrative genre for most students, the leaps that students take and the courage they display in composing them is often the most inspirational part of the projects for me to read. Many experience what Ganz describes as the power to move others through an inclusive calling to shared values. He writes, "By telling our personal stories of challenges we have faced, choices we have made, and what we learned from the outcomes we can inspire others and share our own wisdom. Because stories allow us to express our values not as abstract principles, but as lived experience, they have the power to move others" (1).

The question is, move them to what?

The Story of Now

By the time they turn to part three, the story of now, students are asking the question, what can *we* do about this problem? The story of now is a call to what Ganz calls "hopeful action." This aspect of the public narrative communicates the exigency of the problem and the urgency of doing something collectively to address this conflict. In other words, what needs doing "now"? He contrasts his vision of "hopeful action" with what he describes as shallow "exhortation." He writes, "Leaders who only describe a problem, but fail to inspire us to act together to try to solve the problem, aren't good leaders…a 'story of now' is not simply a call to be for or against something—that's 'exhortation'—it is a call to take 'hopeful' action." Ganz elaborates, "A 'story of now" is urgent, it requires dropping other things and paying attention, it is rooted in the values you celebrated in your story of self and us, and a contradiction to those values that requires action." In other words, for Ganz, there is a significant difference between written texts that argue

---

have a lot of questions and are not sure whom to trust. Next are the "disengaged." The disengaged are the smallest group in the survey, coming in at 5% of those survey. As their name suggests, the disengaged are both uniformed and uninterested in climate science or the issue of climate change. They know very little about the urgency of the crisis, as few are communicating with them about the issue. Finally, on the other side of the spectrum are both the "doubtful" and the "dismissive." These two groups represent 10% and 9% of Americans, respectively. Both groups have been persuaded that climate scientists cannot be trusted on this issue. The doubtful are pretty sure climate change is either not happening, or it is caused by natural forces (and not greenhouse gas emissions). The dismissive tend to believe that climate scientists cannot be trusted. Furthermore, they are nearly certain that the issue is a hoax. As the study suggests, all groups struggle to fully understand or even trust climate science. As the diversity of perspectives in this study highlights, meaningful conversation that builds trust among writers and audiences is essential on this issue.

for a problem and written proposals that both name a problem and inspire readers to join collectively to address that problem.

Ganz's vision for solution-oriented communication represents an "exercise in leadership." Writers exercise this leadership when they first identify solutions to a problem that *they* are willing to organize, join, or support themselves, instead of proposing that readers take action on their own. In other words, writers *invite* readers to *them* in a more collective effort to address the problem. He uses an instructive example to clarify the uniqueness of his vision:

> If you ask me to "change a light bulb," for example, to deal with climate change, do you really think it will happen? Especially if it's among 100 other things I might—or might not—do? But if you ask me to join you in persuading the Kennedy School to change all of its light bulbs by signing a student petition, joining you in a delegation to the dean, and, adding my name to a public list of KSG students who have committed to changing the light bulbs where they live, what do you think the odds are of success?

There are two points worth highlighting in Ganz's advice to writers. First, stories of now should never be reduced to proposals that individual readers must take to solve the problem. The example of the lightbulb clarifies this misconception. Ganz deliberately rejects the individuality of changing a lightbulb because the action is solitary, isolated, and ultimately insufficient for addressing the larger systemic problem of climate change. He contrasts this individualist approach with an example of social organizing. He encourages the writer to initiate a collective effort that is both scalable and multi-faceted. This leads to the second point that in a story of now writers are not sitting idly by and watching from a distance as they tell readers to solve a problem on their own; rather, writers must commit to some new action first, why those actions will address the problem, and why readers should "join" these efforts. Ganz describes the public narrative as a form of leadership that transforms the proposal into an invitation.

When it comes to the climate crisis, the challenges posed by Ganz's story of now are immediately clear to students. What solutions are most needed to address the crisis? What solutions are students committed to taking? To respond to these questions, we read solution-oriented course materials highlighting scientific solutions (Ramanathan and Cole). However, it is common for students to still feel overwhelmed by the size and scope of the problem. Therefore, we focus on the importance of local solutions and scalability (Hayhoe, "Connecting Global Change"); we also read about the power of social movements (Han). Students also research local movements already committed to doing the work that they (and others) may be willing to join.

Two additional challenges regularly present themselves with this part of the unit. One involves the challenge of teaching students how to understand the complexity of solutions in a ten-week quarter so they can identify something they are willing to do and then invite others to join them. As a compromise, I encourage students to focus on stories of now that propose new understandings or ways of thinking. Students often struggle to integrate solutions with stories of self and us. Trust building solutions are those that match the story of self, us, and now and that consider the audience's prior knowledge, attitudes, and beliefs about the crisis. Thus, I conference with students to provide valuable feedback about how to unify the three elements of their projects. We also do a round of peer-review workshops so that students can discuss their ideas and drafts with similarly situated audiences. In other words, peer discussions become a necessary opportunity to learn whether their stories are unified and whether their strategies for building trust are effective.

Conclusion

In my contribution to this special issue, I have argued that narrative storytelling is an effective science communication tool that should be taught with more regularity in colleges and universities, including FYW programs. Public narratives represent a necessary intervention for bridging the larger communication gaps that are widening levels of distrust among scientists and science-skeptical publics across the country. They are built on three elements that undergraduate STEM students need significantly more knowledge and training in as they prepare to engage the public in their areas of professional specialization; these areas include storytelling their own experiences with skepticism and distrust, the rejection of condescension, labeling and dismissiveness, and a compassionate approach to listening and understanding audiences that seem skeptical or even opposed to science. In the coming decades, as science-related crises become even more urgent, educators have a vital role to play in preparing STEM students to communicate meaningfully across differences. Public narratives represent an important part of that bridge, for they help students to take risks with their writing, stand on common ground with others, and motivate others to act on the challenges we face together.

Works Cited

Brownell, Sara E., Jordan V. Price, and Lawrence Steinman. "Science Communication to the General Public: Why We Need to Teach Undergraduate and Graduate Students this Skill as Part of Their Formal Scientific Training." *Journal of Undergraduate Neuroscience Education (JUNE): A Publication of FUN, Faculty for Undergraduate Neuroscience* vol. 12, no.1, 2013, pp. E6-E10.

Christensen, Jon. "Climate gloom and doom? Bring it on. But we need stories about taking action, too." *The Conversation*, 8 Aug. 2017. https://theconversation.com/climate-gloom-and-doom-bring-it-on-but-we-need-stories-about-taking-action-too-79464

Dahlstrom, Michael F. "Using Narratives and Storytelling to Communicate Science with Nonexpert Audiences." *Proceedings of the National Academy of Sciences*. Vol. 111, Supplement 4, 2014, pp. 13614-13620. https://www.pnas.org/content/111/Supplement_4/13614

Deykute, Mariya. "All Scientists Should Write Poetry: Creative Writing as Essential Academic Practice. *The Journal of the Assembly for Expanded Perspectives on Learning*, vol. 27, 2022, pp. 21-38.

DeLuca, Katelynn. "Gaining STEAM: The Integral Role of Composition in an Increasingly STEM World." Kao and Kiernan, pp. 17-29.

Eodice, Michele, Anne Ellen Geller, and Neal Lerner. *The Meaningful Writing Project: Learning, Teaching, and Writing in Higher Education.* Boulder, Colorado UP, 2016.

Ganz, Marshall. What Is Public Narrative: Self, Us and Now. Working paper, Harvard Kennedy School, 2009. http://nrs.harvard.edu/urn-3:HUL.InstRepos:30760283

Han, Hahrie, and Niemann, Michelle. "Your Leadership: Social Movements and Social Solutions to Climate Change." Ramanathan, pp. 5.2-5.21.

Hayden, Adam. "Exploring the citizen-science partnership through narrative-based science communication." *PLOS SciComm Blog.* 11 Oct. 2017. https://scicomm.plos.org/2017/10/11/exploring-the-citizen-science-partnership-through-narrative-based-science-communication/

Hayhoe, Katharine. "Connecting Global Change to Local Impacts & Solutions." *Vimeo,* uploaded by Third Coast Disrupted, 8 Sept. 2021. https://vimeo.com/464643206

Hayhoe, Katharine. "There Must Be More Productive Ways to Talk about Climate Change." *NPR,* Interview with Rachel Martin, 9 May 2017. https://www.npr.org/2017/05/09/527541032/there-must-be-more-productive-ways-to-talk-about-climate-change.

Kao, Vivian, and Julia Kiernan, editors. *Writing STEAM: Composition, STEM, and a New Humanities.* Routledge, 2022.

Kennedy, Brian, ALEC TYSON AND CARY FUNK. "Americans' Trust in Scientists, Other Groups Declines." *Pew Research Center*, 15 Feb 2022, Washington D.C.

Kiernan, J. E. "The assembly and circulation of science: An analysis of the necessity (yet lack) of narrative strategies in STEM curricula." *Communication & Language at Work*, vol. 6, no.1, pp. 16–24. https://doi.org/10.7146/claw.v6i1.113920

Kiernan, Julia E. "Building Socioscientific Trust is a Post-Secondary Obligation: Preparing STEM Students to Communicate and Engage with Public Audiences." Kao and Kiernan, pp. 30-45.

Leiserowitz, Anthony, Edward Maibach, Seth Rosenthal, John Kotcher, Matthew Ballew, Jennifer Marlon, Jennifer Carman, Marija Verner, Sanguk Lee, Teresa Myers, and Matthew Goldberg. *Global Warming's Six Americas, December 2022.* Yale University and George Mason University. New Haven, CT: Yale Program on Climate Change Communication, March 2023. https://climatecommunication.yale.edu/publications/global-warmings-six-americas-december-2022/

Priest, Susanna. *Communicating Climate Change: The Path forward.* Palgrave Macmillan, 2016.

Ramanathan, Veerabhadran. "Climate Change Morphing into an Existential Threat." The Planetary Emergency Lecture Series, 21 Feb 2018, Creighton University, Omaha, NE. Keynote Address.

Ramanathan, Veerabhadran, editor. *Bending the Curve: Climate Change Solutions.* U of California P, 2019.

Ramanathan, Veerabhadran and Cole, Jonathan. "Overview of the Ten Solutions for Bending the Curve." Ramanathan, pp. 4.2-4.44.

Tam, Chui-Ling, "Why We Should Stop Labelling People Climate Change Deniers." *The Conversation,* 3 Dec. 2018. https://theconversation.com/why-we-should-stop-labelling-people-climate-change-deniers-105555

Storying Science: Preparing STEM Students to Engage with Discipline-Specific and Public Audiences through the TED(x) Genre

Erica M. Stone and Sarah E. Austin

Abstract: *Communicating about science with public audiences is becoming increasingly important for STEM students, both during their studies and once they enter a specific scientific workplace. Using two different general education writing courses as case examples, one at Middle Tennessee State University and one at the United States Air Force Academy Preparatory School, this article offers a model for how the rhetorical structure of the TED(x) presentation genre can be used to prepare STEM-focused students to better engage with non-expert audiences. Through narrative reflection and assignment examples, we build on Joshua Schimel's framework for communicating science and provide a replicable model for general education writing faculty to ensure STEM students understand how to 1) Compel audiences to listen/read through engaging content; 2) Compose writing and speech genres in memorable structures; 3) Communicate with non-expert audiences with accessible language.*

Introduction

Recent trends in the production and dissemination of STEM research make it imperative that students of these disciplines are equipped to utilize, critique, and communicate scientific research in accessible and transparent ways.[1] Over the last two decades, approaches to STEM research and teaching have slowly shifted from siloed, discipline-specific publications in prestigious academic journals to interdisciplinary conversations in a variety of media. This onto-epistemological shift in value is due, in part, to stakeholders renewed interest in public impact and engagement. For example, organizations like the National Science Foundation (NSF) and the National Aeronautics and Space Administration (NASA) now require the primary investigators on their funded projects to develop a plan for public engagement. Unfortunately, the result is often less than robust, with researchers meeting the requirement with an afterthought hybrid genre like a blog translation, or a non-linear Twitter thread. Since newcomers to scientific fields largely overlook how technologies and sciences are unequally prescribed, controlled, and delegated (Haas and Eble), teaching communication to STEM students requires a multifaceted approach that enables students to comfortably bridge disparate onto-epistemological traditions (Cagle).

Using case examples from our STEM-populated, undergraduate classes at Middle Tennessee State University (MTSU) and the United States Air Force Academy Prepara-

---

1. At the time of this essay's authoring, Erica was serving as an assistant professor of English and Associate Director of General Education English at Middle Tennessee State University. At the time of publication, she is a content designer and independent scholar.

tory School (USAFAPS), we outline one strategy for teaching STEM students how to communicate with non-expert audiences using the rhetorical structure of the TED(x) genre. Through narrative reflection and an assignment example, we build on Joshua Schimel's work and provide a replicable model for general education writing faculty to ensure STEM students can:

1. Compel audiences to listen/read through engaging content

1. Compose writing and speech genres in memorable structures

1. Communicate with non-expert audiences with accessible language

In the sections below, we summarize the General Education Writing Curricula at each of our institutions, so readers are better able to understand the parameters of our case examples and apply our portable assignment model to their own institutions. Notably, each of our writing sequences utilizes a rhetorical approach to teaching writing, where students are introduced to key rhetorical concepts such as rhetorical situation (audience, context, culture, purpose, author), genre, and rhetorical appeals. Later in our chapter, we share an assignment that offers guidance for how to teach students about the rhetorical structure of a TED(x) talk and how it can be used to discuss complex ideas.

Institutional Profiles

Middle Tennessee State University

Middle Tennessee State University (MTSU) is one of six locally governed public universities in the state of Tennessee and has consistently been ranked as one of the best universities in the nation by the Princeton Review. Founded on September 11, 1911 as a normal school dedicated to teacher training and the public good, MTSU has quickly grown into one of the largest universities in the state with over 80 degree programs, approximately 35 departments, and an annual undergraduate enrollment of approximately 20,000. As a comprehensive university, MTSU's mission focuses on serving Middle Tennessee through research, teaching, and service projects that "develop and sustain academic partnerships, entrepreneurial activities, and public service to support instruction, research, and communities throughout the region" (Mission Statement). Because of its central location and proximity to Nashville, MTSU offers students a wealth of opportunities to pursue careers in the recording and entertainment industries as well as science and technology fields.

United States Air Force Academy Preparatory School

USAFAPS is housed on the same campus as the United States Air Force Academy (USAFA) in Colorado Springs, Colorado. Founded in May of 1961, the Prep School each year enrolls around 240 direct high school graduates and enlisted service members between the ages of 17 and 22. These students are called cadet-candidates (C/Cs). The Prep School program is a ten-month academic, military, and athletic program that prepares promising individuals for the rigors of the USAFA and, ultimately, to be leaders of character and officers in the U.S. Air and Space Forces. The Prep School's most important purpose is to diversify the Air Force officer corps so that it more accurately represents the men and women it leads, as well as the citizens of the United States. The Prep School's academic curricula focuses largely on STEM since the USAFA's curriculum is STEM-specific: all students, regardless of major, graduate with a Bachelor of Science degree.

Filling the Gap in Science Communication Education

Traditionally, science research has been written for scientific audiences (Bazerman). As a result, STEM writing classes have a responsibility to teach students how to consume, critique, and communicate scientific research in accessible and transparent ways. If we ignore this responsibility, we aren't fully educating STEM students for the kind of communication situations they are likely to encounter. While there aren't many models for how to train STEM students to engage with discipline-specific (expert) and public (non-expert) audiences, the rhetorical structure of TED(x) talks offers science communication educators a foundation for thinking about how to shift our writing pedagogies toward a more responsive approach for science communication that values navigating between discipline-specific and public-facing discourse. Based on our lived experiences as both faculty and administrators at MTSU and USAFAPS, we aim to move the current conversation about science communication and STEM-focused writing curricula forward by offering a portable model for engaging STEM students in critical thinking, audience analysis, and rhetorical engagement. Because the American National Academies of Science, Engineering, and Medicine (NASEM) suggests that science communicators need to be prepared to "share the findings and excitement of science," and "increase knowledge and understanding of science" (National Academies 2), we argue that the TED(x) genre provides an ideal rhetorical structure for teaching STEM students to communicate subject-specific ideas and processes with non-expert audiences in an accessible format.

Teacher-scholars across disciplines use TED(x) talks to encourage students to consider the rhetorical structures of the genre (Kendrowicz & Taylor, 2016; Lui, 2017; Masi, 2020) or to locate models for exemplary oral communication (Chang & Huang, 2015; Ludewig, 2017). Within our own discipline of Technical and Professional Communication (TPC), Michele Simmons reminds us that citizens are not necessarily non-experts and should be included in policy decisions. Similarly, scientific research approaches and traditional research publication practices juxtapose with feminist epistemologies, which accept "that knowledge is always provisional, open-ended and relational." This poststructuralist feminist position suggests that we cannot claim single-strategy pedagogies of empowerment, emancipation, and liberation (Luke and Gore 7) particularly within the context of STEM classrooms. Since technologies and sciences are unequally prescribed, controlled, and delegated, a reality that is largely overlooked by newcomers to scientific fields (Haas and Eble), teaching communication to STEM students requires a multifaceted approach that enables students to comfortably bridge disparate onto-epistemological traditions. As we embark on pedagogical practices that seek to teach students how to interrogate, influence, and interject in their communication, we (as educators) need to provide STEM students the support and tools to negotiate the cognitive dissonances that will inevitably arise as they shift among communication purposes and audiences.

Engaging students in open dialogue between science and citizens makes information more transparent and knowledge exchange possible. Using case examples from our STEM-populated general education writing classes at MTSU and the USAFAPS, we narrate the possibilities for teaching students to engage with non-expert audiences on environmental science and responsible reuse practices. In order to teach STEM students how to "transition into professionals that realize and uphold 'scientific citizenship'" (Irwin, qtd. in Nerlich) and value public audiences, we apply the rhetorical structure of TED(x) talks to teaching scientific writing and public engagement. We discuss the rhetorical structure of TED(x) talks further in the next section. In each of our writing classes, students wrote and delivered TED(x) talks followed by conversational critiques that mimic the kind of reciprocal journalism (Lewis, Holton, and Coddington) that occurs in the comments sections of many TED(x) talks and science translation articles. We argue that these types of assignments prepare STEM students to communicate through both discipline-specific and public-facing genres.

Engaging the TED(x) Rhetorical Structure in STEM Writing Assignments

TED (Technology, Entertainment, and Design) is a nonprofit that aims to foster a "global community, welcoming people from every discipline and culture who seek a deeper understanding of the world" that believes "passionately in the power of ideas to change attitudes, lives and, ultimately, the world." Secondary to the global network of intellectuals and artists, TED is working to build TED.com into "a clearinghouse of free knowledge from the world's most inspired thinkers—and a community of curious souls to engage with ideas and each other, both online and at TED and TEDx events around the world" ("How TEDx Started"). TED Conferences are large events held once per year and sponsored by the TED franchise, whereas TEDx events are independently organized and financed by smaller organizations, often nonprofits or universities. Even though TED(x) conferences and events occur all over the world, most people know TED by the short video talks they produce. While these talks are almost always recorded during TED conferences where speakers present their ideas to a live audience, most TED talk fans know the brand and genre by its recorded talks and online presence on YouTube, Facebook, Twitter, Netflix, and of course, TED.com.

By design, the TED(x) genre adheres to a particular cadence and organizational pattern that has become ubiquitous among scholars, entertainers, and advocates. In recent years, TED(x) talks have become a popular media outlet for three groups: public intellectuals, scientists, and academics who want to translate their research for a broader audience; artists who have a unique art form that lends itself to a stage and a time constraint; and people who have experienced trauma and have a universal lesson to share from their lives. When a listener presses play on a recorded TED(x) talk, they have certain expectations: the talk will be between 5-18 minutes long; the speaker will be (somewhat of) an expert on their topic; and, more than likely, the talk will begin with a narrative, a personal story. Because human beings have "always been storytellers or homo narrans" (Young 4), the rhetorical structure of a TED(x) talk offers comforting patterns and predictability. Similarly, TED(x) Talks pay attention to rhetorical style. They "collapse the distance between intellectuals and broader publics" by making information accessible through narratives and a specific organizational pattern (Young 7). By adhering to a predictable pattern, TED(x) has built a brand and genre that is internationally recognized and serves as a venue sharing complicated ideas in plain language using accessible media.

Building on Joshua Schimel's impactful book, *Writing Science*, we argue that a storied approach to communicating science through the rhetorical structure of TED(x) talks offers STEM students a low-stakes opportunity to practice communicating outside of the narrow confines of their disciplines and "become better storytellers" (Schimel 10). Because scientists are often trained to engage technical and subject-specific guidance who are most interested in the results of a study, they often forget to engage in audience analysis and responsive writing practices like anticipating questions or even posing rhetorical questions to provide inquiry and further discussion. TED(x) talks offer a rhetorical structure that encourages students to experiment with data analysis and presentation in a way that is engaging and transparent, two key factors in successful science communication, according to Schimel (12-13). Following Schimel's suggestions, we ask our STEM writing students to "consider the three aspects to effective storytelling: 1) content, 2) structure, and 3) language" (14). First, students are asked to translate their content for a non-expert audience using simpler terminology, metaphors, images, and narrative examples. Next, students model their presentations after TED(x) talks that resonate with them; since TED(x) has a vast repository of scientific and/or disciplinary talks to choose from, the models for students are legion. Last, students are given a lesson in how to draft, edit, and use plain language to describe their ideas. We use examples from Russell Willerton's *Plain Language and Ethical Response: A Dialogic Approach to Technical Content in the 21st Century* and Anna Young's *Prophets, Gurus, and Pundits: Rhetorical Styles and Public Engagement*.

Designing a Replicable TED(x) Assignment Model for STEM Students

Through narrative reflection and an assignment example (see Appendix A), we designed a replicable model for general education writing faculty to ensure STEM students can accomplish the following goals and objectives:

1. Compel audiences to listen/read through engaging content

   SLO 1: Students will be able to use the rhetorical structures of a TEDx talk to engage peer and faculty audiences.

2. Compose writing and speech genres in memorable structures

   SLO 2: Students will be able to accurately write and perform a TEDx speech based on the genre conventions.

3. Communicate with non-expert audiences with accessible language

SLO 3: Students will be able to translate complicated information into legible and user-friendly language that follows the patterns of TEDx.

Following Schimel's process for thinking about science writing as storytelling, our model assignment asks students to conduct primary research to find exemplar TED(x) talks that communicate scientific ideas through engaging content, memorable rhetorical structures, and accessible language. After locating several exemplars, STEM students in our writing courses are required to map the three-part rhetorical structure of each TED(x) talk: 1) personal story, 2) fact-based lesson, 3) call to action using a visual organizer like Figure 1: Mapping the Rhetorical Structure of TED(x) Talks.

TED(x) Talk	Rhetorical Structures		
	Personal Story	**Fact-based Lesson**	**Call to Action**
Bill Gates' (2014) "The next outbreak? We're not ready" is a TED(x) genre model for thinking about engaging graphics and video in addition to simplifying and (*accurately!*) summarizing what might happen if the world were to encounter a deadly respiratory virus that was both airborne and highly contagious.	Bill Gates begins his TED(x) talk with a short, personal anecdote comparing his primary worry about a nuclear war as a kid instead to our current concerns about a global pandemic.	After his anecdote, Gates retrospectively examines the 2013 Ebola outbreak, outlining examples of how governments and healthcare systems failed and discussing the challenges that epidemiologies might face in another pandemic like the Spanish Flu of 1918.	Finally, Gates closes his talk with a call to action and a look toward the future, asking his audience members to we, namely developed, first-world countries, might prepare our local and national budgets, vaccine distribution plans, and healthcare systems to handle a future contagious disease outbreaks or pandemics (e.g., the COVID-19 outbreak and the 2020-2021 vaccine distribution process).

Fig. 1 Mapping the Rhetorical Structure of TED(x) Talks: An Exemplar

Recognizing it as an exemplar for all three areas of the rhetorical structure, one student at USAFA referenced Bill Gates' "The next outbreak? We're not ready" as a TED(x) genre model for thinking about engaging graphics and video in addition to simplifying and (*accurately!*) summarizing what might happen if the world were to encounter a deadly respiratory virus that was both airborne and highly contagious. Since TED(x) talks often begin with a storied introduction, students are easily able to understand the role of storytelling within science communication. Not only does storytelling break down terminology and disciplinary barriers, but it also encourages students to begin to see the intersection between the humanities and the sciences. For example, Bill Gates begins his TED(x) talk with a short, personal anecdote comparing his primary worry about a nuclear war as a kid to current societal concerns about a global pandemic. After his anecdote, Gates retrospectively examines the 2013 Ebola outbreak, outlines examples of how governments and healthcare systems failed, and discusses the challenges that epidemiologists might face in another pandemic like the Spanish Flu of 1918. Finally, Gates closes his talk with a call to action and a look toward the future, asking his audience members, namely developed, first-world countries, how they might prepare local and national budgets, vaccine distribution plans, and healthcare systems to handle a future contagious disease outbreaks or pandemics (e.g., the COVID-19 outbreak and the 2020-2021 vaccine distribution process). Gates' three-part rhetorical structure (personal story, fact-based lesson, call to action) offers STEM students a replicable model for composing their own speech scripts and accompanying media (e.g., slide decks, videos, music) for their TED(x) assignments (see Appendix A: Assignment Sheet).

At the USAFA Prep School the initial assignment in the course Academic Research asks students to identify a current problem that needs solving. All enrolled students have already taken a prerequisite course on Academic Argumentation that outlines Aristotelian rhetoric (to include the rhetorical situation and the rhetorical triangle), Burke's Parlor, and the notion of academic conversations. Students are required to pursue a problem-solution that is academic in nature, rather than philosophical or ethical, exigent, and narrow. That is, they identify an issue that is currently problematic for a specific group of people in a specific place (specific places, demographics, and contexts work best given that our courses are only 9 weeks long).

After conducting primary research and locating at least three exemplar TED(x) talks to emulate, STEM writing students are asked to translate their problem-solution into a TED(x) talk format. We consider the TED(x) format to be part of the students' writing and thinking processes, akin to conference presentations by professors, and encourage students to provide feedback and ask questions of their peers-as-observers. Each TED(x) talk must follow TED genre conventions including an engaging story, fact-based lessons, and a call to action to encourage a paradigm shift among the listeners or readers. Students develop visual aids as well as a fully accessible transcript to accompany their TED(x) talks. The student audience members, and any attending faculty or staff (we always invite our faculty and staff to attend and participate), are asked to complete a short feedback form (see Appendix B) to emphasize the process-oriented nature of research, provide constructive criticism, ask questions, and push students to consider other angles their research might take. The presenting student is allowed to ask follow-up questions, and receives the feedback forms each audience member completes during the following class period so that s/he can utilize the comments to improve their research, their final essay, and their presentation. Many students choose to use their TED(x) story as their essay's "hook" and are able to refine their thesis, hone their problem and solution discussions, and reorganize their argument to make the final written product more effective. Student course evaluations often mention the TED(x) talk as being the moment they really understood what they were arguing and how it should be framed for the final essay.

Adoption and Adaptation of Storying Science with the TED(x) Genre

As we reflect back on our assignment design and pedagogical narratives, we see many possible avenues for adoption and adaptation across STEM fields, digital humanities, and interdisciplinary courses. As Sarah's student demonstrates in his example, scientific problems are also humanitarian problems. When we teach students to engage with science from a rhetorical approach that engages personal story, facts and research, and calls to action, science communication education has the potential to impact students' overall learning experiences in addition to meeting university learning outcomes (ULOs). While we do consider our assignment sheet to be replicable and portable to other institutions and STEM disciplines, we do understand that some adjustments will need to be made to accommodate program outcomes and assessment expectations. To accommodate any limitations or challenges faculty may encounter when adopting or adapting our assignment sheet (see Appendix A), we suggest thinking about the assignment sheet as an editable template that can be changed to meet your own pedagogical, departmental, programmatic, and institutional needs. By using a flexible rhetorical approach, our assignment model engages STEM students with a variety of genres and an opportunity to push and polish their own knowledge of discipline-specific language and public discourse.

Works Cited

"Aerospace." Middle Tennessee State University, 2020, https://www.mtsu.edu/aerospace/

Bazerman, Charles. "Scientific Writing as a Social Act: A Review of the Literature of the Sociology of Science." *New Essays in Technical and Scientific Communication: Research, Theory, and Practice*, edited by Paul V. Anderson, John Brockman, & Carolyn Rude Miller, Baywood Press, 1982, pp. 156-184.

Cagle, Lauren E. "Becoming 'Forces of Change': Making a Case for Engaged Rhetoric of Science, Technology, Engineering, and Medicine." *Poroi*, vol. 12, no. 2, 2017, pp. 2151-2957.

Chang, Yu-jung, and Hung-Tzu Huang. "Exploring TED talks as a pedagogical resource for oral presentations: A corpus-based move analysis." *English Teaching and Learning*, 39.4 (2015): 29-62. Academia.edu.

Core Curriculum. United States Air Force Academy, 2023, usafa.edu/academics/core-curriculum/

Dorpenyo, Isidore Kafui. "Mapping a Space for a Rhetorical-Cultural Analysis: A Case of Scientific Proposal." *Journal of Technical Writing and Communication*, vol. 45, 2015, pp. 226–242.

Haas, Angela M., & Eble, Michelle F., editors. *Key Theoretical Frameworks: Teaching Technical Communication in the Twenty- First Century*. Utah State University Press, 2018.

"How TEDx Started." TEDx WinterPark. https://tedxwinterpark.com/how-tedx-started/.

Kedrowicz, April A., and Julie L. Taylor. "Shifting rhetorical norms and electronic eloquence: TED talks as formal presentations." *Journal of Business and Technical Communication,* vol. 30, no. 3, 2016, pp. 352-377.

Lewis, Seth C., Avery E. Holton, and Mark Coddington. 2014. "Reciprocal Journalism: A Concept of Mutual Exchange between Journalists and Audiences." *Journalism Practice* vol 8, no. 2, 2014, pp. 229–241.

Liu, Zhe, et al. "Fostering user engagement: Rhetorical devices for applause generation learnt from ted talks." *Proceedings of the international aaai conference on web and social media,* vol. 11, no. 1, 2017.

Ludewig, Julia. "TED Talks as an emergent genre." *CLCWEB-Comparative Literature and Culture,* vol. 19, no.1, 2017.

Masi, Silvia. "The multimodal representation of "Ideas worth spreading" through TED Talks." *Lingue e Linguaggi,* vol. 36, 2020, pp. 155-171.

"Mission Statement." Middle Tennessee State University, 2020, https://mtsu.edu/about/mission.php

Schimel, Joshua. *Writing Science: How to Write Papers That Get Cited and Proposals That Get Funded.* Oxford University Press, 2012.

Simmons, Michelle. *Participation and Power: A Rhetoric for Civic Discourse in Environmental Policy.* State University of New York Press, 2007.

Willerton, Russell. *Plain Language and Ethical Action: A Dialogic Approach to Technical Content in the 21st Century.* Routledge, 2015.

Xue Zhao, José Luis Vázquez-Gutiérrez, Daniel P. Johansson, Rikard Landberg, and Maud Langton. *PLoS One,* volume 11, no. 2, 2016, p. e0147791.

Young, Anna M. *Prophets, Gurus, and Pundits: Rhetorical Styles and Public Engagement.* Southern Illinois University Press, 2014.

Appendix A: Assignment Sheet

Purpose

The purpose of this assignment is to teach STEM students to think rhetorically about engaging with disciplinary-specific and public-facing audiences by:

1. Compel audiences to listen/read through engaging content

    SLO 1: Students will be able to use the rhetorical structures of a TEDx talk to engage peer and faculty audiences.

2. Compose writing and speech genres in memorable structures

    SLO 2: Students will be able to accurately write and perform a TEDx speech based on the genre conventions.

3. Communicate with non-expert audiences with accessible language

    SLO 3: Students will be able to translate complicated information into legible and user-friendly language that follows the patterns of TEDx.

Description

This assignment asks students to conduct primary research to find exemplar TED(x) talks that communicate scientific ideas through engaging content, memorable rhetorical structures, and accessible language. After locating several exemplars, STEM students in our writing courses are required to map the three-part rhetorical structure of each TED(x) talk: 1) personal story, 2) fact-based lesson, 3) call to action using a visual organizer like Figure 1: Mapping the Rhetorical Structure of TED(x) Talks.

TED(x) Talk

For this assignment, you will develop a 6-8 minute TED(x) talk on an aspect of your Problem-Solution Essay. Try your best to restructure your paper into the three-part rhetorical structure of TED(x) talk, see Figure 1 for a detailed example. You should spend approximately 1 minute on a personal story, 4-5 minutes on fact-based history/problem/attempted solutions/probable causes, and 1-2 minutes on your call to action/solution.

Delivery & Visual Aids

1. Engage & Involve: Speak conversationally and passionately, and connect (directly and indirectly) with your classmates.

2. Use Visual Aids, Not Visual Crutches: Use simple, elegant, and clean visuals to enhance and illuminate your message; allow your visuals to serve as your memory prompts. Consult with your instructor if you think you'll need more than the computer and projector.

Appendix B: Audience Feedback Form

Problem student poses	
Solution offered	
Thesis/Argument	
What could be better? (Organization, hook, word-choice, flow, depth, clarity of ideas, evidence)	
What worked? (Be specific)	

Fig. 2

Getting Beyond "CRAAP": Scientific Literacy in FYW and WAD

Erica Duran and Lauren Mecucci Springer

Abstract: While first-year writing (FYW) programs often bear the responsibility for teaching students to write across the disciplines (Downs and Wardle), too often students restrict the concepts learned in FYW to the humanities, or even worse, a single class. Moreover, students frequently complete research assignments in FYW which restrict them to scholarly or peer-reviewed sources, hindering their ability to learn how to assess popular sources. This can be especially problematic with scholarly STEM sources, which are laden with unfamiliar technical terms. Although the writing and research skills learned in FYW are often intended to be interdisciplinary, FYW faculty have opportunities to make these courses more relevant and useful to students interested in pursuing STEM majors or careers. We argue FYW is a critical space, allowing us to help students learn how to find, assess, and process scientific information, while simultaneously teaching students how the rhetorical situation (i.e., purpose and audience) is important outside of humanities; since future scientists are tasked, now more than ever, with presenting their information to non-experts in an increasing number of arenas, often competing with pseudoscience. Therefore, our article includes ways to build a STEM-themed FYW course and provides instructors with assignments emphasizing both popular and scholarly sources for all majors, helping demonstrate the value of writing about the sciences in various mediums. Ultimately, FYW provides a unique space where instructors have the chance to help both STEM and non-STEM majors prepare to effectively write and research in today's ever-changing world.

Introduction

Four decades ago James Berlin argued teaching writing is more than helping students develop a "technical skill" ("Contemporary" 776); rather, it is about helping students make sense of the world. Ten years later he would call this producing "literate citizenry" ("Poststructural" 32). But today's critical literacy requires the ability to assess a seemingly endless amount of information quickly and accurately and in ways Berlin could not have imagined over forty years ago.

For instance, there is a proliferation of scientific information shared online via sites like *YouTube* and *TikTok*, so it is understandable how easily non-experts, like college students, might believe credible-looking sources. Take the student who watches a video on a scientific topic from a questionable source, let us say "Dr. M.," who claims to be a "climate change expert." The video does not include a fake news warning from *YouTube*, and since the speaker is a "doctor," the student may assume the person has authority and the information is credible. Further, the *YouTube* profile describes the doctor as a "world renowned expert and speaker on environmental issues." So the student cites the video's information in their essay, but upon reading the quote, the instructor quickly realizes the information sounds inaccurate. The faculty then does the work to vet the source themselves, work the student should have done to begin with, and determines that "Dr. M" is a doctor but in an area wholly unrelated to climate change. In fact, the video is espousing their opinions without any citations or verifiable evidence. The student used what they felt was a credible scientific source, yet the faculty member says it is not credible. Distinguishing between actual science, non-contextualized scientific information, and pseudo-science has always been a challenge, but today it is more critical than ever if we hope to achieve "literate citizenry."

But who is responsible for developing the "literate citizenry," particularly in higher education? What about *scientific literacy*, which Carol Anelli defines as the ability "to weigh options and make informed decisions as individuals and as citizens of democracy"? (243) At most post-secondary institutions, first-year writing (FYW) bears the responsibility for preparing students to write across the disciplines (Downs and Wardle) and is now often tasked with teaching students how to gather, assess, and present research, scientific or not. In fact, FYW is often viewed as the key course to incorporate information literacy (Artman, Frisicaro-Pawlowski, and Monge 94; Sult and Mills 370). Thus, FYW instructors are often relied upon to help students develop skills necessary for success in academe. Today, teaching these skills is complicated by various elements.

With the current ubiquity of fake news, satirical publications, and information overload, ensuring students leave FYW with the skills to accurately assess and comprehend research has never been more important, and for STEM students, this skill set comes with responsibility other disciplines may not encounter. Because information—reliable or otherwise—has never been more accessible, more people are reading scientific information than in previous years, but, too often, scholars write for other scholars, meaning scientific texts are laden with jargon. M. Halliday and J. R. Martin argue children are often turned off by jargon, which engenders a sense of alienation from this discourse; this alienation, according to Halliday and Martin, is carried to adulthood, increasing the likelihood the average reader will avoid jargon-heavy texts. Yet, jargon is something scientists (and other discipline-specific experts) often employ; writing remains critical for sharing scientific knowledge. Therefore, today's scientists often simultaneously write for their peers and the everyday reader—the ones who may stop reading when inundated with jargon.

We argue FYW is positioned to make this specific rhetorical situation clear to students, particularly STEM students, who too often think concerns surrounding audience and purpose are restricted to the humanities; FYW is a space positioned to help both Berlin's "literate citizenry" and Anelli's "scientific literacy" become a reality at a time when science knowledge is especially integral to making sense of the world.

The Relationship Between FYW, WAD, and Information Literacy

Colleges, universities, and even faculty commonly expect FYW faculty to teach college-level writing *and* research skills, including information literacy, in order to prepare students to succeed across the disciplines. Library instruction, in fact, often targets FYW courses as a logical place to teach information literacy since both "writing and researching are viewed as non-linear processes" (Sult and Mills 369). FYW instructors' (unrealistic) course expectations are hampered by a variety of challenges, including time-constraints, students' various skill levels, the available school resources, and the depth of knowledge required by the FYW faculty member to teach both successfully.

While scholars have discussed information literacy in FYW and/or general composition classes (Artman, Frisicaro-Pawlowski, and Monge; Holliday and Fagerheim; Jacobs and Jacobs; Sult and Mills), they're often broad discussions, leaving science literacy in FYW out of the conversation. It's unlikely, then, students, generally speaking, are effectively learning to write and read across the disciplines.

Writing Across the Disciplines

Wardle explains FYW is often criticized for its inability to help students learn to write across the disciplines (WAD) despite the fact WAD is often inherently part of FYW's goals across higher education. Wardle asserts, "the rhetorical situations of FYW courses around the country do not mirror the multiple, diverse, and complex rhetorical situations found across the university in even the most basic ways" (766). If students of all majors leave FYW without the ability to write for different rhetorical situations, it is unlikely FYW STEM students leave with the ability to think about the rhetorical situation outside of academia, either.

Although teaching audience awareness is often a tenet of FYW, assignments can end up presuming a general readership represented by the instructor and perhaps other students in the class. Chris Anson and Jessie Moore explain teaching "genre, purpose, and audience" helps promote the writing transfer that skilled writers need (9). But the general readership paradigm still prevalent in FYW assignments may lead STEM students to conclude such writing is wholly disconnected from that which is required of professional scientists; although science journalism may be presented and used as sources for research papers in their FYW courses, it is unlikely this genre is discussed as a potential career requirement for STEM students. Therefore, it is critical FYW faculty make obvious to STEM students *why* writing with a general audience awareness is valuable for all disciplines. This instruction will help STEM students to envision these assignments as useful across the disciplines rather than a one-off type of assignment in a first-year course. Hyland argues faculty should

> take care in using popular texts as models for scientific writing as differences in constructing proximity mean that they will not help students see how scientific facts can be questioned or modified. Comparisons, however, can have an important consciousness raising function by highlighting features of scientific discourse for learner noticing. Their study, moreover, may help students see something of the importance of audience. (126)

Bringing both popular and scholarly sources into FYW can help students better understand the varying rhetorical choices authors must consider with regard to different audiences.

Thankfully, some students retain the ability to access prior knowledge post-FYW. Jerry Stinnett explains students must "develop metacognitive rhetorical knowledge about writing" to help them transfer writing skills among contexts. In doing so, students develop an "awareness of how writing changes from situation to situation" (357). While it's unlikely students will learn to see every situation outside FYW as rhetorical, the course can initiate this understanding. Simply asking students, for example, to identify differences in writing tasks between their other classes and FYW highlights how audience awareness is not a humanities-specific concept. Helping students understand the rhetorical situation can be difficult, especially as FYW instructors are simultaneously tasked with teaching college-level research skills expected to transfer across higher education and the professional world.

Information Literacy

In order to meet the expectation of equipping students with research skills, instructors often rely on librarians to teach these basic skills in a single class. Leslie Sult and Vicki Mills discuss how library instruction targets FYW courses in an effort to help all students learn information literacy. While this practice has merit, research shows one-time or limited librarian support is problematic, too. Margaret Artman, Erica Frisicaro-Pawlowski, and Robert Monge discuss these "one-shot instruction" moments as ineffective, and other scholars argue first-year students rely (almost solely) on ongoing librarian instruction to develop legitimate information literacy skills (Bowles-Terry and Clinnin 327). Worse, some FYW instructors rely on librarians to help students develop research skills simply at the reference desk without any context (Birmingham et al.). Each of these practices severely limits students' ability to develop their own data literacy, especially as it relates to challenging scientific sources.

Often, then, the onus to find and assess sources still resides with someone other than the student. Librarians are called to support both students and instructors (Bowles-Terry and Clinnin), which increases the likelihood FYW instructors rely on generalized research rules for college-level work, likely amplifying the chances scholarly sources are prioritized. This amplification can lead some instructors to limit the source types students can employ, thus decreasing students' exposure to popular sources and limiting their understanding of the value of popular sources in disseminating information to general audiences.

Due to the time constraints of a roughly 16-week semester wherein they must teach both college-level writing and research, FYW instructors often rely on generalized ways to teach source evaluation basics to their students. One such generalized evaluation process is the CRAAP test. According to Chico State, it is a commonly used checklist provided to first-year students to help them determine the validity and quality of sources. CRAAP is an acronym for five criteria to evaluate in a source: currency, relevance to topic, authority of the source, accuracy of the information, and purpose of the text (Chico State). But due to the proliferation of online sources since its development, the test is outdated. While CRAAP can be a useful tool, it can also be overly simplistic for a process that necessitates critical thinking. Fielding explains why CRAAP does not fully serve students: "While...CRAAP's individual assessments have ongoing value, it has become vitally important to place information into a wider context to adequately evaluate its credibility, as well as teach how information is ranked and presented on search

engines and social media" (622). All criteria in CRAAP are presented as equally important, which is a superficial, misleading approach; the criteria "accuracy" and "authority,"
for example, are often more critical than the other criteria and are especially challenging
for students to understand. Moreover, scholars note students may understand *how* to
evaluate sources but often *do not* rely on the evaluation criteria while choosing sources
(Kim and Sin; List and Alexander). Thus, students may be using other criteria, such as
convenience or urgency, when they decide which sources to use, again, highlighting the
need to help students assess popular sources, too.

Information and Audience Awareness in FYW for STEM Students

Audience awareness and information literacy is especially critical for students engaging
popular STEM sources, such as science journalism. Alongside the proliferation of online
science news sources, STEM reporting by non-scientists has also increased. While
always important, information literacy and audience awareness are arguably even more
critical when it comes to popular STEM sources. In an attempt to avoid the problem of
evaluating such sources, instructors might be tempted to require students use only scholarly STEM material. But these sources, too, are not without their own credibility and
accuracy challenges (Besançon et al.). David Barel-Ben et al. argue there is an ongoing
crisis in scientific journalism due to the ubiquity of online media and an increase in staff
writers assigned to STEM and tech topics when such writers are without the credentials
to take them on; this presents difficulties for students attempting to use basic evaluation
criteria to vet their popular sources. Barel-Ben et al. note that online news outlets may
cut corners on fact-checking simply due to shortened timelines for publication compared
to academic papers. According to the National Research Council, scientific literacy is
the ability to "use evidence and data to evaluate the quality of science information and
arguments put forth by scientists and in the media" (22). This definition, however, relies
on the information the reader is consuming to be accurate, complete, and up-to-date.

The average reader who encounters an online STEM source may not seek out the
original data to "evaluate the quality" of the online source's information, especially if
they believe the source to be credible. For example, it is now common for social media
users, including those working for so-called media outlets, to promote and disseminate
scientific information on platforms like *Twitter*. However, in order to avoid misrepre-
senting scientific studies and research, scientific information communicated via "science
journalists" must be as accurate as possible; scientists have been called upon to help
engender this accuracy. At the AAAS Annual Meeting Communicating Science seminar, science journalist Flora Lichtman noted, "journalists don't often let people look at
the final piece before publication" (par. 12), something often embraced in FYW via
peer-editing. FYW, then, has an opportunity to also illustrate the dangers of publishing
without any editing or peer review. Lichtman recommended scientists make themselves
available for fact-checking following interviews (if they have given them) to help assist
with accuracy. Similarly, FYW may task students with conferences (with peers and/or
their instructor), helping FYW students become comfortable discussing their written

ideas after the fact. Thus, FYW has the space to parallel future scientists' experiences vis- à -vis writing and publishing.

Barel-Ben et al. highlight studies demonstrating how scientists can help fill the gap in communicating science to lay people by writing the articles themselves. In their study of 150 scientific writings for online sources written by both scientists and science reporters, they concluded "in most cases no differences were found between the ways audiences responded to scientific reports written by scientists-as-science-reporters, and stories written by news site reporters" (12). This is encouraging: it means scientists' works, when they learn the rhetorical skills to write *for* a general audience, are read with the same level of interest *by* a general audience. Given this need for more science writing directed at general audiences, FYW offers an early and critical opportunity for students to see these different rhetorical opportunities at the start of their STEM studies so this form of writing can be identified and amplified for STEM students struggling to see connections back to FYW.

Audience Awareness and Popular Sources/Media

While scholarly sources provide a model for STEM students' future research and writing, learning to write for mainstream sources can also be valuable, perhaps for reasons the students haven't considered. For instance, STEM majors typically anticipate working as active scientists, which often requires original research and writing. While the practice of peer-reviewed journal publication will likely remain the cornerstone of scientific research dissemination, outside that community exists a far larger audience who will continue accessing scientific research filtered through mainstream sources like magazines, websites, and social media. This practice, unfortunately, leaves many scientists at the mercy of staff writers and non-scientists who may purposefully and/or inadvertently mischaracterize their research, leading more scientists to mistrust popular sources. In her piece, "The Incredibly True Story of Fake Headlines," author Chi Luu describes a recent example from the *Atlantic*:

> The original headline "The Arrogance of the Anthropocene" accurately described an interesting, well-researched essay on geological time and humanity's role in it, while the more provocative, social media-friendly follow-up headline, 'The Anthropocene Is a Joke,' framed it in the worst possible way. It's not hard to see how subjective and dismissive the informal language of this headline is, but since "anthropocene" is also widely used by scientists as a linguistic shorthand to describe the human-focused crisis we find ourselves in, this was also a fairly irresponsible way to frame what was otherwise a decent story. Unsurprisingly, on social media, it was also shared by climate denialists as support for their beliefs.

Depending on where a reader encounters this article, their perception of its angle, information, bias, and thus its credibility may all be different. This example also illustrates why STEM students need to see the connections between science and rhetoric; a simple word change affected the connotation in the title alone.

Information Literacy and Popular Sources/Media

Scholarly sources for any topic, particularly STEM, can further confuse students who lack the vocabulary and context to translate them. While there are multiple instruments to test STEM students' scientific literacy in scientific courses (Shaffer et al.), these tools are not typically known about or employed in FYW courses, especially if students are non-STEM majors. In fact, before one can become scientifically literate, a minimum degree of general literacy and reading comprehension is required, which many students still grapple with even in college. According to Olney et al.'s study, only 32% of college freshmen read at a 12th grade level (396). This statistic only slightly improved as of 2019 when the National Assessment of Educational Progress annual report card reported 37% of high school seniors were reading at 12th grade level. When these students enter college, they are exposed to a vast number of information sources for which minimal information literacy education is provided unless they take specific courses to help them with this; the information literacy provided in overburdened FYW is often insufficient for many incoming freshmen. Irina Holden notes "a growing concern among secondary educators with the lack of information literacy skills observed in our students" and the need for students to be able to deal with "rapid changes in the information landscapes" (qtd. in McMillen et al.). Faculty and librarians alike bombard students with tips about identifying scholarly sources by jargon or an article's length, but these tips do nothing to strengthen students' reading comprehensions, especially when scientific terms and jargon are difficult for *anyone* outside of STEM to fully understand.

Additionally, struggles to understand researched sources are sometimes compounded when students' own "research is typically addressed in a separate unit, positioned at the end of the course" (Purdy 48). While some FYW faculty introduce research to students from the beginning, weaving it into multiple assignments, most faculty rely heavily on the supplemental instruction of college librarians (Bowles-Terry and Clinnin) and the final research paper. Heidi Jacobs and Dale Jacobs argue that, for a variety of reasons, information literacy is challenging to teach in FYW and note one component typically left out is revision. While composition is taught as a revisionary process, research is not, when the most comprehensive research instruction given is during the "one shot," end-of-term class, which results in "the collection of information more like a scavenger hunt than a critical, self-reflective process" (74). Additionally, Jacobs and Jacobs note faculty are contending with a charge to address a number of competing student needs, so discipline-specific research skills are not a priority when basic research skills provide the most efficient means to an end for a uniform class assignment like a research essay:

> Students taking composition come from all programs, all majors, and all years; an average class might include a visual arts major, a computer science major, a sociology major, and several undeclared students. Thus we (instructors and librarians) are not teaching discipline-specific research methods in the way that we might teach history majors how to do archival research or biology majors how to do scientific research. (76)

FYW faculty might better prepare students writing on STEM topics by teaching them to complete their own scholarly research earlier in the course and by allowing students to utilize more mainstream sources where they are likely to encounter vocabulary they comprehend. This allows students to gradually become more familiar with scientific jargon with a smaller risk of misunderstanding, and exposing students to mainstream writing on STEM topics acquaints students with specific rhetorical situations where technical and scientific knowledge are communicated.

Students who are taught to determine textual authority and accuracy independently often choose not to use that evaluation criteria when choosing sources (Kim and Sin; List and Alexander). Many FYW faculty limit students to peer-reviewed scholarship when conducting research in order to mitigate the problems caused by student choices; however, this ultimately compounds the problem faculty are trying to solve because it limits students' ability to develop the strong critical thinking skills to assess sources on their own (Purdy). The problem occurs when students find a popular source written by a self-proclaimed scientist or doctor: their FYW instructor and librarian may not have covered how to evaluate scientific literature for credibility. If students have only ever been required to use scholarly sources, they have not learned how to evaluate the credibility of these online "experts" beyond a generalized evaluation checklist which they may or may not use (Kim and Sin; List and Alexander). Social media only compounds this problem, especially when scientists and non-scientists alike are using these platforms to share scientific information. J. Holmberg et al. explain how scientists often utilize *Twitter*, for example, to share new scientific publications (qtd. in Boothby et al.). *Twitter* works well since "several features of the scientific paper that are readily transferable to tweets, such as the title, abstract, and figures, are formal cues that may contribute to credibility" (Boothby et al.). Although some information may indeed be accurate, the formula for sharing information to make it appear credible, such as adding charts or graphs and linking to outside sources, can be easily replicated by non-scientists and those who are not experts. Thus, credibility can be even more difficult to determine. This limitation is augmented for FYW students learning about STEM topics primarily through scholarly sources. Thankfully, there are some successful models to follow for credible science online, including the practices of a growing number of celebrity scientists.

Popular Media and Science Communication Artifacts

Celebrity scientists are not new, but their ability to connect with the public is increasing due to the evolution of the web and social media. For example, many are familiar with Jane Goodall, Carl Sagan, and Bill Nye the Science Guy because they regularly appeared on television for three decades. These scientists found great value in direct communication with public audiences while sharing information in layman's terms. Additionally, Goodall and Nye emphasized the importance of sharing their knowledge with younger generations and making science accessible to all ages. While Goodall and Sagan are certainly considered giants among their professional peers, they also managed to successfully communicate beyond the scientific community via regular talk show appearances, public speaking tours, and even their own televised specials.

Today, we see this trend continuing and expanding with figures such as Neil DeGrasse Tyson and Richard Dawkins, who have embraced these same types of popular appearances, in addition to actively participating in new media. Each, for instance, have millions of followers on platforms like *Twitter*. They've also published numerous books for general audiences, appeared on countless television programs and podcasts, and worked continuously to engage mainstream audiences. In fact, mainstream audiences are enamored with today's scientists. In 2014 *ScienceMag* published "The Top 50 Science Stars of Twitter." While discussing celebrity scientists, meteorology scholar and author Marshall Shepherd points out "some critics and 'Ivory Tower' gatekeepers accuse them of being 'popularizers' of science and not serious scholars," but he strongly feels that "scientists should engage more broadly in non-traditional outlets such as the media, policy forums, and social media. If we don't, then people with agendas or limited backgrounds will gladly and strategically fill voids that we leave behind" (par. 2). Tzipora Rakedzon et al. note while "academic writing programs are prevalent in universities around the world, there are few programs that train scientists how to write and communicate with the lay public" (29). Thus, FYW programs should consider how they present writing about scientific topics so students gain introductory knowledge of the many valuable ways in which scientists can and even should write for general audiences. By creating assignments in which non-STEM faculty and students alike can engage with science, FYW instructors can help build both information literacy and audience awareness across disciplines.

The following excerpts come from assignments we developed for our own students, irrespective of majors, to introduce writing about STEM topics for general audiences.

- Find a scientific study on any topic. Then find a mainstream news source summarizing the *same* study. Write a comparison and contrast essay examining the connections between the "conclusion" or "findings" of the scientific study and the mainstream article. Be sure to identify any gaps in the mainstream article that may lead to a reader's misunderstanding of the actual scientific study.

- Choose up to three fake news stories about the *same* STEM topic. Write a 5-to-7-page, thesis-driven essay summarizing the stories, explaining the purpose of the stories (e.g., Do they create fear? Do they have a call to action?), and explaining the risk(s) of someone believing the stories you chose.

- Find an article about a STEM topic in a major newspaper like *The New York Times* or *Los Angeles Times*. Write a letter to the editor responding to the article. Address any concerns you have about the topic relating to one or more of the following: the original author's accuracy or tone, potential impact on your own community, or a dissenting view based on evidence not presented in the article. Support your response with a scientific article (popular or scholarly) on the same topic.

- Using the six conventions of scientific writing (structure, objective, analysis, accuracy, formality, and clarity), write a 5-page, APA formatted, essay explaining one of the lab reports you chose from this semester's research to a general audience. This is your opportunity to take scientific information written by scientists and translate it into digestible and interesting information for a mainstream reader.

- Write a 3-to-4-page rhetorical analysis of one of the science and technology articles we read as a class. In your analysis, identify the audience for the piece, examine how the author's word choice effectively communicates scientific information to that audience, and identify areas where the author was less effective and why.
- Write a 2-to-4-page personal narrative about a time in your life that was significantly impacted by science or technology. Common incidents might include things like your participation in an online gaming community or receiving or witnessing a life-saving medical treatment. Be detailed in your descriptions of both the science/technology and its impact on your life.

These assigments provide opportunities for non-expert FYW faculty to incorporate various STEM-focused writing opportunities that emphasize rhetorical situation. For assistance in developing these, faculty can even look to university websites and samples in WAC/WAD research. Additionally, these assignments provide students opportunities to actively engage both scholarly and popular sources on STEM topics and identify the many differences in how they approach their audiences. Finally, these assignments embed information literacy for STEM topics early in the semester and consistently, so students are applying these skills throughout the course with different types of sources.

Valuing Popular Sources and Media in FYW Research

The term "popular sources" is a loaded one, even for professionals; so the average FYW student can be forgiven for having trouble distinguishing among the good, the bad, the incomplete, and propaganda. The broadest definitions define popular sources as those written for a general audience, including magazines, newspapers, and websites. A source's popularity and ubiquity can also mask its credibility, especially when the source presents scientific information.

Many first-year students enter college with misconceptions about research and their own levels of information literacy (Latham et al.). In their introduction to the college library, most FYW courses include instruction about using college databases, practice developing search terms, an in-depth look at MLA format and citations, and methods for evaluation of source quality (Rinto and Cogbill-Seiders). Both instructors and librarians distinguish between so-called "popular sources" and "scholarly sources." Although there is value placed on each, scholarly sources are often privileged by instructors in FYW and are certainly preferred by instructors across the disciplines; in fact, this is a practice often continued from high school, where teachers prefer scholarly sources as preparation for college-level writing and assignments. Students in turn privilege scholarly sources (Insua et al.), even though many still have trouble understanding them. In fact, James P. Purdy explains college-level instructors frequently caution students about research done via the web, thus compounding this idea that popular sources are less valuable than scholarly ones. While it is prudent to ensure students can identify different types of sources (e.g., scholarly versus popular), according to Purdy, classroom policies restricting students from utilizing technology and sources they are likely familiar with can unnecessarily create classroom barriers for students; it is likely ineffective, too, since instructors ultimately cannot control the research tools students will utilize. Glenda M. Insua et al. argue something similar:

> To address the issue of students adhering to strict guidelines recalled from high school, the research team has moved toward more nuanced instruction regarding popular and scholarly articles. Rather than pitting popular and scholarly articles against each other, a better choice might be to have students engage each type and explore its contribution to research on a topic. (152)

Moving past this idea of "either/or" when it comes to popular versus scholarly sources can strengthen students' ability to locate, assess, and comprehend scientific research.

Because FYW students do not typically read scholarly research, especially scientific publications, outside of a classroom setting, they are more likely to consume scientific information in popular online sources. A 2018 study conducted by the Knight Foundation and Information Literacy Project surveyed nearly 6,000 college students and their newsgathering habits. Remarkably, 93% of respondents said they got their news from peers, 89% from social media, and 76% from online media websites like mainstream news media outlets (Head et al. 5). Educators can take solace in knowing respondents also noted 70% of the time they learned about news from college classes or individual instructors. While these statistics may seem alarming overall, they are unsurprising given that these news-gathering habits mirror that of most Americans. According to a 2017 study, which looked specifically at how people get scientific news, "54% [of respondents] say they regularly get their science news from general news outlets" (Gottfried and Funk par. 2). Interestingly, this study found just 28% of the same respondents felt the science news reported in those general outlets was accurate. When asked why they felt it was inaccurate, 73% of respondents cited "the way the news media cover scientific research" (Gottfried and Funk par. 5). These studies, when related to college students and general news, illustrate that most non-scientists are consuming news from popular online sources, which they acknowledge may not be accurate. Further, the general public's perceptions about popular sources and media are backed up by research on the reputation of specific social media sites, such as *Twitter*. In fact, "Twitter is often considered less credible than other online news media (Schmierbach & Oeldorf-Hirsch). This reputation is often premised in the strong body of recent literature devoted to assessing the spread of misinformation, hostility, or bot-like behavior on *Twitter* (Anderson & Huntington; Robinson-Garcia, Costas et al.; Shao, Ciampaglia et al.; Vosoughi, Roy, & Aral) and to containing and correcting misinformation (Bode et al.; Smith & Seitz). None of this is news to FYW faculty, who have traditionally responded by teaching students to transition their reliance on popular sources to the more academically accepted scholarly sources, at least for the sake of their class assignments and larger research papers, thus reproducing a perceived dichotomy between these genres.

However, by restricting them to scholarly sources, FYW instructors are unintentionally hindering students' ability to understand the concept of audience awareness and are unintentionally creating academic barriers. Students are dissuaded from using what they likely find familiar (Purdy). A recent study on information literacy and college freshmen found that many participants believed "Google to be a sufficient search tool" and "that freely available Internet resources are sufficient for academic work" (Hinchliffe

11). Hinchliffe further argues that student reliance on search engines, however, comes with other risks: students' experiences have led them to see the research process as linear, where questions have just one answer (Hinchliffe). It is not just the students who view research as linear, however: instructors often facilitate research as a linear process rather than a recursive one (Jacobs and Jacobs 74). For example, students develop an argument, find sources, and write the paper. Purdy argues presenting the research process as linear disconnects the research from the writing for students, unintentionally implying "research and writing are wholly separate [and]…uninformed by one another" (48). Separating research and writing contradicts what students are taught about rhetorical situation, especially audience awareness. Additionally, STEM students may encounter research by scientists *only* in scholarly works, curtailing these novices' exposure to non-expert audience models. While traditional FYW research instruction should help students see themselves as burgeoning scholars using scholarly sources, the addition of science communication to the curriculum can and should include non-scholarly sources for mainstream audiences as well. In framing scholarly sources as "experts writing for other experts," instructors may unintentionally leave out the public intellectuals in STEM who often work to translate the raw findings of science for the layperson in palpable and credible ways.

Because of the peer review editing process, audience awareness and information literacy skills are arguably less crucial for students working exclusively with academic sources. STEM students exposed only to scientific articles do not necessarily learn necessary rhetorical principles when encountering other types of science communications. Determining the authority of a traditional, mainstream source can be challenging, even for those with experience vetting sources on a regular basis, but this skill is not typically required or emphasized when students are restricted to scholarly sources. In other words, teaching students to assess sources while simultaneously restricting them to scholarly sources means students are not actually practicing real-world skills needed to make such evaluations.

When we ask novice researchers to assess source authority, faculty must consider how far into the weeds we can ask students to go. Indeed students are in a catch 22 position: evaluation requires knowledge, but knowledge requires reading source material. For instance, both *The Daily Mail* and *The New York Post* are known, at least to academics, as untrustworthy tabloids. Yet online, where search engine results often dictate what appears credible or not, students may not have the background necessary to investigate the authority of either of these sources. Where paper publications used to provide some visual clue as to what was truth versus what was sensational, websites are not always as straightforward. Elise Silva et al. point out, "While [first-year university students] show some hesitancy with design that is too flashy or overbearing, these novices are generally unable to point out what characteristics authoritative sources actually display" (26). Essentially, students believe they can recognize a bad source, but they are not sure what a good one looks like. To distinguish between them, readers must first have a fundamental understanding of who is producing the material they are reading or watching. Thus, without tasking students with rigorous source assessment, they will likely leave FYW without ever having truly employed this skill.

For instructors, the authority of a source is obviously and directly connected to its credibility; however, instructors and FYW students may define credibility very differently, especially for Internet sources. Ideally, traditional news sources have a chain of gatekeepers through which the information must flow prior to publication; this is especially true for scholarly sources. The problem, though, is "as the current information environment online does not often include professional gatekeepers who filter information sources, traditional indicators of authority, competency, and honesty can be hard to spot by consumers" (Silva et al. 25). *YouTube*, for example, makes it easy to find dubious and even dangerous scientific misinformation masquerading as fact. Remember the example of Dr. M from the intro? Unfortunately, as Emma Grey Ellis points out, this type of fake news is not typically picked up by algorithms used to identify other fake news like anti-vaxxing conspiracy theories. Thus, "YouTube and Instagram have built up dozens of resident food scientists, dermatologists, registered dietitians, OB-GYNs, surgeons, astronomers, veterinarians, and biochemists with specialties in beauty-product quality assurance" (par. 7). Human-powered fact-checkers, however, will always be behind the speed of algorithms, especially in an online world where fake stories are generated hourly. This engenders inconsistent flagging of fake videos as false or even dangerous, but because viewers have become familiar with seeing fake news warnings, à la "this post contains information which has been disputed," the lack of a warning on other videos may inadvertently provide FYW students with an unintended perception of approval.

Although scholarly sources should be the standard-bearers of academic writing, prioritizing them above all sources, especially in a world where non-academics do not, is risky, especially for STEM students who will likely be tasked with disseminating scientific information to public audiences throughout their careers.

Conclusion

As we have noted, one critical component to FYW is basic research instruction, including an often less-than-effective introduction to evaluating popular sources, as well as emphasizing scholarly sources for culminating research assignments. Popular sources, especially when related to STEM topics, are often less valued by FYW faculty than peer-reviewed sources. However, when FYW faculty emphasize the quality of scholarly research over popular sources, they limit opportunities for their students to assess and incorporate content for a general audience, a skill they will utilize far beyond FYW. Purdy explains why this is problematic: "In failing to change, we also risk alienating students from valuable practices and resources because we establish the activities and spaces of academic research as inapplicable to their lives outside of the academy" (57). When FYW faculty restrict students to scholarly research, they imply popular sources are inherently less valuable than peer-reviewed research, and this restriction leaves STEM students poorly positioned to effectively evaluate or communicate science to the general population in the future. Instead, FYW students should be shown how to effectively evaluate and utilize both popular and scholarly sources on STEM topics early and often for them to gain guided practice with the assessment and usage of both in their own writing. Additionally, FYW faculty teaching STEM majors should consider assigning writing tasks on STEM topics that not only analyze and engage peer-reviewed scientific research but assignments representing various rhetorical situations, including breaking down complicated scientific information for a general audience. A combination of these practices, a change in research and in the types of writing opportunities assigned, will provide FYW students with a clearer and stronger understanding of the myriad and valuable ways in which science is communicated.

By developing STEM-themed writing assignments, FYW instructors are uniquely poised to expose STEM students, especially, to the craft of writing about science and technology for a general audience in much the same way scientific journalists do. This type of instruction also allows for more in-depth analysis for all FYW students about information literacy and audience awareness across disciplines. Fortunately, these types of assignments need not be exclusive to STEM students; they can provide opportunities for any FYW student to write about science and technology relevant to their own lives. In fact, many WAD courses and programs already employ interdisciplinary writing assignments. For instance, the Writing Across the Curriculum (WAC) Program at SUNY Oswego recommends genre exercises as "one of the most fundamental functions of writing in a WAC course is to introduce students to the language, perspectives, conventions, evidence forms, objectives, and genres practiced in the field" (par. 5) While not all FYW instructors will be part of college-organized WAC/WAD programs, institutional support to help interested instructors take on this task would potentially benefit both students in and outside of STEM.

Works Cited

Anelli, Carol. "Scientific Literacy: What is it, are we Teaching it, and does it Matter?" *American Entomologist*, vol. 57, no. 4, 2011, pp. 235-44, https://doi.org/10.1093/ae/57.4.235.

Anson, Chris M., and Jessie L. Moore. Introduction. *Critical Transitions: Writing and the Question of Transfer.*, edited by Chris M Anson and Jessie L. Moore, University Press of Colorado, 2016, pp. 1-9, wac.colostate.edu/docs/books/ansonmoore/transfer.pdf.

Artman, Margaret, Erica Frisicaro-Pawlowski, and Robert Monge. "Not Just One Shot: Extending the Dialogue about Information Literacy in Composition Classes." *Composition Studies*, vol. 38, no. 2, 2010, pp. 93-110. *JSTOR*, https://doi.org/10.2307/compsud.38.2.0093.

Barel-Ben David, Yael, Erez S. Garty, and Ayelet Baram-Tsabari. "Can scientists fill the science journalism void? Online public engagement with science stories authored by scientists." *PloS one,* vol. 15, no. 1, 2020, e0222250. https://doi.org/10.1371/journal.pone.0222250.

Berezow, Alex. "Will Journalism Destroy Science?," American Council on Science and Health, 8 Feb. 2018, www.acsh.org/news/2018/02/08/will-journalism-destroy-science-12550.

Berlin, James A. "Contemporary Composition: The Major Pedagogical Theories." *College English*, vol. 44, no. 8, 1982, pp. 765–77, https://doi.org/10.2307/377329.

Berlin, James A. "Poststructuralism, Cultural Studies, and the Composition Classroom: Postmodern Theory in Practice." *Rhetoric Review*, vol. 11, no. 1, 1992, pp. 16–33, https://doi.org/10.1080/07350199209388984.

Besançon, Lonni, Elisabeth Bik, James Heathers, and Gideon Meyerowitz-Katz. "Correction of Scientific Literature: Too Little, Too Late." *PLoS Biology*, vol. 20, no. 3, 2022, pp. e3001572–e3001572, https://doi.org/10.1371/journal.pbio.3001572.

Birmingham, Elizabeth Joy, Luc Chinwongs, Molly Flaspohler, Carly Hearn, and Danielle Kvanvig. "First-Year Writing Teachers, Perceptions of Students' Information Literacy Competencies, and a Call for a Collaborative Approach." *Communications in Information Literacy*, vol. 2, no. 1, 2008, pp. 6–24, https://doi.org/10.15760/comminfolit.2008.2.1.53.

Boothby, Clara, Dakota Murray, Anna Polovick Waggy, Andrew Tsou, and Cassidy R. Sugimoto. "Credibility of scientific information on social media: Variation by platform, genre and presence of formal credibility cues." *Quantitative Science Studies*, vol. 2, no. 3, 2021, pp. 845-63, https://doi.org/https://doi.org/10.1162/qss_a_00151.

Bowles-Terry, Melissa, and Kaitlin Clinnin. "Professional Development for Research-Writing Instructors: A Collaborative Approach." *Communications in Information Literacy*, vol. 14, no. 2, 2020, pp. 325–45, https://doi.org/10.15760/comminfolit.2020.14.2.8.

"CRAAP Test Separates Good Resources from Bad." California State University Chico, 21 Sept. 2020, today.csuchico.edu/how-to-craap-test/.

Downs, Douglas, and Elizabeth Wardle. "Teaching About Writing, Righting Misconceptions: (Re)envisioning 'First-Year Composition' as 'Introduction to Writing Studies.'" *College Composition and Communication*, vol. 58, no. 4, 2007, pp. 552–84.

Ellis, Emma G. "The Influencer Scientists Debunking Online Misinformation." *Wired*, 13 Nov. 2019, www.wired.com/story/youtube-misinformation-scientists/.

Fielding, Jennifer A. "Rethinking CRAAP: Getting Students Thinking Like Fact-Checkers in Evaluating Web Sources." *College & Research Libraries News*, vol. 80, no. 11, 2019, p. 620, https://doi.org/10.5860/crln.80.11.620.

Gottfried, Jeffrey M. and Cary L. Funk. "Most Americans Get Their Science News from General Outlets, but Many Doubt Their Accuracy." *PEW Research Center*, PEW Research Center, 21 Sept. 2017, www.pewresearch.org/fact-tank/2017/09/21/most-americans-get-their-science-news-from-general-outlets-but-many-doubt-their-accuracy/.

Halliday, M, and J.R. Martin. *Writing Science: Literacy and Discursive Power*. 2nd ed., Routledge, 2014, pp. 1-35.

Head, Alison, John Wihbey, P. Taxis Metataxis, Margy MacMillan, and Dan Cohen. *How Students Engage with News: Five Takeaways for Educators, Journalists, and Librarians. The News Study Report. SSRN Electronic Journal*, 16 Oct. 2018. https://doi.org/10.2139/ssrn.3503183.

Hinchliffe, Lisa J., Allison Rand, and Jillian Collier. "Predictable Information Literacy Misconceptions of First-Year College Students." *Communications in Information Literacy*, vol. 12, no. 1, 2018, pp. 4–18, https://doi.org/10.15760/comminfolit.2018.12.1.2.

Hyland, Ken. "Constructing Proximity: Relating to Readers in Popular and Professional Science." *Journal of English for Academic Purposes*, vol. 9, no. 2, 2010, pp. 116–27, https://doi.org/10.1016/j.jeap.2010.02.003.

Insua, Glenda M., Catherine Lantz, and Annie Armstrong. "Navigating Roadblocks: First-Year Writing Challenges through the Lens of the ACRL Framework." *Communications in Information Literacy*, vol. 12, no. 2, Sept. 2018, pp. 86–106. *EBSCOhost*, https://doi-org.prox.miracosta.edu/10.15760/comminfolit.2018.12.2.3.

Jacobs, Heidi L. M., and Dale Jacobs. "Transforming the One-Shot Library Session into Pedagogical Collaboration: Information Literacy and the English Composition Class." *Reference & User Services Quarterly*, vol. 49, no. 1, Fall 2009, pp. 72–82. *EBSCOhost*, https://doi-org.prox.miracosta.edu/10.5860/rusq.49n1.72.

Keba, Michelle, and Elizabeth Fairall. "Not a Blank Slate: Information Literacy Misconceptions in First-Year Experience Courses." *Communications in Information Literacy*, vol. 14, no. 2, 2020, pp. 255–68, https://doi.org/10.15760/comminfolit.2020.14.2.5.

Kim, Kyung-Sun, and Sei-Ching Joanna Sin. "Selecting Quality Sources: Bridging the Gap Between the Perception and use of Information Sources." *Journal of Information Science*, vol. 37, no. 2, 2011, pp. 178-88, https://doi.org/10.1177/0165551511400958.

Latham, Don, Melissa Gross, Heidi Julien, Felicia Warren, and Lindsey Moses. "Community College Students' Perceptions of Their Information Literacy Needs." *College & Research Libraries* [Online], vol. 83, no. 4, 2022, p. 593.

List, Alexandra, and Patricia A. Alexander. "Corroborating Students' Self-Reports of Source Evaluation." *Behavior & Information Technology*, vol. 37, no. 3, 2018, pp. 198-216, https://doi.org/10.1080/0144929X.2018.1430849.

Luu, Chi. "The Incredibly True Story of Fake Headlines." *JSTOR Daily*, JSTOR, 20 Nov. 2019, daily.jstor.org/the-incredibly-true-story-of-fake-headlines/.

McMillen, Cynthia, Amy Graves-Demario, and Deb Kieliszek. "Tackling Literacy: A Collaborative Approach to Developing Materials, for Assessing Science Literacy Skills in Content Classrooms through A STEM Perspective" *Language and Literacy Spectrum*, vol. 28, no. 1, 2018.

Melzer, Dan. *Assignments Across the Curriculum: A National Study of College Writing*. Utah State University Press, 2014.

National Science Education Standards: Observe, Interact, Change, Learn. National Academy Press, 1996.

Olney, Andrew M., Raven N. Davis, Breya Walker, and Art Graesser. "The Reading Ability of College Freshmen." *ERIC*, June 2017. *EBSCOhost*.

Purdy, James P. "The Changing Space of Research: Web 2.0 and the Integration of Research and Writing Environments." *Computers and Composition*, vol. 27, no. 1, 2010, pp. 48–58, https://doi.org/10.1016/j.compcom.2009.12.001.

Rakedzon, Tzipora, and Ayelet Baram-Tsabari. "To Make a Long Story Short: A Rubric for Assessing Graduate Students' Academic and Popular Science Writing Skills." *Assessing Writing*, vol. 32, 2017, pp. 28–42, https://doi.org/10.1016/j.asw.2016.12.004.

Rinto, Erin E., and Elisa I. Cogbill-Seiders. "Library Instruction and Themed Composition Courses: An Investigation of Factors That Impact Student Learning." *The Journal of Academic Librarianship*, vol. 41, no. 1, 2015, pp. 14–20, https://doi.org/10.1016/j.acalib.2014.11.010.

Schmierbach, & Oeldorf-Hirsch, A. "A Little Bird Told Me, So I Didn't Believe It: Twitter, Credibility, and Issue Perceptions." *Communication Quarterly*, vol. 60, no. 3, 2012, pp. 317–337. https://doi.org/10.1080/01463373.2012.688723

Shaffer, Justin F., Julia Ferguson, and Kameryn Denaro. "Use of the Test of Scientific Literacy Skills Reveals That Fundamental Literacy Is an Important Contributor to Scientific Literacy." *CBE Life Sciences Education*, vol. 18, no. 3, 2019, pp. 1-10, https://doi.org/10.1187/cbe.18-12-0238.

Shepherd, Marshall. "Should Scientists Be Considered 'Celebrities' to Inspire Kids?" *Forbes*, 11 Dec 2019, https://www.forbes.com/sites/marshallshepherd/2019/12/11/should-scientists-be-considered-celebrities-to-inspire-kids/?sh=70069a4c78c2

Silva, Elise, Jessica Green, and Cole Walker. "Source Evaluation Behaviours of First-Year University Students." *Journal of Information Literacy*, vol. 12, no. 2, 2018, p. 24–43, https://doi.org/10.11645/12.2.2512.

Stinnett, Jerry. "Using Objective-Motivated Knowledge Activation to Support Writing Transfer in FYC." *College Composition and Communication*, vol. 70, no. 3, 2019, pp. 356–79.

Sult, Leslie, and Vicki Mills. "A Blended Method for Integrating Information Literacy Instruction into English Composition Classes." *Reference Services Review*, vol. 34, no. 3, 2006, pp. 368-88, https://doi.org/10.1108/00907320610685328.

"WAC Assignments." State University of Oswego at New York, www.oswego.edu/writing-across-the-curriculum/wac-assignments.

The Nation's Report Card. *How did U.S. students perform on the most recent assessments?*, 2019 https://www.nationsreportcard.gov.

"Tips from Science Journalists ." American Association for the Advancement of Science, 2013, www.aaas.org/programs/public-engagement/tips-science-journalists.

Wardle, Elizabeth. "'Mutt Genres' and the Goal of FYC: Can We Help Students Write the Genres of the University?" *College Composition and Communication*, vol. 60, no. 4, 2009, pp. 765–89.

Embedding the Scientists: Civic Issues as Context for Teaching and Learning

Heather G. Lettner-Rust, Alix D. Fink, Edward L. Kinman,
JoEllen G. Pederson, and Phillip L. Poplin

Abstract: *We teach science as a path to meaningful civic engagement in a partici-patory democracy and as a path that should be open to all; our concern lies in how the next generation of young citizens[1] address challenging civic issues both by apply-ing science to other contexts—public and civic—as well as communicating science to others—peers and the public. To that end, our article seeks to explain an inter-disciplinary capstone course for our general education program that we developed to promote and support science learning and science communication by teaching in the context of important civic issues.*

> *Science is not about big words. It's not about lab coats and safety goggles, and it's definitely not about trying to make yourself sound fancy. Science is not an end in and of itself, but a path. It's a method to help you discover the underlying order of the world around you and to use those discoveries to help you predict how things will behave in the future. (López-Alt 21)*

For 16 years, Longwood University students have traveled to the world's first na-tional park, Yellowstone, to participate in an immersion learning program fo-cused on the stewardship of public lands. Stewardship, a concept applicable in contexts ranging from financial institutions to art museums, offers an approachable framing for students' engagement with complex environmental issues. In the realm of environmental conservation and management, stewardship is rooted in the land ethic of Aldo Leopold and his intellectual descendants, and it offers a "pathway for action" for today's students (Mathevet, et al.). Because Longwood's Yellowstone National Park course (hereafter LU@ YNP) is focused on complex environmental stewardship issues such as management of reintroduced wolves, protected status of grizzly bears, and permissible uses of park lands by visitors, student learning—through explorations, observations, and conversations with peers and local stakeholders—is strongly infused with scientific questions, methods, and concepts.

However, participating students, faculty members, and stakeholders not only have very different disciplinary perspectives and experiences, but also diverse understand-ings of the physical landscape, commonly known as the Greater Yellowstone Ecosystem

---

1. In this chapter, we use the word "citizen" not to denote a person's legal status but rather to refer to residents of U.S. communities who are engaged in civic life. Our collaborators, students, and stakeholders represent diverse communities and come from richly varied backgrounds and experiences. We acknowledge the significant contributions of diverse community members in the Greater Yellowstone Ecosystem and throughout our country; their places of origin and documentation are not relevant.

(GYE), and its human communities. Thus, we embed science students in a learning community in which students from many majors collaboratively discover, digest, and disseminate information about unresolved, and often bitterly divisive, natural resource issues in and around Yellowstone National Park (YNP). This work is facilitated by an interdisciplinary faculty team from biology, geography, mathematics, sociology, art, rhetoric, and other fields, depending on the year. Students construct their learning in key spaces such as the open range, visitor centers, and museums and benefit greatly from the synergy between informal science education and science communication that exists within those spaces as well as from broader disciplinary convergences.

Student learning therefore emerges through real participation in a community of practice that helps students to develop a sense of identity as contributing members of the community, which in turn cultivates in the participants belonging and commitment (Handley et al.). Our goal is for them to transfer the practiced skills to other contexts and communities in their civic lives. In this chapter, we explore the experiences of students steeped in this complex and complicated milieu and make inferences as to the contributions of immersive experiences to students' learning of science communication.

Situated Teaching and Learning: Scholarly Context

In acknowledgment of the pervasiveness of science in modern life and the need for all persons to be able to engage science issues, many countries around the world have invested in efforts to develop "scientific literacy" for all students (Feinstein et al.; Blanco-López et al.). In the United States, the Next Generation Science Standards (NGSS) were developed to address this ongoing and persistent need through K-12 science education reform because "too few U.S. workers have strong backgrounds in these fields, and many lack even fundamental knowledge of them" (National Research Council 1). The goal of the NGSS is that, by the end of secondary schooling,

> All students will have some appreciation for the beauty and wonder of science; possess sufficient knowledge of science and engineering to engage in public discussion on related issues; are careful consumers of scientific and technological information related to their everyday lives; are able to continue to learn about science outside of school; and have the skills to enter careers of their choice, [including science, engineering, and technology fields]. (NRC 1)

Complementary efforts in U.S. higher education have sought to engage students in learning science through the study of "humanity's most pressing current and future challenges" (NRC 1). One articulation of this goal in studying and teaching science, the Science Education for New Civic Engagements and Responsibilities program begun in early 2001, has spawned efforts at hundreds of campuses, all seeking to engage students in connecting "science and civic engagement by teaching 'through' complex and unsolved public issues" (SENCER para. 1). The LU@YNP program exists at this important intersection: post-secondary education, science communication, and civic issues.

To mimic the situational context of a civic body, we placed students in an interdisciplinary course with instructors from multiple disciplines and embedded them in the field to exercise the skills of listening, questioning, dialoguing and researching. This setup subverts the classroom dynamic of sitting and hearing information to be used later. We are not so much filling students with information as we are immersing them in the work of inquiry, research, and understanding. We have brought down the walls between learning environments and invited students to be careful participants of this new place and its issues.

This classroom draws on classic work of John Dewey and Paulo Freire. Freire criticizes the "banking" approach to education in which an expert gifts knowledge to learners with no understanding (*Pedagogy* 72). Freire instead argues for construction through communication: "Knowledge is built up in the relations between human beings and the world, relations of transformation, and perfects itself in the critical problematization of these relations" (*Education* 96). Constructivist Dewey, noting that most students will not become scientists, argued for an approach that connects students "with problems selected from material of ordinary acquaintance" so that "they will be sure and intelligent as far as they do go" (*Democracy* 235). Our approach intentionally avoids the "banking concept" and instead positions students to be the drivers of their inquiry. Thus, we implement these emancipatory pedagogies and strive for a democratization of education that makes learning environments more horizontal and the role of experts less privileged.

In the last several decades, science communication in professional contexts mirrors this shift from the deficit model (i.e., information is transmitted to consumers who are thought to be unaware of it) to an engagement model in which diverse stakeholders participate in dialogue (Bubela et al.). In parallel, many science educators have moved from a focus on content delivery to pedagogical approaches that position students as co-constructors of learning (Davis and Russ).

Another key to learners' active engagement is their affective disposition. Science education scholar Mark Newton considered the emotive reasoning of a cohort of LU@ YNP students and found that they described much more empathetic dissonance (e.g., compassion, guilt, anger, and righteous indignation) for other citizens and for the natural systems after completing the program (Herman et al., "Students"). Newton and his collaborators also describe a realization by students that many ways of knowing should be considered in complex stewardship issues. Through their interactions with diverse stakeholders, students were challenged to consider in concert diverse cultural views, moral and ethical questions, scientific evidence, indigenous knowledge, and more (Herman et al., "Socioscientific"). "Rich" learning environments like this support students' preparation to work to resolve challenging socio-scientific issues (Newton and Zeidler), and, we contend, also help motivate students to do so.

With students primed for action, we ask them to sit and listen just a bit more. For this work, we look to invitational rhetoric (Foss and Foss), which assists speakers with encountering difference, whether it is ideological, educational, or rooted in community history. Invitational rhetoric rests on a set of assumptions, one of which is that a speaker should operate from a position of "power-with rather than power-over" (13). This process suggests that instead of privileging loud or vigorous debate as an active classroom, we make room for careful listening to another's perspective with the goal of understanding rather than waiting to speak. This "rhetorical listening" is a pedagogical strategy designed to make space for the intellectual work of hearing what the speaker is saying within their context and situating the communication within the listener's understanding and interpretive work (Glenn and Ratcliffe). To take up a food metaphor, "There is no production of wine without a gathering and safekeeping of the vintage, just as there is no genuine dialogue without dwelling in another's ideas" (Stenberg 252). The promise of this practice is that the speaker and participants walk away with a richer understanding of multiple perspectives on fraught issues and recognizing the complexity of multiple needs.

To be successful in transferring their knowledge and skills from the ephemeral LU@ YNP community of practice to other civic and professional contexts, though, students must be practiced in communication. Our braided approach to pedagogy supports that development.

The Pedagogy of Braiding

A rope is a useful metaphor to explain our pedagogical approach to promote improved communication of science to various publics and across the majors. Most ropes have three twisted fiber strands, each of which has value independent of the rope. If braided, the strands create an object that is far stronger and of greater value than a loose bundle of the same threads.

The LU@YNP program replicates the rope analogy in a number of ways. One strand is the multidisciplinary faculty team working in collaboration as co-facilitators of the course. The second strand represents students of different majors and minors. The third strand is an interdisciplinary pedagogy enacted onsite in the GYE. The braiding of these strands supports students' exploration and understanding of complex stewardship issues of public lands. Ultimately, each strand is crafted to help students enhance communication of complex issues.

Faculty Strand

Our faculty team is composed of humanists, mathematicians, artists, and natural and social scientists, which parallels the diversity of the legendary Hayden Expedition that, in its mission to explore and document the western territory that would become YNP, employed biologists, earth scientists, a statistician, and artists. In our course, single disciplinary perspectives from faculty members are not emphasized. Formal lectures in the field are minimal. Instead, the interdisciplinary pedagogy goes beyond separate disciplines to form a holistic approach, one in which we are focused on our scholarly expertise in asking questions, making observations, evaluating information, and synthesizing observational research with data. We are not there as experts in wildlife biology, human geography, art, or rhetoric, but rather as intellectual mentors for apprentice investigators who are asking questions, making observations, and communicating their findings.

The GYE with all that it contains, both natural and anthropogenic, serves as the classroom, and we engage a range of local co-teachers—state wildlife biologists, visitor center staff, museum curators, and a host of other stakeholders—to provide instruction and local expertise. In some years, students conducted oral history interviews with citizens whom we consider co-teachers in this endeavor.

Student Strand

The student strand consists of a cohort of many majors. And yet this strand might be considered a three-thread strand within the larger braiding. Each student embodies three identity spaces within the course and is asked to activate those identities extemporaneously as the situation calls for.

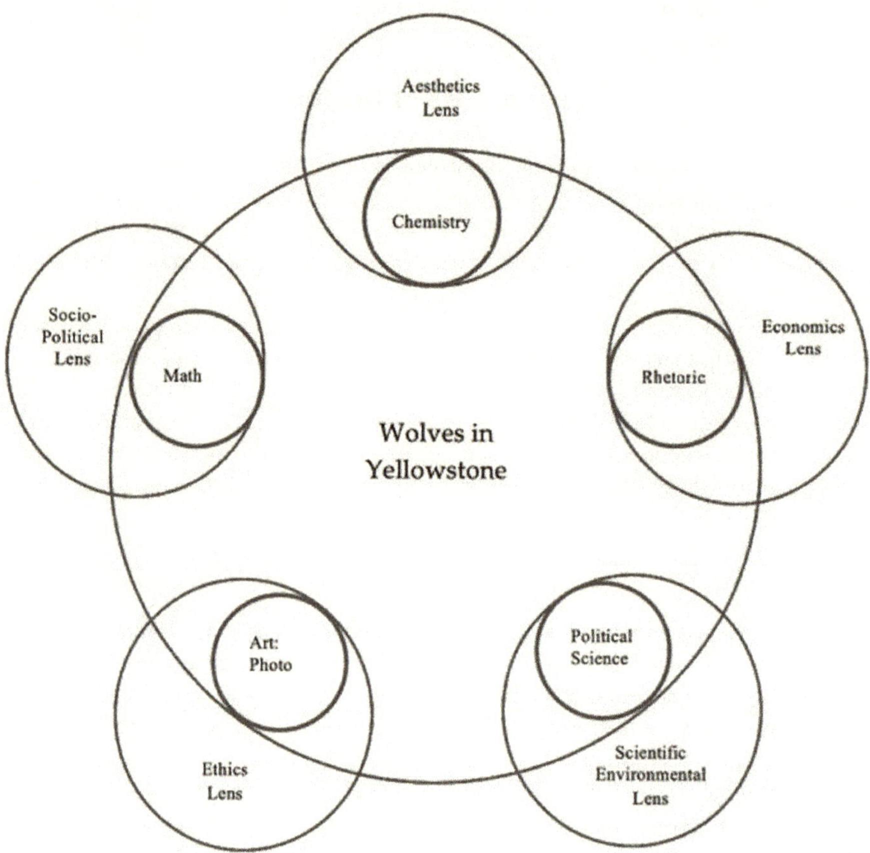

Figure 1: Students' Work Through Lens and Major on Wolves in Yellowstone

First, students are assigned to work with two or three peers in an "Issue" team. That Issue team focuses on one important stewardship issue, such as bison management, invasive species, fire management, water resources, or technology access. This grouping allows students to develop a cache of background knowledge pertinent to topical events affecting the park with regard to that issue. Second, students are asked to bring forward disciplinary knowledge and skills of their majors. We invite students to be intentional in their explorations. How does their discipline interrogate a problem? What evidence do they find useful and where do they look for it? What count as credible conclusions in their field? Each should use the expertise learned in their major to unpack observations, research, and stakeholders' commentary. Finally, we consciously challenge students to think beyond their chosen field by placing them in a "Lens" team. Students are to view issues from their assigned lens: scientific and environmental, aesthetic, economic, ethical.

This three-part combination (see Figure 1) provides students with opportunities to deploy multiple perspectives to address their chosen stewardship issue across multiple audiences, genres, and situations. Using invitational rhetoric to open themselves to diverse perspectives and rhetorical listening to digest what is presented, students mobilize these three strands in order to understand not only their peers' perspectives but the stakeholders' as well.

This process of perspective-taking and listening is practiced daily in debriefing sessions during which students contribute insights on the day's learning activities by alternatively focusing on their lens and their issue. For example, while discussing a wildlife-watching outing, a chemistry major would be expected to introduce the effect of tourism-related air pollution while also considering the aesthetic disruptions of hordes of buses and vans to the wild-ness of the landscape. For discussion of civic issues, students must practice an intentional weaving of multiple perspectives, often extemporaneously, when we deliberate contentious issues in the field and in conversation with local citizens, a practice that ultimately serves them when they publish a document in service of the civic issue. For example, as the number of wolves increase in the Yellowstone ecosystem, the number of domesticated animals harmed or killed by wolves increases. Should hunting be allowed during a longer season or in larger numbers of kills? The art major would be expected to explain the economic benefit from ecotourism while also considering the perspectives of ranchers who have lost valuable livestock. Many of the other students in the art major's lens group may have seen the rhetoric of public communication in anti-wolf bumper stickers on local cars and trucks.

Pedagogy Strand

A fitting pedagogy for this mobile learning community of faculty and co-teachers working with a diverse student cohort is, in a word, flexible. The course unfolds over a six-week period during which students prepare for their immersion in the knowledge base and the communities they are about to enter, develop a portfolio of targeted research, meet stakeholders in the field, and design written, oral, or artistic performances to reflect their understanding and agency based on newfound knowledge and experiences. A critical factor throughout these stages is the act of faculty modeling: model, model, and model again.

For this complex endeavor, we have developed the *Field Immersion Framework*, a four-stage pedagogical scaffolding that guides faculty and students (see Pederson et al.). The first stage, Foregrounding, takes place before the group departs for the field. In this pre-travel period, we actively recognize the diverse perspectives represented in the faculty and intentionally lead teaching sessions with multiple faculty. We are modelling the integration of disciplinary perspectives when the geographer annotates a video clip of the landscape of the Yellowstone ecosystem and an art professor illustrates the use of painting as a tool to persuade Congress to preserve this area as a national park.

Central to student learning during Foregrounding is to have students practice hearing diverse perspectives and synthesizing those views in preparation for field work during the Immersion stage. One such activity is to gather stakeholders representing government interests, private interests, business interests, and university interests to discuss a selected issue with our students at various tables. Over the years, we have used a proposed natural gas pipeline, student housing expansion into the community, and water quality. During a shared meal with community members, students ask thoughtful and respectful questions while also taking notes. After the meal, faculty facilitate a debriefing not only on what they learned but how they learned what they have come to understand. Within these pre-departure days, we also set aside time to coach student research skills both with static sources online and in print as well as meeting invited stakeholders who preview the civic issues involved in the Immersion stage, the physical environment, and various community perspectives.

The second stage, Immersion, takes place in the field. Students are instructed (and faculty continue to model ways) to observe, record, reflect, analyze, focus, and inquire, again, at a moment's notice and in constantly changing environments. Reflection, the third stage, is an iterative metacognitive process initiated in Foregrounding and continuing to the end of the course. Reflective activities reify the actions of interrogating and transforming past knowledge, absorbing and challenging present knowledge during the Immersion stage, and then preparing to put that knowledge to use in the final stage, Agency. In completing the course during the Agency stage, students are challenged to create public documents on their stewardship issues. Students must think about how to use learned interdisciplinary skills to address an issue and to craft documents to elicit a change in thinking and/or behavior for a target audience.

Discussion: Science Communication, Science Education, and Civic Agency

To better prepare undergraduate students of all majors to engage as civic agents, we developed a braided approach that embeds students and faculty members as newcomers and masters in a community of practice (Lave and Wenger) focused on learning skills in context. By co-locating scientists, students of science, and others who use science in their lives as engaged citizens, we created an environment in which science can be talked about, deliberated, and applied in meaningful communicative ways by all involved. The context in which that community of practice functions is key: this all plays out in real time in real communities with real people who are impacted by real issues. It is authentic. It is genuine. It is accessible.

Honoring Diverse Ways of Knowing

Our course situates Virginia students as "outsiders" in the GYE human communities so that students experience a shift in perspective. The insider/outsider context is never more apparent than when they meet Mr. Scott Frazier, a member of the Crow Nation and a Montana resident. As a co-teacher with the LU@YNP program, he shares his community's indigenous ways of knowing and addresses contentious stewardship issues that our students study. Immediately, students gravitate to his literal and figurative narrative. He piques their curiosity as he describes the thousands of years of living his ancestors represent and their indigenous science knowledge—their ways of knowing the land, sky, weather, flora, and fauna.

After meeting with Mr. Frazier and listening to his storytelling about the significance of bison to his people, one of our students, Emily, an elementary education major, describes an integration of his ways with her ways of knowing culture, history, and biology. This integration is evidenced in part by her using the term 'buffalo'—his term—instead of bison as we have used in the course:

> My father is a hunter, who has actually killed a buffalo [with] a regulated, licensed ranch outfitter in Montana. I've eaten the lean, beef-like meat, and the buffalo head is mounted in his barn trophy room. Nonetheless, the Native American tradition and sacred reverence of the buffalo is recognized by my family, but it particularly stands out to me. In studying history, which I hope one day to teach, every part of the buffalo was used, every part. It provided, literally, food, clothing, and shelter for the Lakota Sioux, as well as other tribes. The annihilation, near extinction, [by white hunters] of this species is a stain in American history.

This assignment requires her to choose among the contentious issues of bison preservation, hunting, and societal uses in Yellowstone and to take a side. Emily's reflection evidences her ability to synthesize her family's heritage of hunting animals as trophies, Mr. Frazier's narrative of buffalo as life-giving resources, and U.S. history of slaughter for her own ethical decisions about what should be done with bison and how she will teach in the future. We see her intention to use multiple and conflicting perspectives, rather than choose a single hegemonic perspective in addressing her audiences, as central to science communication. As a future teacher, this ability to listen and invite difference might promise a more integrative teaching approach for the sciences and communicating with other partners, who might be public, non-experts in her sphere.

Situating Science and Communication in Community

Rhetorical listening works well for students as they recognize the importance of a community's history in understanding and synthesizing current issues. Calli, a chemistry major, recognizes that there must be understanding of how a community has come to be and to know the issues before one can consider how to address matters of public concern. She explains that "These ranchers and wildlife biologists interact with their community and the surrounding community in ways that we could only understand by asking questions and listening, not assuming that we knew their way of life." In these ways, Calli sees the ranchers and biologists as masters in a community-of-practice, and this opportunity is her apprenticeship in understanding in order to communicate effectively.

Diane, a biology major, extends that acknowledgement of expertise to many diverse community members:

> The biggest aspect of the class and trip in my opinion was communication. I spoke with many different people…locals in shops, shop owners, or even the bartender. A lot of topics [we are studying]…are sensitive topics to the people who live there. The skills I've learned through practice in my general education curriculum prepared me to acknowledge the person's position so I could have a healthy conversation with them.

Acknowledging the person in conversation, a form of "power-with rather than power-over" (Foss and Foss 13), is the first step so urgently needed in public discourse about civic issues, and, by extension, a necessary social practice for young scientists speaking in community. The complexity of stewardship issues requires all voices be present at the collective table and, as demonstrated by Calli, the asking of complex questions through invitational rhetoric.

Transfer of Learning

As educators who work to promote strategies for transfer, our hope is for students to carry the lessons with them—when they return to family, coworkers, and peers —in their communications with myriad public, non-expert audiences. In the following reflection, Shawn, an integrated environmental sciences major, demonstrates his learned research and communication skills with family members. He is a translator of research, synthesizing complex concepts and terminology, then explaining for understanding rather than preparing for a debate.

> When my parents or siblings have a question related to science…, I can sift through the dense language of scientific articles, but my family members may struggle comprehending the same information…. Since it would not be effective to relay the information to them verbatim, I have to acquire, organize, and present the information clearly and precisely so that they can understand too.

Thus for Shawn, science communication is not a summary of scientific principles or findings but a connection of his audience's concerns to his re-organization and explanation of research that encourages a dialogue, where his family members may continue to have questions. This process mimics one of our pedagogical moves to place students and stakeholders in tandem as they grapple with complex issues in the field. Our intention is that students understand learning to be a dialogic process combined with active listening skills to understand who is speaking and from what frame of reference.

Recommendations for Transfer and Adaptation

We see science as a path forward to broader and more inclusive dialogues about the many complex issues that affect our local communities and that unfold on the global stage. Climate change, pandemic response, biodiversity loss, legacy chemicals: citizens need more than scientific literacy to be engaged with these challenges. They also need to be practiced in communicating about them with fellow citizens who are different in culture, education, and socio-historical signifiers.

We contend that braiding science communication and science education in the context of key civic issues is an effective approach to preparing the next generation of citizen leaders. In form and function, the LU@YNP program engages students in learning science by practicing key competencies of science and science communication. They do so in a mobile community of practice that immerses faculty members and undergraduate students in our own consilience (à la Wilson) to draw on diverse disciplines and interrogate ideas, evidence, arguments, and proposals. In this disciplinary milieu, students are consumers and producers of science communications through a "bottom-up" process of dialogue (Blanco-López, et al.) in the community of practice and in the human communities they explore. Through conversations with local citizens, students' own written reflections, formal discussion with peers, faculty, and staff members, and formal written assignments, students build proficiency in science competencies through communication and in a context that calls on them to practice civic agency.

Even without substantial institutional or departmental support, the model of transdisciplinarity can be started with a pairing of two courses scheduled at the same time. Perhaps it is a summer course or, during the traditional semester, the course can be co-constructed to share assignments or simply have students communicate at choice times for an interdisciplinary conversation. Regardless of the level of braiding, the following recommendations for teaching science communication are made with an interdisciplinary population of instructors and students in mind.

Teach the Conflict

We believe that introducing students to the heart of the problem early on will whet their appetite for course learning. This introduction should be facilitated by competing and complementary disciplinary voices to share in the development of information. Our course is led by a number of instructors from different fields, and we also include expert and non-expert stakeholders involved in the issue. In addition, we suggest transparency of expectations early and often: students need to know that they will co-construct their learning, which relies on their initiative, rather than waiting for material to be delivered. To that end, instructors must model good questions and make time for said questions and reflection. For instance, LU@YNP's Foregrounding stage, which occurs three days before the course moves out West, focuses on engaging students with local civic issues and facilitating the explorations of conflicts. By embedding the students in sample conflicts in our campus town, we can coach students through the identification and research of a civic issue, processes they will need as soon as they hit the ground in Montana. We find there is a lot less passivity on the part of the students using the conflict as a catalyst.

Use Organic Writing Genres

Rather than creating assignments based on "mutt" genres, which work to deliver information for teacher review and to transmit what the learner has learned (Wardle), we select assignment genres based on the rhetorical situation of student work. Typically, mutt assignments only function in the classroom and bear little-to-no resemblance to the writing found in professional or even personal spaces. While mutt genres can be useful for information delivery or checking student comprehension, those genres do not work well for engaging students in the real work of science communication or public work. For example, it is unlikely that a letter with citations or a five-paragraph essay would be an effective means to communicate with a stakeholder.

We believe what is best for the learner, especially operating in the civic, public sphere, is to use genres used in workspaces organic to the challenge of the complex issue in question. For example, if the goal is for students to record their observations or collect data, a field notebook might be a good choice. We might show them examples of how scientists or other operators in the field—anthropologists, archeologists, social workers—take notes on their work. The name "field notebook" signals to the student where the genre is used (the field), where the content is collected (the field), and the level of formality required (it is a notebook, a rough draft, a ledger, but it needs to be legible for later use or the review of outsiders). Adopting and adapting genres from outside the classroom allow students to work with types of writing that function with a sense of agency beyond the classroom; furthermore, they are practicing the very adaptivity they will need when approaching public audiences to communicate complex and contentious issues.

Maximize Reflection

Reflection has had a long history as a strategy for learning (Dewey, *How We Think*; Freire, *Pedagogy*), a record of change in thinking (Schön; Kolb), and a tool for assessment (White; Yancey). Our use takes up all three approaches.

In engaging students in this practice, the first goal is to have them use reflection as a tool of science. Notetaking in the field notebook channels both Darwin and Dewey. Mimicking Darwin, students take notes in certain physical and intellectual spaces in Yellowstone. We encourage their use of visual, linguistic, and spatial skills for these notebooks. Students might create a graphic display of information, draw the animal in its environment and label its parts, or sketch the new cultural geography before them. Dewey's influence in the field notebook is encouraging learning from experience with the process of reflection. Thus, we ask students to place their reflections in proximity to these visuals so a record of learning and thinking is integrated.

These notebooks also are used as a point of learning during and after an activity. Donald Schön has proposed that learners reflect during and after an activity as a way to solve complex problems in the workplace. Given that we have embedded apprentices in the environment of local stakeholders sharing their expertise, we are intentional about the tools that allow the apprentice to get up to speed. The field notebook is part organizational tool for cognition and part debrief as they navigate the messy boundaries of complex civic issues.

This process of learning and reflecting is a crucial fiber in our pedagogy strand of the braid. We continue the practice of reflection as students examine different ways in which scientific information is discussed in diverse settings. Listening and recording what they hear, see, and think facilitates looking deeper, and students distill the frames, terms, and perspectives that build understanding and cause increased conflict. For instance, because students have read during our pre-departure the seminal publications of Truman Everts' 1923 narrative "Thirty-Seven Days of Peril" that galvanized the public's imagination as well as the 1916 *National Geographic* that spurred Congress to preserve Yellowstone, students have prior knowledge of how well science was communicated in that context to the public. That prior in Foregrounding reading allows us to repeatedly recall those models as one way to write to different audiences about complex contentious issues, incorporating science using diverse source material.

Finally, students' reflections in the field notebook along with submitted documents make visible the learning and application of science as well as the rhetorical flexibility they have exercised in developing communication skills to a wider set of audiences. This metacognitive transparency is a key aspect of our community of practice as it supports critical dialogue among students and faculty members and also contributes to our real-time adaptive management of pedagogical activities. We assess student learning in this dynamic context through formal and informal reflection to evidence the often-invisible process of learning and to help students recall, organize, and name their learning (Adler-Kassner and O'Neill; Beaufort; Yancey). Reflection that requires students to reference their experiences or written work encourages them to document rather than invent the evidence of their learning (VanKooten; White; Yancey). We ask students to reflect on what they have seen, heard, read, applied, and learned. The resulting student work used herein was taken from two sources: field notebooks and a final reflective analysis (students are identified by pseudonym and major). This reflective material reveals some useful insights for our evolving pedagogical approaches as students document strengths and challenges to their learning.

Though an adventure in the wilds of the West is not feasible for all students, every community faces key civic issues that involve science—in the root causes, in the dialogues, and in the paths forward. Undergraduate students of all majors can be immersed in these challenging issues and therein apply their science knowledge and practice communicating it. Science is a path to discovery and to a view of the future, and undergraduates—all undergraduates—are a vital link to a future that includes richer dialogue about science in our lives.

Works Cited

Adler-Kassner, Linda, and Patti O'Neill. *Reframing Writing Assessment to Improve Teaching and Learning.* Utah State University Press, 2010.

Bearzi, Maddalena. "5 simple tips for communicating science." *National Geographic.* https:// blog.nationalgeographic.org/2013/10/11/5-simple-tips-for-communicating-science/.

Beaufort, Anne. *College Writing and Beyond: A New Framework for University Writing Instruction*. Utah State University Press, 2007.

Blanco-López, Angel, Enrique España-Ramos, Francisco José González-García, and Antonio Joaquín Franco-Mariscal. "Key Aspects of Scientific Competence for Citizenship: A Delphi Study of the Expert Community in Spain." *Journal of Research in Science Teaching*, vol. 52, no. 3, 2015, pp. 164-198.

Boswell, Helen. C. and Tasha Seegmiller. "Reading Fiction in Biology Class to Enhance Scientific Literacy." *The American Biology Teacher*, vol. 78, no. 8, 2016, pp. 644-650.

Brownell, Sara E.; Price, Jordan V. and Lawrence Steinman. "Science Communication to the General Public: Why We Need to Teach Undergraduate and Graduate Students this Skill as Part of Their Formal Science Training." *Journal of Undergraduate Neuroscience Education*, vol. 12, no. 1, Fall 2013, E6-E10.

Bubela, Tania, et al. "Science Communication Reconsidered." *Nature Biotechnology*, vol. 27, no. 6, 2009, pp. 514-518.

Davis, Pyrce R. and Rosemary S. Russ. "Dynamic Framing in the Communication of Scientific Research: Texts and Interactions." *Journal of Research in Science Teaching*, vol. 52, no. 2, 2015, pp. 221-252.

Dewey, John. *How We Think*. D. C. Heath, 1933.

Dewey, John. *Democracy and Education*. Myers Education Press, 2018.

Everts, Truman C. *Thirty-Seven Days of Peril: A Narrative of the Early Days of the Yellowstone*. Grabhorn Press, 1923.

Feinstein, Noah, Sue Allen, and Edgar Jenkins. "Outside the Pipeline: Reimagining Science Education for Nonscientists." *Science*, vol. 340, 2013, pp. 314-317.

Foss, Sonja, and Karen Foss. *Inviting Transformation: Presentational Speaking for a Changing World*, 4th ed., Waveland Press, 2019.

Freire, Paulo. *Education for Critical Consciousness*. Bloomsbury Academic, 2013.

Freire, Paulo. *Pedagogy of the Oppressed: 50th Anniversary Edition, 4th ed.* Bloomsbury Academic, 2018.

Glenn, Cheryl, Radcliffe, Karen, editors. *Silence and Listening as Rhetorical Arts.* Southern Illinois UP, 2011.

Handley, Karen, Andrew Sturdy, Robin Fincham, and Timothy Clark. "Within and Beyond Communities of Practice: Making Sense of Learning Through Participation, Identity and Practice." *Journal of Management Studies*, vol. 43, no. 3, 2006, pp. 651-653.

Herman, Benjamin C., Dana L. Zeidler, and Mark Newton. "Students' Emotive Reasoning Through Place-Based Environmental Socioscientific Issues." *Research in Science Education*, vol. 50, 2018, pp. 2081-2109.

Herman, Benjamin C., Troy D. Sadler, Dana L. Zeidler, and Mark H. Newton. "A Socioscientific Issues Approach to Environmental Education." *International Perspectives on the Theory and Practice of Environmental Education: A Reader*, edited by G. Reis and J. Scott, Springer International Publishers, 2018, pp. 145-161.

Kolb, David A. *Experiential Learning*. Prentice Hall, 1984.

Lave, Jean and Etienne Wenger. *Situated Learning: Legitimate Peripheral Participation*. Cambridge University Press, 1991.

Lehr, Jane L., Ellen McCallie, Sarah R. Davies, Brandiff R. Caron, Benjamin Gammon, and Sally Duensing. "The Value of 'Dialogue Events' as Sites of Learning: an Exploration of Research & Evaluation Frameworks." *International Journal of Science Education,* vol. 29, no. 12, 2007, pp. 1467-1487.

Lewenstein, Bruce V. "Identifying What Matters: Science Education, Science Communication, and Democracy." *Journal of Research in Science Teaching,* vol. 52, no. 2, 2015, pp. 253-262.

López-Alt, J. Kenji. *The Food Lab: Better Home Cooking Through Science.* W.W. Norton and Company, 2015.

Mathevet, Raphaël, François Bousquet, and C. Raymond. "The Concept of Stewardship in Sustainability Science and Conservation Biology." *Biological Conservation,* vol. 217, 2018, pp. 363-370.

National Research Council. *A Framework for K-12 Science Education: Practices, Crosscutting Concepts, and Core Ideas.* The National Academies Press. 2012.

Newton, Mark. H. and Dana L. Zeidler. "Developing Socioscientific Perspective Taking." *International Journal of Science Education,* vol. 42, no. 8, 2020, pp. 1302-1319.

Pederson, JoEllen G., Heather G. Lettner-Rust, and Jessi B. Znosko. "The Field Immersion Framework: A Transformative Pedagogy Experiential Civic Education." *Journal of Transformative Learning,* vol. 20, no. 3, June 15, 2022.

Schön, Donald. *The Reflective Practitioner: How Professionals Think in Action.* Basic Books, 1983.

SENCER. *Science Education for New Civic Engagements and Responsibilities: SENCER Ideals.* 2017. http://sencer.net/sencer-ideals/.

Stenberg, Shari. "Cultivating Listening: Teaching from a Restored Logos." *Silence and Listening as Rhetorical Arts,* edited by Cheryl Glenn and Krista Radcliffe, Southern Illinois UP, 2011, pp. 250-263.

VanKooten, Crystal. "Identifying Components of Meta-Awareness about Composition." *Composition Forum,* vol. 33, 2016.

Wardle, Elizabeth. "'Mutt genres' and the Goal of FYC: Can We Help Students Write the Genres of the University?" *College Composition and Communication,* vol. 60, no. 4, 2009, pp. 765-789.

Welp, Martin, Anne de la Vega-Leinert, Susanne Stoll-Kleemann, and Carlo C. Jaeger. "Science-based Stakeholder Dialogues: Theories and Tools." *Global Environmental Change,* vol. 16, 2006, pp. 170-181.

White, Edward. "The Scoring of Writing Portfolios: Phase 2." *College Composition and Communication.* vol. 56, no. 4, 2005, pp. 581-600.

Wilson, Edward O. *Consilience: The Unity of Knowledge.* Knopf, 1998.

Yancey, Kathleen B. *Reflection in the Writing Classroom.* Utah State University Press, 1998.

Yancey, Kathleen B. *Teaching Literature as Reflective Practice.* NCTE, 2004.

Coastal Communications: Teaching Civic Scientific Literacy in English and Environmental Science and Resource Management Classes

Stacey Stanfield Anderson and Kiki Patsch

Abstract*: Named after the national park that lies just off of our Ventura County shores, California State University Channel Islands draws faculty who are committed to integrating the coast into their teaching and research. This context has inspired our interdisciplinary collaboration as teacher-scholars who hail from separate departments (English and Environmental Science and Resource Management). Our work together is designed to amplify civic scientific literacy in our classrooms as a means of elevating discourse on the growing challenges that threaten our coastal communities.*

Introduction

This article explores our collaborative, interdisciplinary approach to amplifying civic scientific literacy for undergraduates across disciplines as a means of elevating scientific communication on issues relevant to the California Coast. We hail from separate departments—Stacey Anderson from English, Kiki Patsch from Environmental Science and Resource Management—at California State University Channel Islands (CSUCI) in Camarillo, California. Founded in 2002, CSUCI is the newest campus in the country's largest state university system and a Hispanic Serving Institution, with a student population that is 60 percent Latinx. Almost 60 percent of students are the first in their families to attend college ("Spring Enrollment Snapshot"). Many CSUCI students are second-generation Americans whose families work the agricultural fields that connect our Ventura County campus to the coastal shores that lie just five miles away.

Both our university and respective departments encourage interdisciplinary collaboration in teaching, scholarship, and service. As the name of our campus suggests, CSU Channel Islands also draws faculty who are committed to integrating the coast into their teaching and research. While California State University campuses are typically named after the cities or counties in which they are located, we are named after the National Park that is visible from our shores and just a short boat ride away. This institutional and geographic context inspired us to merge our respective areas of expertise as teacher-scholars who are committed to empowering students to communicate how and why we value our coast across disciplines and to articulate and address the growing challenges that threaten its preservation and public access.

Our work together prioritizes civic scientific literacy and communication as essential not just for aspiring STEM (Science, Technology, Engineering, and Mathematics) practitioners and educators, but for an engaged citizenry that will be increasingly faced with navigating civic scientific pathways. We approach our collaborative efforts through a framework of "civic scientific literacy" that empowers students to engage in public scientific discourse (Johnson 371; Miller 29). Science education expert Wendy R. Johnson recognizes that not all students will choose STEM careers, but "all citizens of our society need the skills to continue to learn about science outside of school and the ability to apply their understanding to make personal decisions and engage in public discussion of socio-scientific issues" (371). Research scientist Jon D. Miller goes further, considering civic scientific literacy as crucial to safeguarding democracy in the United States (33). Miller, a lifelong advocate for civic scientific literacy, underscores the urgency of a basic level of literacy to at least be able to "read the science section of the Tuesday *New York Times* or to watch an episode of *Nova* on public television" (32).

Interdisciplinary Collaboration

We have developed an interdisciplinary scholarly and creative collaboration centered on civic scientific literacy of the California Coast that works in reciprocity with our classroom teaching and community outreach (Curtis et al. 3; Gunawardena et al. 214). Our collaborative efforts in both scholarship and teaching underscore that advocating to the general public for the protection and preservation of California's coast includes conveying complex scientific data through compelling and innovative vehicles to reach both hearts and minds (Lemarie 5; Schwab 47). We approach our work with an interdisciplinary mindset and a shared understanding that natural sciences often intimidate the general public, particularly those who feel uneducated or insecure with their knowledge base in the sciences (Schwartz 275). This article delineates the framework of this pedagogical and scholarly collaboration and underscores the value of making such partnerships visible on campus and in the community to model the collective, interdisciplinary approach to wrestling with the increasing strains placed upon our coastal communities.

Our efforts rely on a shared understanding that California's beaches can be valued through diverse yet intersecting disciplinary lenses that collectively highlight how much relies on the preservation of California's coast. Economically, sandy beaches generate over $5 billion a year in direct revenue to the state (King and Symes 3). Wide beaches and dune complexes serve as natural buffers to storm surge, protecting back beaches and low–lying ecosystems as well as human development and hardscape (Griggs et al. 46). Ecologically, beaches are integral to nutrient cycling in terrestrial and marine systems; function as natural biological filters; serve as habitat for imperiled and endemic species; and support the breeding, migrating, and wintering of many other creatures (James 506; King et al. 45-46; Lafferty 1949-50; Schlacher et al. 557-58). Recreational and commercial fishing also depend on beaches as habitat and an essential component of the food web. Psychologically, beaches encourage outdoor recreation and improve mental health and well–being (Nichols; Pilkey and Cooper xi-xii). Culturally, California's beaches have inexorably shaped trends and genres in music, art, fashion, dance, and recreation to create what we characterize as the "California imaginary." Our teaching and scholarship strive to cultivate civic scientific literacy of this prismatic array of disciplinary lenses that is integral to engaging in informed discourse among everyday citizens and policymakers on the issues facing California's beaches and what is at stake if we fail to address them.

Our interdisciplinary collaboration is rooted in curriculum development. In the spring of 2017, Kiki taught for the first time an upper-division, interdisciplinary, writing-intensive course proposed by the Environmental Science and Resource Management Department, *ESRM 335: The Beach*, an "[i]nterdisciplinary course that explores the sociocultural importance of sandy beaches in Southern California, integrates diverse perspectives on California's beach culture and society, and focuses on issues pertaining to coastal development and sustainability" ("2023-2024 University Catalog"). This class fulfills the upper-division general education requirement for scientific inquiry and reasoning and is populated by students across nearly all majors. Between 2017 and 2023, the enrollment of the class grew from one section of thirty students to two sections totaling over 200. Kiki's expertise is in coastal geomorphology, processes, and hazards as they relate to coastal resilience in the face of climate-induced sea level rise. This general education class, however, sought to unpack the significance of California's sandy beaches beyond buffering houses and infrastructure from storm surge and sea level rise or providing a space to throw down one's towel and lie in the sun.

Interdisciplinary Teaching, Take One

In preparing for *The Beach* class, Kiki recognized that people view and value the beach through a variety of lenses, including those delineated above. Empowering students in ESRM 335 as scientific communicators would entail cultivating both a baseline literacy of scientific processes and policies regarding California's coastal zone as well as an appreciation of the diverse lenses through which stakeholders could be engaged in issues concerning its protection and preservation. Ecologists see the sandy beach as a complex ecosystem that depends on the rise and fall of the tides and the movement of sand along the coast to provide habitat and nutrients for critters that live in the sand and form the bottoms tiers of the ocean food web. Economists perceive the sandy beach as an important economic driver, generating necessary dollars from tourism for localities. Dance and music historians observe the influence of California's beaches on the fluid movements of evolving dance styles and on the surf music often associated with California culture. Families enjoy the beach as a place to play and make memories splashing in the waves, building sandcastles, and digging for crabs. Amateur athletes and everyday exercisers seek out the beach as a place for solo and social activities such as surfing, skateboarding, and volleyball. Those craving mental wellness flock to the beach for the restorative sensory experience of crashing waves and ocean breezes. Reflecting on this range of lenses, Kiki realized that communicating the value of the sandy beach went far beyond her own geological lens of how sand arrives at the beach and is influenced by the waves.

As valued as beaches are, they are still under attack due to climate-induced sea level rise. The US Geological Survey predicts that up to 67% of southern California's beaches will disappear by 2100 (Vitousek et al. 782). Coastal armoring (e.g., seawalls and jetties) and replenishing the supply of sand to the beaches with outside sources are widely perceived to offer a solution to beach erosion, but these short-term solutions further exacerbate the issue through environmental degradation and other problems (Defeo et al. 3; Dugan et al. 193; Griggs 13; Griggs and Patsch 1061; Griggs et al. 72; Runyan and Griggs 336). In *The Beach* class, Kiki aimed to convey to students the importance of managing the coastal zone in a way that prioritizes the protection and preservation of sandy beaches and the importance of engaging the public in this process. This meant exploring the beach through a variety of lenses to ideally touch on those that would resonate with students. Most students in this class grew up near the coast yet did not fully grasp the interdisciplinary ways we can study and explore the beach. The goal was thus to allow the students to reclaim their relationship with the natural world by taking the familiar location of the beach and exploring the many ways we can understand its dynamism and value. By personalizing and broadening the understanding of this known and loved place through multiple disciplinary lenses and then using that as a springboard to discuss the complex issues of policy and management in the face of climate-induced threats, students learn to engage with a "comfortable" scientific topic while understanding the viewpoints of a multitude of stakeholders. Understanding the complexity of an issue from the perspective of different stakeholders is a valuable tool to teach students effective civic scientific literacy. Kiki knew that she could not be the "sage on the stage" for every topic in this course, so she invited guest speakers to share their disciplinary perspective in relation to California's beaches. Kiki's goal for the class was to create an active learning environment where students would be inspired to care about beach protection and cultivate their civic scientific literacy. The semester was divided into four overarching sections: *The Physical Environment and Processes of the Sandy Beach*; *The Ecological Functioning of the Sandy Beach*; *The Cultural Importance of the Beach as it relates to the "California Imaginary"*; and *Threats to California's Sandy Beaches*. Exposing students to each aspect of the beach would allow them to develop their own perspective of what is at stake with climate change and sea level rise, empower them to broadly communicate such threats to the public using course assignments, and reveal to them that they all have a stake in the protection of California's beaches.

Each week of *The Beach* class included a documentary, reading, and guest speaker to convey the significance of the beach from diverse disciplinary perspectives and through a range of sensory experiences. For example, Javier Gonzales, musician and CSUCI global languages professor, integrated songs associated with or inspired by the "California sound" to explore the influence of the beach on music worldwide. Dancer and CSUCI performing arts professor Heather Castillo pulled students out of their seats to engage them in the physicality of how the beach and ocean shaped modern American dance. Philip King, an economics professor from San Francisco State University, discussed the importance of the beach to local and state economies. Ethan Estess, an environmental advocate, marine scientist, and artist, revealed how he uses art to communicate environmental threats to our beaches and oceans. Kiki's fellow CSUCI ESRM professors demonstrated the diversity of lenses that could be explored even in the same academic department: Dan Reineman discussed beach access equity and the future of California's beaches, Clare Steele emphasized the importance of the sandy beach ecosystem, and Sean Anderson homed in on public perceptions, threats, and stressors to the beach.

Every week, students were asked to think critically about the sandy beach from the "disciplinary lens of the week" and reflect on this perspective through discussion boards and/or blog posts. The goal was to build civic scientific literacy and communication by using a setting that students were already familiar with and comfortable exploring. Public-facing blog assignments required that students visit a beach and discuss the significance of that location using the disciplinary lenses discussed in class. This assignment encouraged students to think critically about their environment and expand their communication skills to a public forum. Science students were engaging with the arts and art students were now looking at the beach as an ecologist or geologist and communicating their observations with the general public through their writing. The alternate, or previously unexplored disciplinary lenses, were truly eye-opening to students. Asking students to experience the beach through different disciplinary lenses required a level of critical thinking expected in an upper division course. Students were presented with disciplinary topics and asked to assimilate information gleaned from readings, documentaries, and lectures on how this topic, or lens, could be applied to the beach.

Students were then challenged with not only understanding the topic as it related to California's beaches, but to apply that understanding to a specific California beach as well as an international one. The culminating project required either an in-class or recorded presentation on the Coastal Imaginary of a location outside the continental US. Working in groups, students drew upon their weekly writings to explore threats to their selected country's beaches using multiple disciplinary perspectives in order to convey the importance of the sandy beach environment and the effects of management choices on this important, vanishing ecosystem. They were charged with essentially creating a public service announcement to engage and communicate with classmates about our global coasts in crisis, with an ultimate goal of conveying to the general public the plight of the world's beaches.

Interdisciplinary and Collaborative Scholarly and Creative Activities

The success of *ESRM 335: The Beach* opened our eyes to the potential of forging an interdisciplinary collaboration centered on fostering informed discourse on the issues facing the California Coast. We applied for and received an internal interdisciplinary Research, Scholarship, and Creative Activities (RSCA) grant for the summer of 2017 aimed at facilitating collaboration between faculty in STEM and Arts and Humanities. Drawing upon our respective backgrounds in coastal science (Kiki) and composition and rhetoric (Stacey), we launched *Beaches on the Edge*, a website dedicated to exploring and communicating the significance of California's beaches. This project included conducting video interviews on location at Point Mugu State Beach with members of the campus and local community about the significance of the coast and its influence on music, dance, culture, and our identity as Californians. Interviewees included CSUCI faculty Javier Gonzalez (on music) and Heather Castillo (on dance) as well as California State Parks Lifeguards Stephanie Crane and Colin Simon, who shared their insights on issues facing California beaches, from environmental challenges to recreational usage.

The perspectives of the lifeguards were particularly revealing regarding the potential of civic scientific literacy in engaging the public on coastal issues. These lifeguards have witnessed firsthand how the beach functions as the outdoor playground and gathering place for inland, urban residents who do not have yards of their own or crave the sea breezes in the heat of summer. Indeed, it appeared that the increasing periods of excessive heat associated with climate change yielded increased demand for the coastal locations that are also threatened by climate change and the resulting sea level rise (Patsch and Anderson). Engaging in conversations such as this underscored the potential to draw upon the current moment and this collective affection for California's beaches to speak directly to the challenges they face and promote advocacy for addressing them.

Interdisciplinary Teaching, Take Two

Taking our interdisciplinary collaboration a step further, in the fall of 2017, Stacey adapted the topics explored in *The Beach* class and in *Beaches on the Edge* when she taught an online version of *English 330: Interdisciplinary Writing* for the first time. This class focused on "[i]ndividual and collaborative writing that integrates research from a variety of disciplines. Students will work on projects that incorporate various forms of research, including electronic, and which result in both oral presentations and academic papers. Each section will be based on a theme appropriate for interdisciplinary research and writing" ("2023-2024 University Catalog"). Anderson built this course around the theme of "The California Coast." Students engaged in a variety of reading, research, and writing activities that asked them to delve into the multiple disciplinary lenses through which the coast can be viewed and valued, including completing collaborative and multimedia projects. As with Kiki's *The Beach* class, Stacey found that a framework of civic scientific literacy within the context of an interdisciplinary writing course spoke to students across disciplines as they prepared to negotiate evolving political, cultural, economic, and media terrain that inevitably shape public discourse on issues of scientific relevance.

David Helvarg's *The Golden Shore: California's Love Affair with the Sea*, one of several texts Kiki drew upon in *The Beach* class, served as the primary text in English 330. The book examines California's coast through a range of disciplinary perspectives. Written in a style that is accessible and personal yet still informative and persuasive, Helvarg's book appealed to the wide array of students the English 330 course served, including those majoring in English, business, and liberal studies. The course began by asking students to compose weekly journal entries on Helvarg's text, which included exploring the intertwining natural and human–induced influences that have shaped the California Coast, analyzing the diverse lenses through which the California Coast is perceived by various stakeholders, and evaluating the benefits the California Coast provides and the challenges it faces.

Students proceeded to create presentations on the theme of "What the Coast Means to Me." This assignment asked students to draw upon what they had learned through reading and writing in response to Helvarg's *The Golden Shore* as they visited the coastal site of their choice and reflected on the various disciplinary lenses through which they were perceiving it. Students captured their perceptions through photographs and notes and used those to build a slide deck. They then uploaded that slide deck to VoiceThread, a digital platform embedded in our Learning Management System that enables users to create interactive, multimedia presentations to promote asynchronous discussion among presenters and viewers via recorded audio or video responses. Presenters narrated their own VoiceThread slides to communicate what the coast meant to them as understood through the perspectives they had selected, which could include psychological, economic, political, educational, environmental, musical, cultural, ethnic, literary, artistic, biological, commercial, international, multicultural, community-oriented, cinematic, intellectual, emotional, familial, and so on. Classmates then viewed and responded to the presentations in VoiceThread via audio and video comments, building conversations based on what the presenter had shared and/or previous comments from other classmates. In this manner, presenters developed experience in articulating with their peers why the coast matters to them and fostering dialogue on why it is worth protecting and preserving, and audience members learned to see the coast through the eyes of others and to communicate their own perceptions in response.

This led to the next multimedia project, "Coastal Perspectives," which asked students to conduct video interviews to discern the perspectives of others on the value of the coast. While VoiceThread presentations gave students the chance to communicate their understanding of the coast with their classmates, these videos were posted publicly to YouTube, expanding potential audience reach. This assignment built upon students' prior experience with the ubiquitous YouTube platform that had played a formative role in shaping how their generation accesses and interacts with content relevant to their personal interests and academic needs. At the same time, the assignment challenged students technically and stylistically, as they came to recognize the complexities of communicating in this medium in a manner that is polished, professional, and engaging for the intended audience. This assignment asked students to share what they had learned in the class with potential interviewees, record interviews that discussed the value of the coast as viewed through any of the lenses we had been exploring, and edit their material for a video to be published on YouTube (see Figure 1). While students understood that YouTube videos were powerful ways to communicate with and impact viewers, they also learned that creating an effective video to interest an audience beyond their own class was not as easy as simply whipping out their smartphones and hitting Record. Many submitted videos did not meet students' own expectations for quality, and the instructiveness of the assignment came from reflecting on the nuances of communicating in this medium that they had taken for granted in all of their own years of YouTube binging. While video quality varied, students appreciated the opportunity to create using a platform they had only engaged with as consumers in the past. Students also watched and responded to one another's videos via the discussion board, broadening their exposure to a range of perspectives and approaches to communicating their insights. Students were then asked to reflect on what they learned that they would take with them when producing a video in the future. They recognized the value of location (with a preference for coastal sites that aligned with the theme, as in Figure 1), relevant coastal images (as in Figure 2), clear and audible sound, and integrating a range of lenses and interview subjects. Students were particularly affected by interviews that exposed them to new knowledge (such as a Ventura County resident who had a passion for photographing bioluminescence) or novel perspectives (including an 84-year-old grandmother who attributed her longevity to living by the coast). All recognized that producing a video that could authentically reach its target audience was far more demanding than they had anticipated.

Figure 1: A screenshot of the Seal Beach pier from a student YouTube video for ENGL 330 (Velasco). Successful videos were filmed on location at coastal sites along the Southern California Bight, either as background during the interview or as B-roll footage.

Figure 2: A screenshot from a student YouTube video for ENGL 330 (Willingham). The video transitioned to this photo of the interview subject bodyboarding in front of an iconic Ventura County coastal site (Mugu Rock) after the subject had shared how much this beach activity means to him.

The class concluded with a collaborative interdisciplinary project on "The Value of the California Coast." Students formed groups after watching and responding to each other's YouTube videos and identifying potential partners. Groups then collaborated to produce three research-based texts in different genres and for distinct audiences focused on a particular issue or topic of mutual interest regarding the value of the California Coast. These texts included an op-ed aimed at Ventura County residents, a blog entry directed at California readers, and a letter to the California Coastal Commission, a state body that "plans and regulates the use of land and water in the coastal zone," including beach access, development, and habitat protection ("Our Mission"). Each group worked in a shared Google Drive folder to facilitate asynchronous, remote collaboration in this online class. The module included guidelines and resources for approaching each communication scenario and crafting each text for its targeted audience. This project required groups to build their own civic scientific literacy on their chosen topics—urban runoff, oil spills, pollution, and wetland restoration—and to compose texts that integrated resources relevant to each rhetorical situation. The op-eds used very spare, direct, argumentative language and communicated in the limited space allotted by submission guidelines, while the blog posts traded in images, web design, and more personal, inviting language and tones. The letters to the California Coastal Commission were written on letterhead and followed the stringent guidelines for *ex parte* communications set forth by the Commission. Each of these genres offered unique opportunities for groups to write persuasively to specific audiences, to communicate what they had learned about their chosen topics, and to advocate for attention and action on these issues. Students also worked independently to compose a reflective essay that synthesized what they had learned throughout the semester about the value of the California Coast. This gave students the chance to cite their own contributions to the class to communicate their own civic scientific literacy journeys. These reflective essays were composed in a Google Doc that included both newly written reflections as well as text, images, and multimedia content from their previous assignments, either embedded directly or hyperlinked in the essay. The intended audience for this piece was the English Composition Faculty, who read and evaluated each project through a blind, holistic assessment process. This further expanded the readership of student work to an audience that is trained in rhetoric and writing and attuned to the conventions and expectations of the diverse genres.

Future Directions

As we teach additional iterations of these upper-division, general education ESRM and English courses, we continue to draw upon our shared knowledge and commitment to cultivate civic scientific literacy and engagement in our students and empower them to communicate clearly and confidently on the issues facing the coast that is so integral to our identity as a campus and as a community. The importance of clear scientific communication, interdisciplinary collaboration, and multimedia engagement has only become more palpable since we began our work together, and particularly over the course of the COVID-19 pandemic that placed online, digital platforms at the center of how we engage with each other, both inside and outside academia. The multimodal dimensions of *The Beach* class enabled the course to evolve and adapt as the course cap rose to serve the growing number of students who were drawn both to the coastal orientation of the course and the fact that it was a highly accessible and relevant way for them to fulfill their upper-division, general education requirement in the area of scientific inquiry. These aspects also eased the shift to teaching the class online and asynchronously, a modality that will continue even as other courses at our campus have returned to in-person instruction. Similarly, the initial foray of teaching ENGL 330 online and asynchronously, and the focus on an array of digital and visual texts in a variety of genres and contexts, presaged the direction of this and other writing courses, which have continued to empower students to engage with real-world issues of scientific relevance and to communicate the significance of those issues in ways that will reach audiences far beyond the classroom. Again, this is the power of a general education, interdisciplinary, writing intensive course that reinforces and rewards the significance of collaboration, dialogue, and consensus building.

As we continue to engage with this work, we have come to understand that feelings of insecurity and "imposter syndrome" permeate our underserved student population at CSUCI when it comes to both civic scientific literacy and communication. The familiar and evocative setting of California's beaches offers us a chance to engage students with science and with writing in a way that speaks authentically to their perspectives and experiences and connects them to the natural world. This, in turn, empowers students to share what they have learned with their own families and communities and to engage more directly with the "wicked problems" such as climate change and sea level rise that can otherwise seem so far out of their grasp and beyond their control. Our interdisciplinary collaboration serves as a model for how we can begin to chip away at these seemingly intractable challenges and the importance of accessible, evidence-based means of communicating these challenges and fostering buy-in from the general public so that they too can serve as instruments of outreach and advocacy (Curtis 183; Curtis et al. 3).

Works Cited

"2023-2024 University Catalog." California State University Channel Islands. https://catalog.csuci.edu/.

Curtis, David J. "Creating Inspiration: The Role of the Arts in Creating Empathy for Ecological Restoration." *Ecological Management & Restoration*, vol. 10, no. 3, 2009, pp. 174-84.

Curtis, David J, Nick Reid, and Guy Ballard. "Communicating Ecology through Art: What Scientists Think." *Ecology and Society*, vol. 17, no. 2, 2012.

Defeo, Omar et al. "Threats to Sandy Beach Ecosystems: A Review." *Estuarine, Coastal and Shelf Science*, vol. 81, no. 1, 2009, pp. 1-12.

Dugan, J. E. et al. "Generalizing Ecological Effects of Shoreline Armoring across Soft Sediment Environments." *Estuaries and Coasts*, vol. 41, no. S1, 2017, pp. 180-96.

Griggs, Gary. "The Impacts of Coastal Armoring." *Shore and Beach*, vol. 73, no. 1, 2005, pp. 13-22.

Griggs, Gary and Kiki Patsch. "The Protection/Hardening of California's Coast: Times Are Changing." *Journal of Coastal Research*, vol. 35, no. 5, 2019, pp. 1051-61.

Griggs, Gary, Kiki Patsch, and Lauret Savoy. *Living with the Changing California Coast.* University of California Press, 2005.

Gunawardena, Sidath, Rosina Weber, and Denise Agosto. "Finding That Special Someone: Interdisciplinary Collaboration in an Academic Context." *Journal of Education for Library and Information Science*, vol. 51, no. 4, 2010, pp. 210-21.

Helvarg, David. *The Golden Shore: California's Love Affair with the Sea.* Reprint edition ed., New World Library, 2016.

James, Rodney J. "From Beaches to Beach Environments: Linking the Ecology, Human-Use and Management of Beaches in Australia." *Ocean & Coastal Management*, vol. 43, 2000, pp. 495-514.

Johnson, W. R. "Why Engaging in the Practices of Science Is Not Enough to Achieve Scientific Literacy." *The American Biology Teacher*, vol. 78, no. 5, 2016, pp. 370-75.

King, Philip G. et al. "Valuing Beach Ecosystems in an Age of Retreat." *Shore & Beach*, vol. 84, no. 4, 2018, pp. 45-59.

King, Philip and Douglas Symes. "The Potential Loss in Gross National Product and Gross State Product from a Failure to Maintain California's Beaches." A Report for the Department of Boating and Waterways, 2004. https://citeseerx.ist.psu.edu/document?repid=rep1&type=pdf&doi=e0c48384cc8d44471b1cf1e872b930dc137838f9

Lafferty, Kevin. "Birds at a Southern California Beach: Seasonality, Habitat Use and Disturbance by Human Activity." *Biodiversity and Conservation*, vol. 10, 2001, pp. 1949–62.

Lemarie, Jeremy. "Rhythms and Cycles in Surf City USA®: Commercializing Surfing in Southern California." *Academia.com*, 2015.

Miller, J.D. "What Colleges and Universities Need to Do to Advance Civic Scientific Literacy and Preserve American Democracy." *Liberal Education*, vol. 94, no. 4, 2012.

Nichols, Wallace J. "A Conversation with Dr. Wallace J. Nichols." Interview by Kiki Patsch, Environmental Science and Resource Management, 2021, https://youtu.be/pwja3n_fG-E.

"Our Mission." California Coastal Commission. https://www.coastal.ca.gov/whoweare.html.

Patsch, Kiki and Stacey S. Anderson. "Guardians of the Shore." *Beaches on the Edge.* https://beachesontheedge.sandshed.org/.

Pilkey, Orrin H. and J. Andrew G. Cooper. *The Last Beach.* Duke University Press, 2014.

Runyan, Kiki and Gary B. Griggs. "The Effects of Armoring Seacliffs on the Natural Sand Supply to the Beaches of California." *Journal of Coastal Research*, vol. 19, no. 2, 2003, pp. 336-47.

Schlacher, Thomas A. et al. "Sandy Beaches at the Brink." *Diversity and Distributions*, vol. 13, no. 5, 2007, pp. 556-60, doi:10.1111/j.1472-4642.2007.00363.x.

Schwab, Gabriele. *Imaginary Ethnographies: Literature, Culture, and Subjectivity.* Columbia University, 2012.

Schwartz, Brian. "Communicating Science through the Performing Arts." *Interdisciplinary Science Reviews*, vol. 39, no. 3, 2014, pp. 275-89.

"Spring Enrollment Snapshot." California State University Channel Islands.https://oneci.csuci.edu/t/IRPEGuest/views/FallEnrollmentpublic/EnrollmentDashboard?%3Aiid=1&%3AisGuestRedirectFromVizportal=y&%3Aembed=y.

Velasco, Giovanni. "Coastal Perspectives: Engl 330: Interdiscuplinary Writing Fall 2017." *YouTube*, 27 October 2017, https://youtu.be/Xy0v0I_q7v4.

Vitousek, Sean, Patrick L. Barnard, Patrick Limber, Li Erikson, and Blake Cole. "A Model Integrating Longshore and Cross-Shore Processes for Predicting Long-Term Shoreline Response to Climate Change." *Journal of Geophysical Research: Earth Surface*, vol. 122, no. 4, 2017, pp. 782-806.

Willingham, Christine. "Reasons Why Our Coast Is Special." *YouTube*, 29 October 2017, https://youtu.be/RwK0lnj5j7s.

Weaving Science Communication Training through an Undergraduate Science Program with a Focus on Accessibility and Inclusion

Adina Silver, Zoya Adeel, Tim Li, Abeer Siddiqui,
Alexander Hall, Sarah Symons, and Katie Moisse

Abstract: *Science communication training can help scientists engage diverse audiences with the promise and process of science, helping to strengthen science literacy and preserve public trust in science. But not all scientists have access to such training. To address this shortfall, we have embedded a suite of science communication courses in the Life Sciences Program, the largest undergraduate science program at McMaster University in Hamilton, Ontario. A foundational course focuses on making science accessible through inclusive language and media, while more advanced courses emphasize the importance of understanding and centering the values, beliefs, questions, and critiques of audiences, and using narratives and rhetoric to inform, inspire, and ignite change. Throughout the curriculum, students engage with and contribute to the scholarship of science communication. They graduate with skills that serve them in diverse careers. In this article, we outline the structure of our curriculum and detail key components of our science communication courses. We also describe a student-led assessment of our curriculum that highlights strengths and opportunities for improvement. Ultimately, we strive to provide a compelling rationale for teaching science communication at the undergraduate level by sharing a framework of replicable pedagogical practices for engaging large cohorts of students with both the theory and practice of science communication.*

Introduction

We have more *access* to scientific information than ever, and that access brings great promise and peril. There is an assumption that open science will foster public dialogue, improve understanding, and grow confidence in science (Nemer). But *access* alone does not make science *accessible*. If we, as citizens, cannot decipher open science articles, we cannot enjoy them, critique them, or confidently apply their knowledge within our lives. Even when science is made more accessible, citizens must still look for it and identify it in a growing sea of misinformation. We are then challenged with whether and how to act upon it.

Science communication training is helping to address this challenge. There are approaches, backed by evidence, for engaging diverse audiences—the young and the old; the skeptics and the "sciencephiles"—with the promise and process of science (Jensen and Gerber; Schäfer et al.). Importantly, there is now empirical evidence refuting the deficit model of science communication, which posits that one merely needs *access* to scientific information to make science-based decisions (Simis et al.). It is now widely accepted that our beliefs, values, self-identity, and social contexts influence how we seek out, scrutinize, and apply information (Nadkarni et al.).

Science communication training within higher education can help scientists reject the deficit model and engage more intentionally with diverse audiences in varied forums and genres. Indeed, 85% of the general population say they trust scientists and 82% say they want to hear more from scientists about their work (3M State of Science). Yet, in Canada few institutions provide formal training in science communication (Brownell et al.). While there is one Canadian graduate program in science communication at Laurentian University, there remains a need for wider access to science communication training for scientists at all career stages (Laurentian University; Akin et al.) Embedding science communication training into undergraduate programs is ideal because students can gain transferable skills relevant to a wide range of traditional and non-traditional careers in science, not to mention exposure to the latter (Rosenzweig et al.)

Science communication training also provides opportunities for students to examine how science shapes society and vice versa. No longer can educators separate science from its social contexts in our curriculum. The COVID-19 pandemic made clear the extent to which personal beliefs and values, as well as societal histories and politics, affect how we make sense of science and apply it in our lives. Other recent events, such as the racist attack that killed 10 Black people in Buffalo, highlight the power of science to shape beliefs and values—the shooter used genetics research to justify his hate crimes. Students should have opportunities to explore how science can be dismissed or misused to fuel agendas, as this affects public trust in science.

In this article, we describe the successful integration of science communication training into the Life Sciences program at McMaster University. We outline the structure of our curriculum and detail key components of our science communication courses. We also describe a student-led assessment of our curriculum that highlights strengths and important areas for improvement. Ultimately, we strive to provide a compelling rationale for teaching science communication at the undergraduate level by sharing a framework of replicable pedagogical practices for engaging large cohorts of students with both the theory and practice of science communication.

Connecting Science and Society

The Life Sciences Program at McMaster University is the largest undergraduate program in the Faculty of Science, with 1,619 students. Instructors in the program value innovative pedagogies, interdisciplinary perspectives, and experiential learning. The program is distinct from a biology program in its emphasis on the societal contexts of science. Many of our courses feature community-informed or -partnered projects. For instance, students have worked with municipal staff and non-profit organizations to co-create solutions for real-life community challenges. These partnerships provide opportunities for students to build relationships and prioritize reciprocity, equity, and sustainability—core tenets of community engagement ("Principles of Community Engagement").

Many of our courses include written, oral, and multimedia communication assessments, which serve several important purposes. For instance, they require students to demonstrate higher order learning (Armstrong), invite students to practice transferable skills, adopt a creative mindset, connect course content to contemporary challenges and their own lived experiences, and take a critical stance on science. However, in many science courses with a disciplinary focus there is little room for students to learn best practices in communication. For this reason, in 2018 we sought to codify our commitment to communication in the form of a science communication curriculum. We now have four science communication courses in the Life Sciences Program. Students taking these courses practice communicating scientific concepts and findings for different audiences and purposes using varied media and communication strategies. They also critically analyze examples of science communication and engage with the growing field of science communication research, which aims to identify barriers to science literacy and opportunities to engage underserved or skeptical audiences. Scaffolded activities encourage students to connect theory and practice via consistent reflection on their work.

Over the years, our science communication courses have provided a forum for students to view science through a social justice lens. The introduction of "inclusive science communication" as a concept in the science communication literature in 2020 helped to formalize this focus (Canfield et al.). The core traits of inclusive science communication—intentionality, reciprocity, and reflexivity—now form the backbone of our curriculum. We encourage students to communicate with purpose, actively listen, and routinely check their assumptions. Course discussions and activities push students to reject deficit models, practice humility, and embrace difficult conversations (Canfield and Menezes). Students are encouraged to recognize historical oppressions, discrimination, and inequities, and value the knowledge, experiences, questions, and criticisms that audiences—particularly marginalized audiences—bring to conversations about science.

Science Communication Curriculum

Our science communication curriculum spans the second-, third- and fourth- year of the Honours Life Sciences Program (students enter the program their second year). Currently, only our second-year course is required. But beginning in Fall 2023, Life Sciences students will also be required to take one of two third-year science communication courses. Our fourth-year science communication courses are electives. Life Sciences students are also required to take a number of discipline-specific science courses, many of which have communication assessments (papers, presentations, creative projects, etc.) accounting for at least 20% of the final grade.

Within our core science communication courses, we've designed our instructional approaches and assessments to minimize grade-based motivation and encourage students to take ownership of their own learning. We view our curriculum as an inclusive community of practice, wherein students connect theory to practice, take creative risks, and reflect on the process together. We incentivize students to value and incorporate instructor and peer feedback by providing opportunities to reflect on and in some cases resubmit work. Most importantly, we strive to build community in the classroom and foster a sense of belonging in science.

We designed our second-year course to prepare students for science communication activities that are common in upper-level courses, graduate science programs, and careers in science. In each of these scenarios, one is tasked with making science accessible to non-experts. For instance, upper-year undergraduate students may need to create text or video content for a community partner; graduate students may need to create a 3-minute thesis for peers in other labs or disciplines; and scientists often need to write lay summaries for journals and funding agencies. Students enter our second-year course with a desire to make science accessible, but realize through activities and discussions the limitations of the deficit model mindset. Ultimately, they propose ways to move beyond information-sharing, which keeps the onus on audiences to seek out information, and toward more intentional and reciprocal engagement.

In their third year, students work to actively dismantle the deficit communication model. They become increasingly focused on specific goals and audiences, as well as the biases we all bring to conversations about science. They reflect on the assumption they made at the start of second year, that making science accessible will result in meaningful engagement. They must now make sense of science while applying the science of sense-making—considering how people notice information, find meaning within it, and act on it (Weick). Activities challenge students to practice intentionality, reciprocity, and reflexivity, and assessments privilege measurement of the strategic development process over the final product.

In their fourth year, students apply their knowledge and skills in the context of narrative storytelling, a form of science communication that can nurture comprehension, interest, and engagement (Dahlstrom). Here, students practice humility and empathy as they connect directly with audiences to inform their communications. Through iterative, independent work, they recognize storytelling as a powerful way of knowing and a promising avenue for reaching disengaged and passive audiences for science communication.

We acknowledge that our curriculum is a work in progress. We think about our students as audiences and continue to practice the intentionality, reciprocity and reflexivity that we preach. Below, we summarize the learning outcomes for each of our core science communication courses (Table 1). We then highlight select pedagogical practices in each course. We choose to focus on practices that scaffold across our curriculum, though each course has multiple unique learning activities and assessments. Importantly, our instructional approaches and assessments have been developed and refined through meaningful partnerships with students.

Table 1. Core science communication course learning outcomes. Our science communication courses are intentionally scaffolded across second, third, and fourth-year to introduce key competencies in science communication and provide opportunities for students to practice and master these competencies.

Year	Course Name	Learning Outcomes
2	Foundations in Science Communication	1. Critically evaluate scientific papers and articulate the most salient information using accessible language 2. Communicate scientific concepts and data in different formats for different audiences of purposes 3. Critically analyze examples of science communication in the context of misinformation and politicization of science 4. Read, apply, and contribute to the scholarship of science communication 5. Describe alternative careers in science, including careers in science communication
3	Communicating Science for Public Audiences	1. Critically evaluate primary research in science and science communication 2. Apply principles of inclusive science communication to create text and visuals that inform, inspire and ignite positive change 3. Center equity, diversity and inclusion in discussions about how knowledge is created and shared 4. Merge creative and analytical skills to communicate complex ideas 5. Prioritize the process of science and science communication over the final product
4	Science & Storytelling	1. Explore a diverse range of science stories and discuss how they educate and inspire their target audiences 2. Identify neglected narratives and audiences and create new opportunities for inclusion through storytelling 3. Develop fundamental storytelling skills and apply them to different mediums 4. Shed jargon and formulaic writing in favor of creative, engaging prose without sacrificing accuracy

		5. Share our science stories with the community
	Science Communication in the Media	1. Critique diverse examples of science journalism and consider their potential to shape public opinion and policy 2. Discuss opportunities for science to be misconstrued and think proactively about the social and political contexts of science 3. Extend and apply our toolkit for communicating science through popular media 4. Seek out and integrate diverse expert perspectives into our communications 5. Read, apply, and contribute to the scholarship of science communication

Year Two: Foundations in Science Communication

In this foundational course, students practice critically reading research articles and summarizing the most salient information using inclusive language—avoiding jargon and the use of the passive voice, for instance. They do this in the context of scholarly articles that support best practices in science communication (Shulman et al.; Chan and Maglio). One important activity is the "lay summary," a plain-language distillation of a scientific paper for a non-expert audience. Lay summaries (also known as lay abstracts, plain-language summaries, digests, and more) have grown more common—and more important—with the rise of open access to scientific research. In this course, we call them "inclusive summaries" to better reflect their intention, which is to welcome non-scientists into research.

We created an inclusive summary rubric [see Appendix A] based on existing author guidelines for lay summaries and traits of inclusive science communication. We use this rubric in two activities. In one activity, students write an inclusive summary (first with peers and then independently) and receive a grade and feedback through the rubric. In the other activity, the students use our rubric to assess the quality of published lay summaries from four different journals. In winter 2022, 323 students assessed 200 lay summaries (50 from each journal with three independent scorers per summary). We pooled our data and used an ANOVA (Analysis of Variance) to compare scores between the journals (Figure 1).

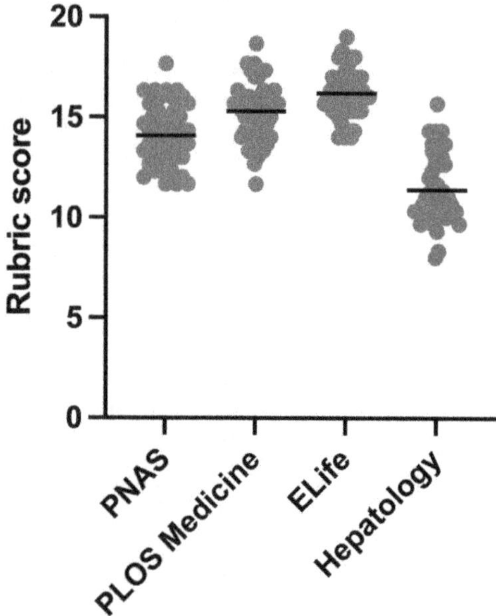

Figure 1: Overall lay summary rubric scores for four selected journals (n=200 lay summaries per journal with n=3 independent raters per lay summary).

The journals eLife and PLOS Medicine score significantly higher on the rubric than PNAS and the Journal of Hepatology (p<0.0001; ANOVA with Tukey post-hoc). All data were collected by students in our second-year science communication course.

This activity has four goals: It exposes students to a wide range of lay summaries, helping to inform their own writing; it requires students to understand and critically apply the rubric that will be used to assess their writing; it provides data from which students can draw conclusions about the usefulness of lay summaries and whether they serve their intended purpose; and it provides us, as instructors, with valuable insight on the inter-rater reliability of our rubric (this is important as we strive to make our expectations explicit and our grading equitable).

Through their research, students learn that the quality of published lay summaries varies greatly across journals. They also realize that the guidelines for authors vary, as do the levels of editing support. The students describe their research findings in an accessibly-written manuscript that includes a review of the relevant literature, including literature on inclusive best practices. They then propose a knowledge mobilization initiative, aimed at transforming their findings into positive change. Proposals have included universal lay summary guidelines for authors, lay summary workshops for researchers, and future explorations into the audiences for—and impact of—lay summaries. (For instance, does a well-written lay summary lead to better comprehension and more positive perceptions of science/scientists than a poorly-written one? Are there better formats and forums for welcoming non-scientists into research?) Students share their research and their proposals with their peers at an end-of-term showcase.

Year Three: Communicating Science for Public Audiences

Our third-year course builds on the activities and discoveries of our foundational course. Students reflect on lay summaries and how, even when done well, they require audiences to look for and find them. Students realize that the traditional structure of scientific communication—leading with the background and ending with what's new and why anyone ought to care—does not align with how non-scientists search for, vet, and share information today. They realize that less is often more, that visuals can be more impactful than text, and that effective communication respects the values, knowledge, experience, questions, and critiques of audiences.

One important activity in our level three course is the research translation which, unlike a lay summary, leads with the most salient information for a given audience. In about 300 words, students must describe the main takeaway or conclusions of a study (what's new), the implications of the work (why an audience ought to care), the approach, the specific findings, and the limitations. They are assessed using a research translation rubric [Appendix B], which prioritizes clarity, conciseness, accessibility, and engagement. Many students assume the research translation will be easy, given their experience with lay summaries, and are surprised by how awkward the new format feels. But after multiple attempts and feedback, their communications become increasingly creative, inclusive, and tailored to their audience.

Students realize through required readings that the format of their research translation aligns with the format of science news articles. One of the first research studies they 'translate' is a randomized controlled trial exploring the effects of spin in health news articles. The study concludes that audiences who read science news articles that do not accurately capture the methods and limitations of research are more likely to believe the research will help them or a loved one than are those who read more accurate, nuanced articles. Students go on to critique published science news articles that are guilty of spin and reflect on how this affects public trust in science.

In the fall of the 2023-24 academic year, students in our third-year course will build on the research they started in level two and run their own randomized controlled trial. They will identify a poorly written lay summary in medical literature, revise it to score better on our inclusive summary rubric, and then rewrite it again as a research translation. We will then recruit students in a large first-year science course to read one of the three summaries and answer survey questions gauging their comprehension, ease of reading, and perceptions of the authors (are they elitist, for instance). Our third-year students will describe their findings in a commentary written in the style of *The Conversation,* an online network for researchers and journalists to publish research commentaries.

Students in our third-year course are also asked to think critically about different audiences for science communication and, importantly, the expertise, lived experiences, questions, and critiques these audiences bring to conversations about science. We review the traits of inclusive science communication—intentionality, reciprocity and reflexivity—and reflect on how they apply in different scenarios. For instance, students read a commentary by Ty Fletcher-Beals titled "How I advocate the importance of vaccines to my Black family" and analyze how the author applies traits of inclusive science communication. We also reflect on our own privilege, as science students, and recognize that the mentors, museums, courses, camps, and clubs that engaged us with science are not universally accessible. Finally, we work with a community partner to address a science communication challenge in our community. Students share their work with their peers and our community partner at an end-of-term showcase.

Year Four: Communicating Science Through Stories

We have two elective fourth-year science communication courses, both of which have a focus on storytelling. Students are only eligible to take one of these courses.

4E03: Science & Storytelling. "Science & Storytelling" is a 30-student seminar course built around the premise that effective science communication concurrently considers audience, purpose, and narrative structure. This course continues the conversations that began in "3P03: Communicating Science for Public Audiences," centering relationship- and trust-building as necessary components for effective science communication. Students engage with dialogic science communication practices, rather than models built on a unidirectional flow of information. Additionally, students learn the importance of communicating science both as a process and as a product; building trust with their audiences by inviting them into the messy, behind-the-scenes parts of scientific knowledge production.

Students engage in a term-long project to create a science story for a particular audience. Past projects have included children's books, documentary films, and interactive narrative-based games. To encourage students to take creative risks and take ownership of their learning, students develop their own rubrics for their final projects in collaboration with the instructor. Grading criteria is tailored to the student's selected story, medium, genre, and audience. For example, an art installation about the health impacts of solitary confinement was assessed on its ability to make the audience feel anxious in a confined space.

To incentivise students to value and incorporate instructor and peer feedback, we have established a resubmission/regrading policy for key formative assessments. Students also meet weekly with their peer check-in groups to share rough drafts and solicit feedback on the final project. While this component is ungraded, students keep track of their discussions in an online notebook. The notebook also allows instructors to catch up on students' progress over the course of the semester. Furthermore, peer check-in groups help create a sense of community within the class–students can work together to troubleshoot problems, share resources, and celebrate successes without the incentive (or indeed, the threat) of being graded. Students in check-in groups are often working on drastically different final projects, ranging from short stories to documentaries to board games, and can therefore apply key principles of science communication to various formats and contexts.

In another assessment, students interview a member from their own respective communities about a specific topic and create a photo essay to share their story. A recent topic was science misinformation; students interviewed community members, friends, family members, etc., about whether they trust science, and why. Here, students practiced listening with empathy to understand where their interviewees' hesitations and misconceptions originate, and subsequently reflected on how we, as science communicators, can (re)build trust.

4J03: Science Communication in the Media. "Science Communication in the Media" is another 30-student seminar course in which students bring the science communication skills and theory they've amassed in years two and three to the practice and critique of science journalism. They engage with professionals who have different roles in the media: public information officers, journalists, and scientists with media experience. They compare and contrast the parallel roles of these science communicators in terms of their audiences and goals. Through engaging in these activities, they come to realize how divergent pressures and priorities create the potential for messages about science to get distorted.

An important focus in this course is the reported article, which combines elements of research translations and explanatory writing, and further integrates the perspectives of credible subject matter experts. Students engage with weekly activities focusing on each of these elements and have the semester to integrate them into a 1,000-word article for a non-scientist audience. There are many opportunities for one-on-one consultation with the instructor, just as there are in a writer-editor relationship. We publish exceptional student work on *The Macroscope*, a website featuring reported articles and commentaries by our science communication students.

Students in this course also engage in science communication research with a focus on media representations of science and scientists. They work in groups of five to come up with a research question that they can answer during the semester using existing data, such as online news articles (accessible through the online database Factiva), public funding databases, and more. They first submit a proposal, on which they receive feedback. They later submit a manuscript and present their findings to the class. In winter 2022, groups focused on topics including media representations of psilocybin research and coverage of men's mental health. The investigations revealed interesting differences between right- and left-leaning media organizations in terms of depictions of evidence and sources of expertise. In winter 2021, one group published their paper on media representations of postpartum depression (Benepal et al.).

Beyond the Classroom

To supplement our classroom offerings, we also create opportunities for students to participate in science communication activities through applied work placements and participate in research through independent studies and thesis experiences. These for-credit experiences, offered during third- and fourth-year, allow students to build their portfolios under the mentorship of an individual or community organization or contribute to the science communication literature under the mentorship of a faculty member.

One of our instructors, Dr. Katie Moisse, has supervised students in experiential placements engaging in a wide range of science communication activities, including writing science news articles, co-creating projects for science communication courses, illustrating pathogens, and painting portraits of women to spotlight women's health issues. Dr. Moisse has also supervised research practicum, independent study, and thesis students doing science communication research, including explorations of media coverage of preprints, comparisons of print and visual media for communicating epidemiological concepts, assessments of the impact of science communication workshops, and investigations of gender and racial bias in science news coverage. These independent projects allow students to dive deeper into the science communication literature and apply the research and data analysis skills they've learned in new ways. Many of these projects use surveys, providing students with the opportunity to engage in the ethics review process and learn qualitative analysis techniques. Students have presented their work at conferences, such as the Science Writers and Communicators of Canada annual conference (Adeel and Moisse) and published in peer-reviewed undergraduate science journals (Wadie).

Student Experience

In July 2020, Dr. Moisse received a Leadership in Teaching & Learning Grant from the MacPherson Institute for Leadership, Innovation and Excellence in Teaching and Learning at McMaster University. The grant provided funds to partner with current and former students (Adeel, Silver, and Li) to map our course offerings against core competencies in science communication (Mercer-Mapstone and Kuchel) and assess student perceptions of our science communication training (Table 2).

In April 2021, we invited students who had taken one of our core undergraduate science communication courses during the 2020-21 academic year to participate in a survey co-designed by students and science communication instructors. The exit survey invited students to reflect on their experiences with the curriculum and their comfort with various science communication activities (n=93). Our results suggest our curriculum provides transferable skills and gives students the confidence to communicate with diverse audiences for a range of purposes. Most students reported they were more comfortable applying oral, written, and multimedia science communication skills as a result of taking a science communication or communication-intensive course. For example, students were more comfortable completing certain communication-focused assessments for non-expert audiences, commentaries/opinion pieces (90%), social media posts (95%), and research translations (94%) in particular. Confidence levels for completing communication assessments almost always increased with each academic year. Our students' self-perceived ability to communicate science to non-expert audiences also increased with each academic year — confirming that our curriculum scaffolds its learning objectives as intended (Figure 2).

Table 2. Integration of the 12 core competencies of science communication in core courses and experiential electives. As students progress through our science communication curriculum, they are introduced to (light gray), actively apply (dark gray), and master (black) the 12 core competencies of science communication.

Core competencies	Year 2	Year 3	Year 4	Experiential electives
Identify and understand a suitable target audience	light gray	light gray	dark gray	dark gray
Use language that is appropriate for your target audience	light gray	light gray	dark gray	dark gray
Identify the purpose and intended outcome of the communication	light gray	light gray	dark gray	dark gray
Consider the levels of prior knowledge in the target audience	light gray	light gray	dark gray	dark gray
Separate essential from non-essential factual content in a context that is relevant to the target audience	light gray	light gray	dark gray	dark gray
Consider the social, political, and cultural context of the scientific information	light gray	light gray	dark gray	dark gray
Use a suitable mode and platform to communicate with the target audience		light gray	light gray	dark gray

Use/consider style elements appropriate for the mode of communication (such as humor, anecdotes, analogy, metaphors, rhetoric, images, body language, eye contact, and diagrams)				
Understand the underlying theories leading to the development of science communication and why it is important				
Promote audience engagement with the science				
Encourage a two-way dialogue with the audience				

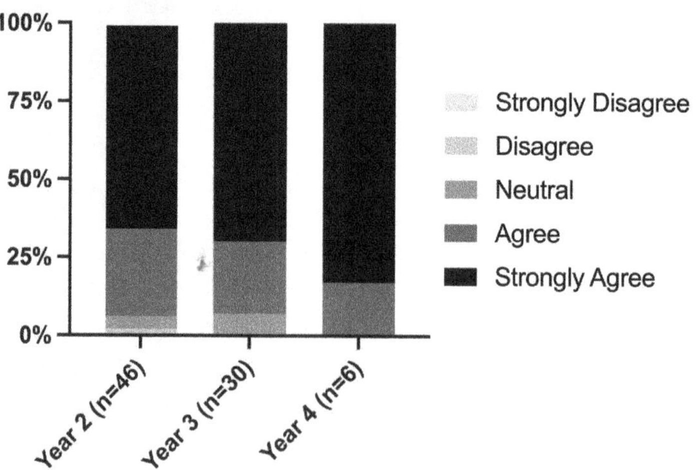

Figure 2: Students report their level of agreement with the statement, "My ability to communicate science to non-expert audiences has improved as a result of this course." At all undergraduate years, the majority of students strongly agreed that their science communication skills improved by taking a science communication course.

Our results also identified some curricular gaps. Students reported discomfort with performing a debate (55%), being interviewed by the media (46%), and engaging in policy communication (33%). We intend to fill these gaps through curriculum revisions such that students have an opportunity to develop these skills, which were affirmed as critical during the COVID-19 pandemic (Caulfield et al.; Gross).

We further captured student perceptions of the importance and relevance of science communication training at the undergraduate level. Many students shared that they believe science communication training should be mandatory for all undergraduate scientists (80%), expressing their recognition of the necessity of accurate and accessible communication in the field of science. They also agreed that it's important to include activities that develop science literacy and science communication in the curriculum (95%) and that it highly applies to their future careers (90%). When students have the opportunity to formally engage with science communication training, they recognize its importance and develop an interest in actively pursuing future opportunities to learn/practice science communication both informally and formally.

The Life Sciences Program encourages students to explore career paths beyond the traditional sciences. We found that the experience our students gain from these courses impacts their interest and willingness to pursue employment in science communication. Almost half (47%) of the student respondents reported that they are open to a career in science communication, while almost one-third (31%) said they would consider pursuing a Master of Science Communication degree. By embedding science communication training in our undergraduate program, we are addressing the need for students with training in both science and science communication to enter sectors outside of research and academia, from public policy and health communications to outreach and advocacy (Brownell et al.; Davies and Horst). Below are some excerpts from our qualitative survey that highlight positive student experiences with the science communication curriculum.

> "I never liked writing... But once I took [the third-year science communication course], my mind completely flipped. That course made writing fun and engaging for me. I have realized that I prefer writing for non-academic audiences because I want to simplify explanations of things and make it more accessible for everyone to understand. After the course, I felt accomplished and proud of my abilities... I think [science communication training] should be mandatory because, being in the science field, it is vital to be able to make science available and accessible to everyone, not just academic audiences." —Fourth-year student

> "I start medical school soon and I can't stress the importance of the skills I've learned over the last four years. I can only imagine the crucial role science communication will play in explaining complicated medical knowledge in easy to understand terms for my patients." —Fourth-year student

> "The science communication courses I took, and the pandemic and global warming, have shown me the importance of knowing how to explain science. That's why I wish to engage in science communication activities." —Third-year student

This evaluative survey has been key in refining our curriculum, within each course and across our offerings. Our students tell us they're learning transferable skills they can confidently apply in varied contexts. This survey was sent out again in April 2022, providing us with a growing longitudinal dataset of student perspectives that we can use to further refine our curriculum.

Looking to the Future

We are proud of the science communication curriculum we have built over the past four years and the ways our students are applying what they have learned. But we must continue to be intentional, reciprocal, and reflexive in our pedagogies. This coming fall, we will add a second third-year course, "Communicating Science for Professional Audiences" (see Figure 3). In this new course, students will practice communicating for clinicians, investors, regulatory bodies, and policymakers. They will debate solutions to climate change and outbreaks with other professionals, such as economists, and practice media interviews to address curricular gaps. We will also open up our science communication courses to undergraduate students across campus—not just science students—and further open up to graduate students our fourth-year experiential courses, in which students can engage with the theory or practice of science communication with an academic or community supervisor.

We will also introduce a concurrent Certificate in Science Communication open to students in any undergraduate program. Students can complete the certificate by taking our second-year course, one of our third-year courses, one of our fourth-year courses and three electives from an interdisciplinary course list. The list includes courses from all faculties that have a focus on bioethics, education, persuasion, policy, advocacy, media studies, or the sociology of science.

Finally, we are in the process of developing a new course-based Master of Science Communication graduate program. This 14-month program aims to engage students from the sciences, social sciences, and humanities with the theory and practice of science communication. Instructors are an interdisciplinary team of science communication scholars and practitioners. Students will practice evidence-based strategies for communicating a range of concepts, findings, and lines of inquiry to diverse audiences—public and professional. Here, too, the traits of inclusive science communication will provide the framework within which students collaborate, create, critique, and reflect.

We hope that by sharing some of our pedagogical practices and reflections on our curriculum, we can inspire others to embed science communication training and opportunities for students to connect theory to practice in their courses and programs. We are eager to engage with other instructors and contribute to a community of practice in Canada and beyond. We welcome all comments, questions, and critiques, and thank the editors for the opportunity to share our practice and process.

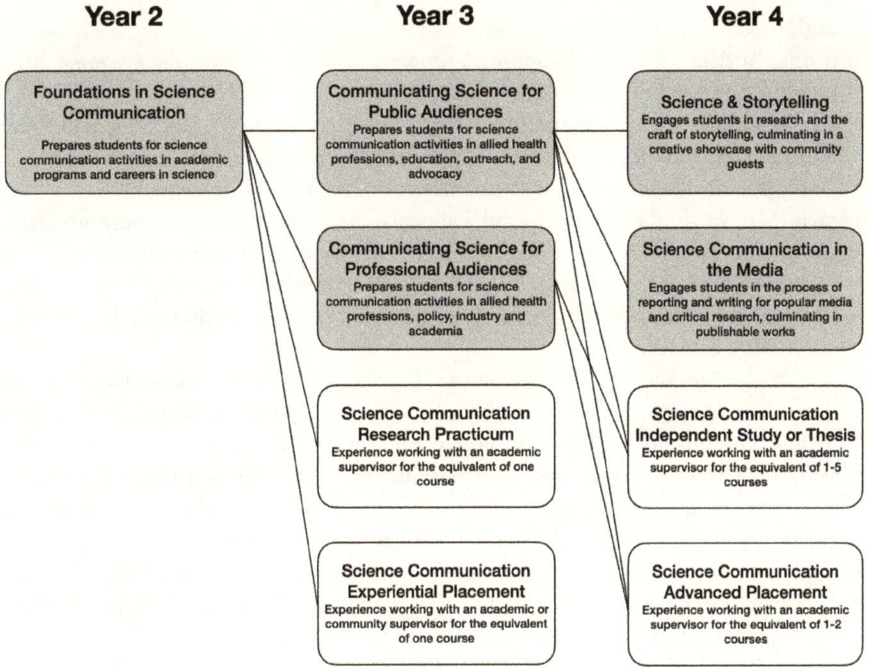

Figure 3: Flowchart schematic of the science communication curriculum with existing and forthcoming courses. Our updated curriculum will have five science communication courses (gray) and four experiential courses (white) through which students can engage in science communication activities or research.

Acknowledgments

The research described was funded by a Leadership in Teaching and Learning Fellowship from the Paul R. MacPherson Institute for Leadership, Innovation and Excellence in Teaching and Learning. Curriculum development was supported by an IDEAS (Inclusion, Diversity, Equity, Accessibility, and Sustainability) Grant from the MacPherson Institute.

Works Cited

Adeel, Zoya, and Katie Moisse. "The Portrayal of COVID-19 Preprint Publications in the News." Science Writers & Communicators of Canada 2021 Virtual Conference, 15 Jun. 2021, Virtual. Poster Presentation.

Akin, Heather, Shelly Rodgers, and Jack Schultz. "Science Communication Training as Information Seeking and Processing: A Theoretical Approach to Training Early-Career Scientists." *Journal of Science Communication*, vol. 20, no. 5, 2021, https://doi.org/10.22323/2.20050206.

Armstrong, Patricia. "Bloom's Taxonomy." *Vanderbilt University Center for Teaching*, 2010, https://cft.vanderbilt.edu/guides-sub-pages/blooms-taxonomy/.

Benepal, Manmeet, et al. "Postpartum Depression Reporting Within Canadian News Sources (2010-2019)." *Sciential - McMaster Undergraduate Science Journal*, vol. 7, 2021, pp. 10–15, https://journals.mcmaster.ca/sciential/article/view/2916.

Brownell, Sara E., Jordan V. Price, and Lawrence Steinman. "Science Communication to the General Public: Why We Need to Teach Undergraduate and Graduate Students This Skill as Part of Their Formal Scientific Training." *Journal of Undergraduate Neuroscience Education*, vol. 12, no. 1, 2013, https://www.ncbi.nlm.nih.gov/pmc/articles/PMC3852879/.

Canfield, Katherine, and Sunshine Menezes. "The State of Inclusive Science Communication: A Landscape Study." *Digital Commons at University of Rhode Island*, 2020, https://digitalcommons.uri.edu/cgi/viewcontent.cgi?article=1186&context=nrs_facpubs.

Canfield, Katherine N., et al. "Science Communication Demands a Critical Approach That Centers Inclusion, Equity, and Intersectionality." *Frontiers in Communication*, vol. 5, no. 2, 2020, https://doi.org/10.3389/fcomm.2020.00002.

Caulfield, Timothy, Tania Bubela, Jonathan Kimmelman, and Vardit Ravitsky. "Let's Do Better: Public Representations of COVID-19 Science." *Facets*, vol. 6, no. 1, 2021, pp. 403-423, https://doi.org/10.1139/facets-2021-0018.

Chan, Eugene Y., and Sam J. Maglio. "The Voice of Cognition: Active and Passive Voice Influence Distance and Construal." *Personality and Social Psychology Bulletin*, vol. 46, no. 4, 2020, pp. 547-558, https://doi.org/10.1177/0146167219867784.

Dahlstrom, Michael F. "Using Narratives and Storytelling to Communicate Science with Non Expert Audiences." *Proceedings of the National Academy of Sciences*, vol. 111, no. 4, 2014, pp. 13614-13620, https://doi.org/10.1073/pnas.1320645111.

Davies, Sarah R., and Maja Horst. *Science Communication: Culture, Identity and Citizenship.* Palgrave Macmillan London, 2016.

Fletcher-Beals, Tyler. "How I Advocate the Importance of Vaccines to My Black Family." *Nature*, 8 Mar. 2021, https://www.nature.com/articles/d41586-021-00480-7.

Gross, Michael. "Communicating Science in a Crisis." *Current Biology*, vol. 30, no. 13, 2020, pp. R737–R739, https://doi.org/10.1016%2Fj.cub.2020.06.052.

Jensen, Eric A., and Alexander Gerber. "Evidence-based Science Communication." *Frontiers in Communication*, vol. 4, no. 78, 2020, https://doi.org/10.3389/fcomm.2019.00078.

"Science Communication (M. S. Com or G. Dip.)", *Laurentian University*, https://laurentian.ca/program/science-communication.

Mercer-Mapstone, Lucy, and Louise Kuchel. "Core Skills for Effective Science Communication: A Teaching Resource for Undergraduate Science Education." *International Journal of Science Education Part B*, vol. 7, no. 2, 2017, pp. 181-201, https://doi.org/10.1080/21548455.2015.1113573/.

Mercer-Mapstone, Lucy, and Louise Kuchel. "Teaching Scientists to Communicate: Evidence-Based Assessment for Undergraduate Science Education." *International Jour-*

nal of Science Education, vol. 37, no. 10, 2015, pp 1613–1638, https://doi.org/10.1080/09500693.2015.1045959.

"Principles of Community Engagement." *McMaster University*, https://community.mcmaster.ca/about/strategic-priorities/principles-of-community-engagement/.

Nadkarni, Nalini M., et al. "Beyond the Deficit Model: The Ambassador Approach to Public Engagement." *BioScience*, vol. 69, no. 4, 2019, pp. 305-313, https://doi.org/10.1093/biosci/biz018.

Nemer, Mona. "Roadmap for Open Science." *Government of Canada*, Feb. 2020, https://www.ic.gc.ca/eic/site/063.nsf/vwapj/Roadmap-for-Open-Science.pdf/$file/Roadmap-for-Open-Science.pdf.

Schäfer, Mike S., Tobias Füchslin, Julia Metag, Silje Kristiansen, and Adrian Rauchfleisch. "The Different Audiences of Science Communication: A Segmentation Analysis of the Swiss Population's Perceptions of Science and Their Information and Media Use Patterns." *Public Understanding of Science*, vol. 27, no. 7, 2018, pp. 836-856, https://doi.org/10.1177/0963662517752886.

Shulman, Hillary C., Graham N. Dixon, Olivia M. Bullock, and Daniel Colón Amill . "The Effects of Jargon on Processing Fluency, Self-Perceptions, and Scientific Engagement." *Journal of Language and Social Psychology*, vol. 39, no. 5-6, 2020, pp. 579-597, https://doi.org/10.1177/0261927X20902177.

Simis, Molly J., Haley Madden, Michael A. Cacciatore, and Sara K. Yeo. "The Lure of Rationality: Why Does the Deficit Model Persist in Science Communication?" *Public Understanding of Science*, vol. 25, no. 4, pp. 400-414, 2016, https://doi.org/10.1177%2F0963662516629749.

Rosenzweig, Emily Q., et al. "Inside the STEM Pipeline: Changes in Students' Biomedical Career Plans Across the College Years." *Science Advances*, vol. 7, no. 18, 2021, https://doi.org/10.1126/sciadv.abe0985.

Wadie, Juliana. "Health in Bite Sized Pieces - Discovering Lack of Accessibility and Engagement in Lay Summaries." *Sciential - McMaster Undergraduate Science Journal*, no. 8, 2022, pp. 2–9, https://journals.mcmaster.ca/sciential/article/view/3014.

Weick, Karl E., Kathleen M. Sutcliffe, and David Obstfeld. "Organizing and the Process of Sensemaking." *Organization Science*, vol. 16, no. 4, pp. 409-421, 2005, https://doi.org/10.1287/orsc.1050.0133.

"State of Science Index Survey." *3M State of Science*, 2022, https://www.3m.com/3M/en_US/state-of-science-index-survey/interactive-3m-state-of-science-survey/.

Appendix A: Inclusive Summary Rubric

Content	Level 5 5 points	Level 4 4 points	Level 3 3 points	Level 2 2 points	Level 1 1 point	Criterion Score
Did you accurately summarize the study methods, results and conclusions?	You excelled at this task, providing information that was consistently on-point.	Your summary is mostly accurate but sometimes ambiguous.	Your summary is mostly accurate but incomplete, introducing the potential for confusion.	Your summary raises multiple questions or lacks focus and was difficult to unpack.	Your summary contains multiple inaccuracies.	/ 5
Did you accurately summarize the study rationale, implications and limitations?	You excelled at this task, providing information that was consistently on-point.	Your summary is mostly accurate but sometimes ambiguous.	Your summary is mostly accurate but incomplete, introducing the potential for confusion.	Your summary raises multiple questions or lacks focus and was difficult to unpack.	Your summary is off-point.	/ 5

Style	Level 5 5 points	Level 4 4 points	Level 3 3 points	Level 2 2 points	Level 1 1 point	Criterion Score
Is your writing clean, clear and logically organized?	Your writing is free of typos and grammatical errors and easy to follow, with smooth transitions that carry your reader from one thought to the next.	Your writing is clean and your sentences are strong, but the overall organization could be improved.	Your writing contains one typo, grammatical error, confusing sentence or awkward transition or it lacks some clarity in terms of sentence structure and organization.	Your writing contains more than one typo, grammatical error, confusing sentence or awkward transition.	Your writing has multiple mistakes or minimal flow.	/ 5
Is your writing tailored to its audience and purpose?	Your writing is a joy to read. You make complex concepts relatable and consider your audience from start to finish, in terms of the language you use and the organization of your thoughts.	Your writing is accessible and contains elements that will engage your audience.	Your writing is generally accessible and contains at least one element aimed at engaging your audience, but some parts fall flat.	Your writing is generally accessible but it lacks elements that will engage your audience and keep them reading from start to finish.	Your writing contains words or descriptions that are inaccessible to your audience or may bore them.	/ 5

| Total | | | | | | / 20 |

Appendix B: Research Translation Rubric

Content	Level 5 5 points	Level 4 4 points	Level 3 3 points	Level 2 2 points	Level 1 1 point	Criterion Score
Did you accurately convey the main takeaway and implications?	You excelled at this task, providing accurate information that was consistently on-point.	Your descriptions were accurate but buried or hard to identify.	Your descriptions were accurate but incomplete or raised new questions that went unanswered.	Your descriptions lacked focus or were difficult to unpack.	Your descriptions were inaccurate or missing.	/ 5
Did you accurately describe the methods and results?	You excelled at this task, providing accurate information that was consistently on-point.	Your descriptions were accurate but raised new questions that went unanswered.	Your descriptions were accurate but incomplete, creating confusion.	Your descriptions lacked focus or were difficult to unpack.	Your descriptions were inaccurate or missing.	/ 5
Did you accurately capture the limitations and indicate appropriate next steps?	You excelled at this task, providing accurate information that was consistently on-point.	Your descriptions were accurate but raised new questions that went unanswered.	Your descriptions were accurate but incomplete, creating confusion.	Your descriptions lacked focus or were difficult to unpack.	Your descriptions were inaccurate or missing.	/ 5

Style	Level 5 5 points	Level 4 4 points	Level 3 3 points	Level 2 2 points	Level 1 1 point	Criterion Score
Is your writing clean and clear with a logical flow?	Your writing is free from typos and grammatical errors and easy to follow, with smooth transitions that carry your reader from one thought to the next.	Your writing is clean and your sentences are strong, but the overall organization could be improved.	Your writing is clean, but lacks some clarity in terms of sentence structure and organization.	Your writing has multiple typos, grammatical errors, confusing sentences or awkward transitions.	Your writing has multiple mistakes or minimal flow.	/ 5
Is your writing accessible and engaging?	Your writing is a joy to read. You make complex concepts relatable and consider your audience from start to finish, in terms of the language you use and the organization of your thoughts.	Your writing is accessible and contains elements that will engage your audience.	Your writing is generally accessible and contains at least one element aimed at engaging your audience, but some parts fall flat.	Your writing is generally accessible but it lacks elements that will engage your audience and keep them reading from start to finish.	Your writing contains words or descriptions that are inaccessible to your audience or may bore them.	/ 5

| Total | | | | | | / 25 |

Addressing Gaps in Science Competencies: Incorporating Science Communication into Existing Classes

Amy J. Hawkins, Melissa Rowland-Goldsmith, and Nicole C. Woitowich

Abstract: *Regardless of which career path a scientist decides to take, they must be able to communicate effectively with broad audiences. As such, science communication training has become an essential component of STEM professional development. While multiple national scientific societies have articulated the need to address these skills as in fundamental training, few undergraduate scientific training programs have formally addressed this in their degree programs. Here we present an innovative approach to teach this skill set by blending an online science communication course with existing curricula in the biomedical sciences. Online content from the American Society for Biochemistry and Molecular Biology (ASBMB) Art of Science Communication (ASC) course was integrated into an undergraduate setting. This new iteration utilized components from the successful online course format blended with an institutional course to foster science communication skills. We provide key insights into blended-course development and its impact on learners' professional development and science communication skills. We contextualize our approach with what others have learned from blended courses and online professional development opportunities for STEM students.*

Introduction

Dialogues between scientists and non-experts likely date as far back as the beginning of science itself. Certainly public understanding and appreciation of science are essential underpinnings of modern society, and scientific literacy provides benefits that span individual, community, and organizational levels. Yet gaps in public understanding of science as a process and profession persist, and the resulting misconceptions and mistrust of science have significant consequences across our society. Anti-science sentiments and growing mistrust of science have real-world implications on a global scale as recommendations from climate scientists are ignored, anti-vaccination movements are highly visible and vocal, and pseudo-scientific medical treatments, which have no scientific or clinical basis, are increasingly popular.

The activities which promote knowledge, interest, and understanding of science are broadly categorized into the fields of science outreach and communication, and may incorporate components of formal or informal education (American Association for the Advancement of Science). We contend here that the deficit model of communication historically used by the scientific community in its interactions with non-experts has significant limitations. Active listening and mutual learning between scientists and non-experts, where the emotions, beliefs, motivations, and interests of all parties are considered, become critical for effective communication. Communicators of science must learn how to engage their audience and to translate scientific content into accessible language with three goals in mind: (1) increase awareness of science by generating interest and positive attitudes, (2) create understanding of science, and, eventually, (3) foster an appreciation of and participation in science.

One of the main goals of science communication is to increase public engagement, awareness, and understanding of science (AAAS). In this text, we refer to our audience as non-experts, rather than non-scientists, general public, or lay public for several reasons. Using the terms non-scientists and general public establishes a barrier and unfavorable power dynamic which assumes scientists are in a distinct category of individuals separate from anyone else. The term lay public is typically used synonymously with genetical public but can also reference members of a religious organization, and we avoid using the term for both these reasons. The tern non-expert also encompasses science communication which occurs across scientific disciplines. Geophysicists and biochemists are both scientists, but they are not likely to be experts in both fields. Taking these nuances into consideration fosters inclusive communication that encourages the audience to be an active participant in science.

The realization of a need for effective science communication has led to a growing body of research in the theory and practice of science outreach and communication within academia and beyond, as demonstrated by the explosion of scholarly literature related to this emerging field. The next challenge is to incorporate these findings and this knowledge into the formal educational programs of scientists and to provide continuing education for those in the scientific workforce. Here we describe an approach to incorporate an online science communication course into existing classrooms and discuss lessons learned from these approaches.

Communicating Science

Scientists rely on various modes of communication in order to conduct, advance, and disseminate their research. Strong communication skills are necessary to establish collaborations, form research teams, obtain funding, and share research findings (Feliú-Mójer). Moreover, many scientists are required to demonstrate the broader impact of their work in order to obtain extramural funding (National Science Board). The addition of "Broader Impacts" to the criteria used to formally evaluate competitive National Science Foundation (NSF) grant proposals establishes an expectation that taxpayer-funded scientific research must engage the public and contribute more broadly to achieving societal goals (National Science Foundation).

Indeed, scientists overwhelmingly agree that public engagement with science is essential (Dang and Russo; Ecklund et al.; Johnson et al.; The Wellcome Trust). Yet discomfort with science communication techniques may limit scientists' participation in outreach (Committee on the Science of Science Communication: A Research Agenda et al.). Moreover, science communication efforts often fail to represent the diverse spectra of individuals involved with or impacted by science (Bevan et al.; Canfield et al.). As described by the Center for the Advancement of Informal Science Education (CAISE) task force on broadening participation in STEM (Bevan et al.): "Representations and instantiations of science are typically informed by the dominant cultural norms of STEM, which are mostly white, western, and male." In order to meet the need for effective science communication conducted by a diverse group of scientists, broadly accessible training should be available and required as part of undergraduate science curricula and training (Brownell et al.; Jandciu et al.; Kuehne et al.). Without an investment in culturally-relevant science communication training, created by and for members of diverse communities, we are faced with propagating outdated stereotypes of who can access, participate in, and benefit from science.

Furthermore, the call to develop science communication curricula has been articulated by stakeholders at every level of formal education. In 2011, The AAAS released *Vision and Change in Undergraduate Biology: A Call to Action* (American Association for the Advancement of Science). This report represents a seminal consensus from faculty, researchers, students, and representatives from professional societies. Together with pedagogy experts, these stakeholders articulated a vision for how undergraduate biology education must transform to meet the needs of the 21st century (McLaughlin and Metz). This includes a list of competencies that students must acquire in order to become biologically literate and practice science. Notably, two of the six core competencies include: "the ability to communicate and collaborate with other disciplines," and "the ability to understand relationships between science and society," underscoring the importance of science communication training as a critical component of undergraduate education.

Despite these recommendations, few undergraduate courses address science communication. While college courses on rhetoric and technical communication are plentiful, they are most often found in English or Communication departments and have not become standard components of scientific training. These "turf wars" between disciplines over certain competencies are doing a profound disservice to students, pulling in the opposite direction of where education needs to be headed, towards scientific literacy forged by interdisciplinary cooperation. As a result, students entering the scientific workforce will be unprepared to communicate effectively with broad audiences and may not have an opportunity to pursue such training at further points in their careers.

Course Context: The ASBMB's Art of Science Communication

To address the lack of oral science communication training geared towards non-expert audiences, the American Society for Biochemistry and Molecular Biology (ASBMB) Science Outreach and Communication Committee developed an online course entitled "The Art of Science Communication" (ASC) (Greer et al.). The ASC course was designed to provide scientists with the fundamental skills required to effectively communicate their research and scientific interests to non-expert audiences. The goal of the course is to increase learners' confidence and competence in science communication. The course is open to self-identified, "scientists and STEM professionals." There are no prerequisites and individuals of all career and educational stages may participate. While the course is hosted by the ASBMB, participants need not be society members.

The ASC curriculum was originally described by Greer and colleagues (Greer et al.). Briefly, the online course spans seven weeks, in which learners are assigned to small weekly group sessions, held online via a web conferencing platform, and moderated by experienced science communicators (Figure 1). The general format is the flipped classroom model: Learners access the pre-recorded, professionally produced lectures, homework assignments, and supplementary content on an online Moodle platform hosted by the ASBMB asynchronously, then utilize the synchronous virtual group meetings for discussion of the course content and assignments.

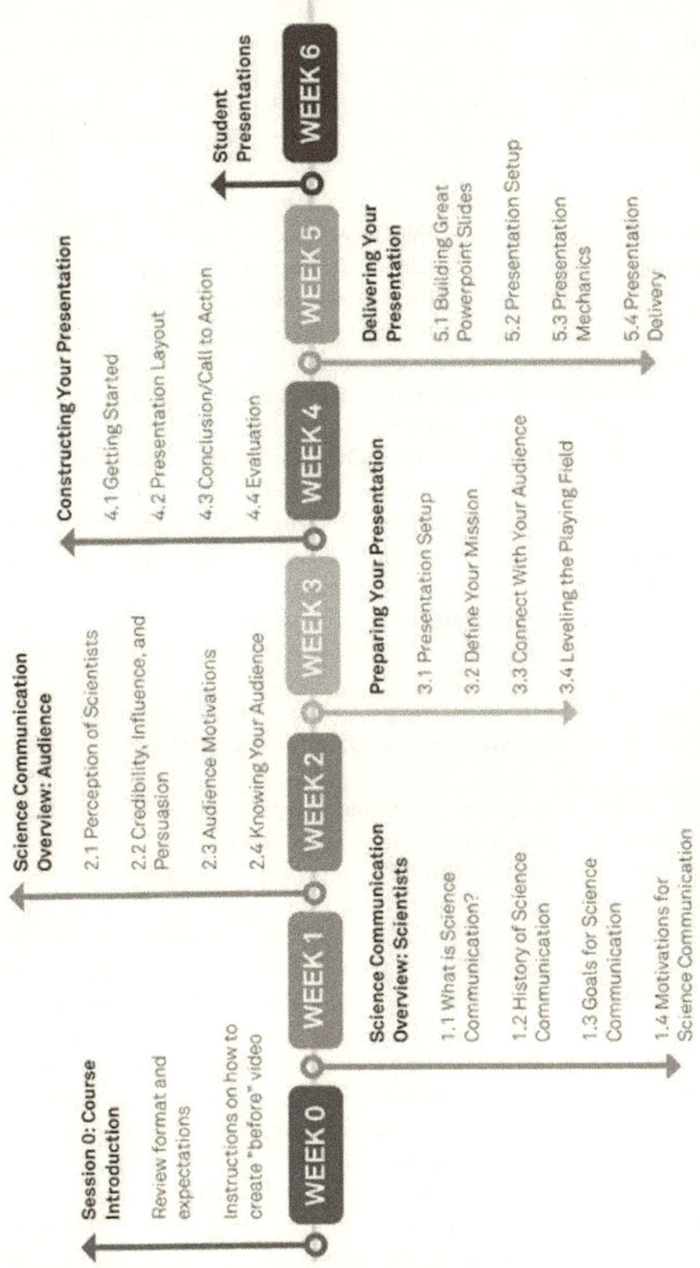

Figure 1: Timeline of the ASBMB Art of Science Communication Course. Adapted from Greer et al., 2018.

To start, learners receive detailed instructions on the format and expectations of the course, which include the production of a five-minute long pre-recorded oral presentation about their own research or a topic of their choice, *tailored to a non-expert audience*. The video recordings serve as a basis on which to apply concepts and ideas that are introduced throughout the course (Figure 1). The following weeks address major themes in oral science communication including framing, the use of analogies and metaphors, accessible language, and storytelling techniques. Each theme is evaluated within the context of the learners' pre-course presentation, which makes it immediately relevant to the students.

The course culminates with learners preparing and delivering a five-minute post-course video presentation of their topic, incorporating course concepts and group-feedback. These presentations are generally much improved and demonstrate the learners' newly acquired communication skills. Likewise, learners are more cognizant of their intended audience(s) and have tailored their post-course video accordingly.

Developing and hosting an online course through a scientific society offers considerable benefits. The course exists independent of an academic institution and remains open and accessible to all who are interested in participating, regardless of location, affiliation, or career stage. Unlike the traditional MOOCs, the course benefits from weekly interaction with expert mentors, skilled in science communication, and with members of the discussion group. This allows for feedback and discussion in real time and has proven very beneficial to the participants. From 2015 – 2022, there have been 35 sessions of the course, interacting with a cumulative participation of 905 learners, employing 110 trained mentors, and achieving an average course completion rate of 74%. Most participants hail from the biological or life sciences, with graduate students being the most common type of learner.

Transitioning to Blended Learning

Early in ASC course development, it became clear that academic institutions could utilize the course within their scientific training programs by offering a blended version. The online content would be fused with in-person discussion groups and integrated into existing courses at academic institutions. Offering the course in both blended and online-only formats further extends the accessibility of science communication training.

Since the onset of the COVID-19 pandemic, the teaching world has undergone a rapid revolution. Educators are no longer engaged in a theoretical discussion on the merits of online and/or blended learning. Rather, we addressed an immediate need for adopting existing curricula to what was rapidly becoming the most prominent mode of teaching. To this end the ASC provides an innovative and integrative approach to blend online science communication training with existing biomedical curricula.

While there is no single accepted definition for blended learning, here we evoke this definition: blended learning courses (1) thoughtfully integrate different instructional methods such as lecture, discussion group, self-paced activity; and (2) contain both face-to-face and computer-mediated portions (Alammary et al.). The accepted understanding of what qualifies as blended learning is variable, and different practices have been studied for their effectiveness. In general, meta-analyses indicate that blended learning may be more effective than either online learning or face-to-face instruction since it takes advantage of some of the best aspects of both synchronous and asynchronous activities: synchronous learning offers spontaneity and the opportunity for a participant to feel "in sync" with a community of learners, while asynchronous activities allow for flexibility (Means et al., "Effectiveness"). When designing blended versions of the ASC course, we adopted some of these best practices such as focusing on synchronous activities within a small community of learners and utilizing asynchronous time for delivery of didactic content. We designed educational interventions that would be useful to students, given resource constraints of both the instructors and students.

Approaches to blended learning can be categorized as "medium-impact," in that activities are integrated into an existing face-to-face course. The activities described in this blended ASC course aim to meet the goals of creating specific materials (a 5-minute presentation), active learning (continually improving the presentation by applying newly acquired knowledge and skills), community building (each student's work is critiqued by each member of the class in a thoughtful and respectful manner), and participant reflection (by continually re-examining their work as the course progresses). By (1) recording an initial presentation on a scientific topic, (2) participating in interactive science communication training where they evaluate outside materials, (3) receiving feedback on their own scaffolded attempts at science communication, and (4) recording a revised final presentation, students build their own understanding of a scientific topic and learn to avoid using jargon in their explanations. By completing the communication exercises, conducting peer-to-peer feedback, and building off of their initial presentation, students also participate in metacognition by engaging in reflection and recognizing the conceptual change in their communication.

Here we describe a case study in which the online ASC course is blended within an existing classroom setting at the undergraduate level. We describe the development and evolution of the blended course and its impact on participants. Throughout this collaborative project we learned that the online ASC course lends itself to many different iterations, and hope that this example will inspire the science teaching community to adopt some of these concepts and techniques into their own classrooms or programs.

Case Study: Integrating the ASC into an Undergraduate Biology Course

Developed by Melissa Rowland-Goldsmith, Schmid College of Science and Technology at Chapman University

Course Context

The ASC course was integrated into an upper division undergraduate "Biology of Cancer" course at Chapman University. The class is offered to junior and senior biochemistry and biology majors and covers the fundamentals of cancer biology. Specifically, this course focuses on the biological mechanisms of cancer formation and progression. It is an interactive course where students read primary literature and deliver presentations to the class. Since most students plan for careers in biomedicine, the skill of communicating complex scientific topics to non-expert audiences is an indispensable necessity. Here, I describe the development of the blended ASC, Biology of Cancer course from 2018–2020 and its impact on students.

Course Structure

Prior to the first class, students completed homework that provided a framework for the importance of learning science communication skills. This included watching the Ken Burns PBS miniseries "Cancer: Emperor Of all Maladies;" reading Rebecca Skloot's book, "The Immortal Life of Henrietta Lacks;" and reading Anna Leahy's book, "Tumor."

During the first few weeks, students were required to read three journal articles co-authored by a physician-scientist who specializes in pancreatic cancer. Each student selected an article and a key figure that would serve as their research topic for the ASC section of the course and recorded a 5-minute pre-course presentation, explaining their literature-based research topic. Next, students met with the physician-scientist who co-authored the papers. They explained the methods and results of each paper and emphasized concepts of accessible and effective communication in relation to their career. After this meeting, students participated in the ASC portion of the course and developed strategies to present their selected figure to a non-expert audience. Upon completion of the course, each student generated an improved version of their presentations and delivered them to a non-expert audience consisting of a panel of pancreatic cancer survivors and caregivers.

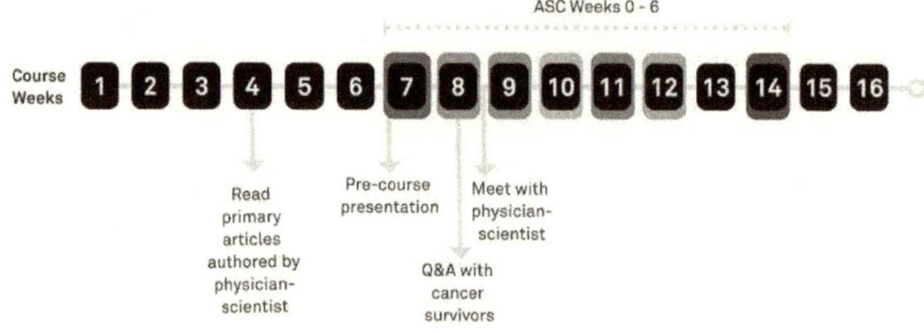

Figure 2: Timeline of Iteration 1 - ASC Course Blended in the Biology of Cancer Course

Year One. In year one, the course included seven in-person, one-hour sessions that took place outside of the scheduled cancer biology course. Students were required to read three articles (Ankeny et al., 2016, Girgis et al., 2011, Elliott et al., 2017) co-authored by Dr. Mark Girgis, a physician-scientist at the University of California, Los Angeles. Students chose a figure from one of the articles as their focus for the ASC course. The articles were relevant to the content they were studying in the cancer biology course. The students met with Dr. Girgis after week two of the ASC course (Figure 2). Students were required to watch the online lectures, complete homework assignments, and review the additional materials offered by the online ASC course platform. During the in-person class sessions, students discussed highlights from the online course content, mirroring the small group sessions of the online version of the course. Significant time was dedicated each week to discussion and interpretation of the homework assignments. These discussions were extremely useful when students started to work on their final presentations. First, students shared their proposed presentation title and discussed ways to remove jargon and/or make it creative and enticing. In addition, students discussed their "mission statement" and "leveling the playing field" statements and received individualized feedback. Since students were required to read all of the articles associated with the presentation topics, they felt comfortable giving constructive feedback to their peers. The collaborative nature of this course also helped students learn from one another in order to modify their presentation content accordingly.

Each student met with me privately prior to the final presentation to discuss additional ways to make the presentation understandable and interesting to a non-expert audience. Students were not allowed to use slides during their presentations but were encouraged to use visual aids to explain their topic. During these consultations, several students developed creative demonstrations. One student used a Velcro shoe to illustrate a device called the NanoVelcro Chip which captures circulating tumor cells from a blood sample. During their presentation, the student showed the Velcro portion of a strap on a shoe, and stated it was similar to the NanoVelcro chip. He demonstrated that Velcro only binds to specific material on the other half of the strap and does not bind to any other part of the shoe, establishing an analogy as to how the NanoVelcro chip only binds to circulating tumor cells and not to other kinds of cells in the body. These types of analogies are encouraged by the ASC course and this specific example demonstrates how everyday objects can be used to distill complex biological topics.

Year Two. Year two built on the experiences acquired during year one. I invited three former students who took the initial course to serve as co-instructors for year two. This follows the instructor recruitment model from the online ASC course, where outstanding learners are invited to become future instructors. Each co-instructor was assigned a cohort of three students. Once again, students read articles co-authored by Dr. Girgis as described above and met with him in week two of the course. In year two, all ASC instruction took place via Zoom. Importantly, this was prior to the Covid-19 pandemic, and Zoom was chosen because it allowed more flexibility with students' schedules. Students reported that the small cohorts provided them with individual attention from their co-instructor, that they encouraged participation and were convenient to attend. As former students, the co-instructors also provided key insights and agreed that the small cohorts allowed for more personalized feedback during class. Lastly, in year two, the ASC-related material was delivered in five meetings instead of seven: the content from weeks three and four was merged (see Figure 2), and the pre-course orientation was eliminated.

Year Three. As a result of the Covid-19 pandemic, the Fall 2020 iteration of this course was taught fully online to 18 students. Five ASC co-instructors were selected from the year two class section. Just like in year two, each co-instructor taught the course to groups of three-to-four students via Zoom. For this iteration, I created groups within the online course learning management system of the college. Each group had their own home page where they could post discussions, collaborate, and establish additional student-led meetings. The students read a total of four scientific articles co-authored by Dr. Girgis and Dr. Murray Korc from the University of California, Irvine (Girgis et al.; Gore et al.; Stuparu et al.). Including another co=author during year three allowed the students to have more choices about which paper and figure to select as their research focus for the ASC course. As in years one and two, I worked with each student at the end of the course to refine their final presentation. The final presentations were delivered via Zoom and attended by cancer survivors or caregivers. Other than these changes, year three followed the general organization and timetable of year two.

Final Presentations

All three years of the blended ASC-Biology of Cancer course provided students with an opportunity to practice their science communication skills with non-experts. To humanize an otherwise molecular biology-focused course, I invited pancreatic cancer survivors and caregivers to share their experiences with the class and asked them to help grade the students' final presentations. Each year, reviewers graded presentations using a rubric that was adapted from the 2018 ASC Instructor Manual. For each question, the reviewers provided a numerical score and written feedback. At the end of the semester, each student received approximately ten evaluations from both their instructors as well as the non-expert stakeholders. Students indicated that they would make changes based on this feedback to deliver better presentations in the future. At the end of the course, all participants received a certificate of completion from the ASBMB. We believe that this blended course leads to a substantial improvement in student presentations and promotes science communication with non-experts.

Discussion

While the broadscale adoption of science communication training at the undergraduate level has remained minimal, the ASC course serves a useful resource for students and faculty, and if adopted, can benefit their respective departments and academic institutions. The ASC course can be seamlessly integrated into a variety of classroom settings or workshop formats and provides professional development opportunities to its students.

Reflections from Blended Course Students

A mixed-methods survey of ASC alumni found that their participation increased their comfort in communicating science with non-expert audiences (ASBMB Science Outreach and Communication Committee, *in preparation*). As one student from Chapman University (ASC) notes:

> After taking the course, I have felt more confident in my ability to properly explain scientific topics to all crowds and types of people with varying backgrounds. I feel like I can apply the knowledge I learned to other public events.

While another Chapman University student (ASC) highlights their newfound awareness of the intersectionality of science and society:

> Through the course, I realized how important science is for people in general. Science is not for scientists; it is for all people, no matter what their background is. What is the point of doing science if the people you are performing the studies for don't understand why or how it [is] important to them.

In addition, the majority of surveyed ASC alumni from blended courses indicated that their participation in the course helped them achieve some type of personal (96%, n=26) or professional (85%, n=23) goal. Another Chapman University student (ASC) shared their personal goal of communicating science with their non-expert family members:

> While I am a first-generation college student, and the rest of my family does not come from a science background at all. My personal goal was to be able to better explain my research to my family, and this course definitely taught me useful skills that help me do so every day.

Other students' professional goals focused on employment or the development of long-term skills. A student from Chapman University (ASC) shares:

> I got my dream job doing research that combines bench work and community engagement based on my experiences in the course.

Taken together, these reflections highlight the impact of the blended ASC course on students' professional development.

Pedagogical Strategies to Engage Students

We posit that key aspects of the blended ASC course contribute to positive student outcomes via several pedagogical approaches. With regards to many aspects, the experience undergraduate students had with the blended ASC course reflects the professional development initiatives developed for STEM graduate students and postdoctoral scholars (see Hokanson et al.). Members of the Center for the Integration of Research, Teaching and Learning Network designed and implemented several online synchronous professional development workshops which integrated active learning, participant reflection, skill development, and commitments to follow-up actions. For example, the workshops focused on helping participants to create specific materials that pertained to career development. Workshop participants indicated that they chose to participate "because they wished to take ownership of their own professional development and career trajectory," and "completing a tangible assignment and building a sense of community through structured time for reflection were the principle elements of our ICE [inform-create-evaluate] workshop design that they valued" (Hokanson et al.). The CIRLT workshop participants highlighted that they particularly valued time for reflection, echoing what was reported as the practice with the strongest evidence for learning effectiveness in blended learning (Means et al., "Evaluation"). This same meta-analysis also reports on a body of preliminary evidence that supports the hypothesis that conditions in which learners have control of their learning (via active learning experiences) produce larger learning gains than do instructor-directed conditions (such as expository learning experiences) (Means et al., "Evaluation"). We used some of these strategies in achieving successes in our blended ASC course: students had the opportunity to take ownership of their learning by choosing their scientific topics and developing a tangible product (e.g., a five-minute presentation).

We argue that our results support those of others who have applied a social constructivist theory of learning to the online environment, according to which human development is socially situated and knowledge is constructed through social interaction with others (Huang). The facilitated, small group learning communities that are intrinsic to the structure of the ACS course are critical for fostering the students' motivation. Similarly, other research suggests that student interaction with an instructor affects MOOC learner retention, a format that has elements in common with our online course (Hone and El Said). In the online ACS course, personalized mid-week reminders, or "nudges," and individual feedback from an experienced instructor deliver the positive reinforcement to sustain motivation to engage in the asynchronous content, knowing that once a week, they'll encounter a synchronous social learning environment with peers who expect their engagement (Manturuk). Students' self-directed learning is empowered through the weekly assignments and final presentation, learning tasks that others describe as supporting constructivist collaboration in both physical and virtual learning spaces (Sze-yeng and Hussain).

Suggestions for ASC Integration

Potential blended course instructors should spend several months preparing to teach this course due to the logistics involved with its execution. Faculty members are required to take the online ASC course three to six months in advance of the blended course. In addition, instructors must work with their departments to ensure a funding model is available for the course, as the ASBMB charges a small fee per student taking the course.

Sharing expectations and coordinating the timing of the blended ASC course is critical and includes several key points. The course description should highlight the ASC component and indicate that five to seven additional sessions will be held outside of the traditional class hours. This can be reiterated by the instructor prior to the start of classes, so that students who do not wish to participate in this component can enroll in a different course. These expectations should be reiterated in the syllabus and describe what portions of the ASC course are graded. For example, the final presentation in the ASC-Biology of Cancer course was worth 15% of the overall grade.

Another difficult task is finding appropriate time within the semester to integrate the ASC course content. Students need to have enough foundational knowledge in the scientific content area in order to develop their presentation. While instructors can let students choose their own scientific presentation topics, we suggest using primary research articles that align with the course topic and learning objectives. To create added value, the faculty member can arrange to have the co-author(s) of each assigned paper meet with the class. This meeting should take place early within the ASC course so that the students have the remaining time to work on their final presentation.

It is also useful to recruit outstanding former students to serve as co-instructors. By doing so, the class can be divided into smaller learning environments. Though they may not get paid for this role, they gain teaching experience which can be leveraged for professional development purposes. Lastly, if possible, the instructor should invite a panel of non-experts to grade each presentation. These suggestions help create a blended course which is differentiated from the online version and provides numerous aspects to humanize science by working with their peers, meeting the scientists who author publications, and communicating with non-experts impacted by science. Together, these emphasize the important relationship between science communication and society.

Conclusion

The blended ASC course exemplifies the statement that, "It takes a village to educate our students." The robust partnership between the ASBMB and the academic institutions which have blended the ASC course into their existing curricula has led to a bespoke method of teaching science communication to undergraduate students. Faculty teaching other discipline-based science courses can use this model to successfully blend ASC into their curriculum. There are several key logistical considerations that faculty should be aware of which require coordination and planning between the ASBMB and the partnering institution. As blended and virtual learning becomes more commonplace, following the COVID-19 pandemic, this strategy to promote science communication training may appeal to a broader number of stakeholders within the STEM education ecosystem.

Science communication is no longer considered a soft skill, but rather a linchpin of the scientific enterprise, connecting science and society. The development and dissemination of effective science communication training is of critical importance and must rapidly evolve to meet learners and educators needs in a technology-driven environment. As more academic institutions seek to formalize science communication as a key component within their curricula to meet the recommendations set forth by the scientific community, the ASC course, and its blended iteratives, provide one example of how to successfully scale and sustain science communication training.

Works Cited

Alammary, Ali, Judy Sheard, and Angela Carbone. "Blended learning in higher education: Three different design approaches." *Australasian Journal of Educational Technology,* vol. 30, no. 4, 2014.

American Association for the Advancement of Science. *Vision and Change in Undergraduate Biology Education.* American Association for the Advancement of Science, 2011.

"Why Public Engagement Matters." *American Association for the Advancement of Science (AAAS),* https://www.aaas.org/pes/what-public-engagement.

Ankeny, J. S., et al. "Circulating tumour cells as a biomarker for diagnosis and staging in pancreatic cancer." *British journal of cancer,* vol. 114, no.12, 2016, pp. 1367-1375.

ASBMB Science Outreach and Communication Committee, forthcoming.

Bevan, Bronwyn, Angela Calabrese Barton, and Cecilia Garibay. "Broadening perspectives on broadening participation: Professional learning tools for more expansive and equitable science communication." *Frontiers in Communication,* vol. 5, 2020, p 52.

Brownell, Sara E., Jordan V. Price, and Lawrence Steinman. "Science communication to the general public: why we need to teach undergraduate and graduate students this skill as part of their formal scientific training."
Journal of undergraduate neuroscience education, vol. 12, no.1, 2013, p.E6.

Canfield, Katherine N., et al. "Science communication demands a critical approach that centers inclusion, equity, and intersectionality." *Frontiers in Communication*, vol. 5, 2020, p. 2.

Dang, Lisa, and Pedro Russo. "How astronomers view education and public outreach: an exploratory study." *arXiv preprint arXiv:1507.08552*, 2015.

"Don't Give up on the Nudge--It Can Still Help Students." Inside Higher Ed, 2019. https://www.insidehighered.com/digitallearning/views/2019/11/13/dont-give-nudge-it-can-still-help-students-opinion.

Ecklund, Elaine Howard, Sarah A. James, and Anne E. Lincoln. "How academic biologists and physicists view science outreach." *PloS one* vol. 7, no. 5, 2012, p. e36240. https://doi.org/10.1371/journal.pone.0036240

Feliú-Mójer, M. I. "Effective communication, better science." *Scientific American,* 2015. https://blogs. scientificamerican. com/guest-blog/effective-communication-better-science.

Girgis, Mark D., et al. "Oncologic outcomes after robotic pancreatic resections are not inferior to open surgery." *Annals of surgery,* vol. 274, no. 3, 2021, pp. e262-e268.

Gore, Jesse, et al. "TCGA data and patient-derived orthotopic xenografts highlight pancreatic cancer-associated angiogenesis." *Oncotarget*, vol 6, no. 10, 2015, p. 7504.

Gore, Jesse, et al. "Combined targeting of TGF-β, EGFR and HER2 suppresses lymphangiogenesis and metastasis in a pancreatic cancer model." *Cancer letters*, vol. 379, no.1, 2016, pp. 143-153.

Greer, Susanna, et al. "The art of science communication—A novel approach to science communication training." *Journal of microbiology & biology education*, vol. 19, no. 1, 2018, p. 1–3.

Hokanson, Sarah Chobot, et al. "A study of synchronous, online professional development workshops for graduate students and postdocs reveals the value of reflection and community building." *Innovative Higher Education* vol. 44, no. 5, 2019, pp. 385-398.

Hone, Kate S., and Ghada R. El Said. "Exploring the factors affecting MOOC retention: A survey study." *Computers & Education*, vol. 98, 2016, pp. 157-168.

Huang, Hsiu-Mei. "Toward constructivism for adult learners in online learning environments." *British journal of educational technology*, vol. 33, no.1, 2002, pp. 27-37.

Jandciu, Eric, et al. "Bridging the Gap: Embedding Communication Courses in the Science Undergraduate Curriculum." *Journal on Excellence in College Teaching*, vol. 26, no. 4, 2015, pp. 103-123.

Johnson, David R., Elaine Howard Ecklund, and Anne E. Lincoln. "Narratives of science outreach in elite contexts of academic science." *Science Communication*, vol. 36, no. 1, 2014, pp. 81-105.

Kuehne, Lauren M., et al. "Practical science communication strategies for graduate students." *Conservation Biology,* vol. 28, no. 5, 2014, pp. 1225-1235.

McLaughlin, Jacqueline, and Anneke Metz. "Vision & change: why it matters." *The American Biology Teacher*, vol. 78, no. 6, 2016, pp. 456-462.

Means, Barbara, et al. "The effectiveness of online and blended learning: A meta-analysis of the empirical literature." *Teachers College Record*, vol. 115, no. 3, 2013, pp. 1-47.

Means, Barbara, et al. "Evaluation of evidence-based practices in online learning: A meta-analysis and review of online learning studies." 2009, ERIC.

National Science Foundation's Merit Review Criteria: Review and Revisions (NSB/MR-11-22). National Science Board, 2011. https://www.nsf.gov/nsb/publications/2011/nsb1211.pdf

Perspectives on Broader Impacts. National Science Foundation, 2015. https://www.nsf.gov/od/oia/publications/Broader_Impacts.pdf

Stuparu, Andreea D., et al. "Targeted alpha therapy in a systemic mouse model of prostate cancer-a feasibility study." *Theranostics*, vol.10, no. 6, 2020, p. 2612.

Sze-Yeng, Foo, and Raja Maznah Raja Hussain. "Self-directed learning in a socioconstructivist learning environment." *Procedia-Social and Behavioral Sciences*, vol. 9, 2010, pp. 1913-1917.

The Role of Scientists in Public Debate. The Wellcome Trust, 2000. https://wellcome.org/sites/default/files/wtd003425_0.pdf.

Negotiating Scientific Identity and Agency: Graduate Student Perspectives on a Public Communication of Science Course

Lillian Campbell

Abstract: *Drawing on interviews with nine graduate science students, this article explores perspectives on a Public Communication of Science (PCS) course designed to help students translate their research for a public talk given at a local town hall. I first outline the history of the student-run course and then discuss three course components—public rhetoric of science; improvisation; and audience awareness. Within each component, I describe one student's particular experience with the course. I describe how students transferred rhetorical lessons from the course to their academic writing but could also transfer rigid views of communication from their scientific work back into their public talks. I also argue that the PCS course helped students to embody flexible scientific identities, but also had the potential to alienate them from norms of communication in their field. Meanwhile, their strategies for imagining and speaking to the public remained constrained by limited access to a range of audience perspectives. Findings demonstrate that there is much to be gained in challenging science students to translate their findings for new audiences. At the same time, instructors must continue to think critically about how we can help students to imagine and access a range of publics.*

> *Part of the public communication training is thinking about who might encounter this and what preconceived notions are they probably going to have about me, and how do I want to change those. I mean in some ways, I'm trying to manipulate their idea of who and what a scientist is.*

> – Graduate Instructor Kara

In the above excerpt, Kara, a graduate student in Environmental Science who has been involved for several years as a designer and instructor for a graduate Public Communication of Science (PCS) course at a large public university, describes some of her aims when communicating her research publicly. Most notable is Kara's focus on identity. She recognizes how her position as a scientist might create a barrier between her and her listeners, but she also sees that barrier as malleable. While previous research on public science communication in graduate programs has provided programmatic and curricular overviews (i.e. Crone et al.; Druschke et al.), scholars have yet to address how participating in PCS courses impacts graduate science students' identity and agency during a critical moment in the development of their professional personas. This research can also help us to better understand undergraduate science student preparation for future scientific communication, inside the academy or beyond.

This article will explore perspectives on a graduate PCS course designed to support students in translating their research for a public talk given at town hall. I first outline the history of the student-run course and then discuss three course components—public rhetoric of science; improvisation; and audience awareness. Within each component, I describe one student's particular experience with the course. I describe how students transferred rhetorical lessons from the course to their academic writing, but could also transfer rigid views of communication from their scientific work back into their public talks. I argue that the PCS course helped students to embody flexible scientific identities, but also had the potential to alienate them from norms of communication in their field. Meanwhile, their strategies for imagining and speaking to the public remained constrained by limited access to a range of audience perspectives.

Overall, this research has the potential to inform future initiatives to incorporate scaffolding for a public talk into undergraduate or graduate science training, whether through formal curriculum changes (Moskovitz; Rakedzon et al.) or extra-curricular programs (Crone et al.; Simpson et al.). These findings demonstrate that there is much to be gained in challenging science students to translate their findings for new audiences. At the same time, instructors must continue to think critically about how we can help students to imagine and access a range of publics.

Graduate Writing Pedagogy and the Public Communication of Science

Graduate school presents a period of significant identity transformation for many students. Transitioning from outsiders to insiders within disciplinary discourse communities often necessitates that they take up both the language and worldviews of their field. Several studies highlight the challenges students encounter when learning to write at the graduate level as well as the entanglements between writing and disciplinary enculturation (Berkenkotter, Huckin, and Ackerman; Colbeck). As graduate students progress in their programs, they often come to self-identify as scholars, simultaneously becoming distanced from the language and values of laypeople. Alternatively, they may fail to assimilate into disciplinary culture, which can be accompanied by academic failure as well (Gardner).

Recent years have seen an increased interest in the unique needs of graduate student writers and a variety of programs to provide support, from the dissertation boot camp to programs that position students as "ethnographers of the writing in their fields" (Sundstrom). These courses recognize that graduate students are often still novice writers, struggling to decode the obscure genres of academia and carrying unfounded assumptions that "writing up" their research should be a transparent process (Kamler and Thomson 1-14). Thus, many graduate writing courses endeavor to demystify the genres of academia—from the dissertation abstract to the scholarly article—with a rhetorical focus on audience, purpose, and disciplinary context (Kucan).

While challenges exist across disciplines, graduate students in the sciences face several unique hurdles. For one, scientific discourse is often characterized by rigid organization, nominalization, and passive voice, which scholars have aligned with ideological perspectives like objectivity and antagonistic stance, that allow little room for personal voice (Halliday and Martin). Meanwhile, the little (if any) feedback that students receive on their writing during their undergraduate studies often focuses primarily on grammar and form rather than larger rhetorical context and aims (Moskovitz). At the graduate level, writing instruction frequently involves co-authoring articles with mentors, which may not occur until late in students' programs (Florence and Yore).

While there is little research on graduate students involved in public communication of science, Druschke et al.'s initiative is a notable exception. Their NSF-funded curriculum aimed to develop graduate science writers' rhetorical skills across scholarly and public genres. A challenge for participants in their program was "convinc[ing] their major professors that [writing] participation is a worthwhile investment of time and energy that would otherwise be spent directly on their scientific research" (11). Similarly, research on the identity negotiations of professional public science writers shows a dominant perception within scientific fields that public communication efforts are "not widely accepted as legitimate forms of scholarship" (Jacobson et al. 248).

Still, considerations about identity and public communication training are rarely a consideration for PCS education at the graduate level, even while there is a growing recognition that fewer doctorates than ever will move into tenure track research positions in the sciences. By considering both the affordances and limitations of students' experiences in this PCS course, I hope to inform future courses and programmatic design. On a broader level, ensuring that science students gain these skills early on in their careers can improve the public's access to and comprehension of scientific research in the future.

History of the PCS Course

The PCS course described in this article emerged out of a 2009 reading group organized by graduate science students across a range of disciplines to discuss several books on the topic. The group decided to launch a speaker series, where graduate students had an opportunity to share their work with interested audiences in a classroom on campus. During the initial 2010 speaker series, students recognized the difficulty of translating their research. Thus, several members spent the summer re-designing curriculum based on the shortcomings they observed in those initial presentations. The following year, the group piloted a three-credit PCS class that met for two hours weekly and was taught by several of the initial presenters. Course outcomes were described as:

1. To assist graduate students with developing skills to communicate with the public about science and engineering;

2. To provide opportunities for graduate students to present their area of research to the public; and

3. To promote public awareness of research conducted by graduate students at [the university] (Clarkson et al.).

The same year that the group first conceived of the PCS course, they also received city support to move the speaker series to a town hall, where it was more easily accessible to the public. The town hall is centrally located in an urban location and regularly hosts public readings, performances, and other cultural events. The science speaker series was held weekly, publicized as part of the town hall's monthly calendar, and free to attendees. During each event, two students would tell the story of their research alongside a Powerpoint for 20-25 minutes with time for questions at the end. The PCS class continued to run during Winter quarter for several years, taking applications each Fall and aiming to keep the incoming cohort to about 16 students. The course was volunteer-taught until 2013, when the leaders garnered college support to fund a TA. However, the group continued to grapple with institutional buy-in, struggling to find a department to list the course and to maintain funding for their instructor. As of this writing, the course is no longer being regularly offered.

Methods

Research for this project was undertaken over a ten-week quarter at a large, public Northwestern university in winter 2013. At the time, I was a graduate student in English with research interests in the rhetoric of science, participating in a certificate program in public scholarship. Through that program, I designed a project that involved talking with participants of the PCS course about their course experiences. I never took an instructional role in the course.

I conducted semi-structured interviews, ranging in length from twenty to sixty minutes with nine graduate science students involved in the course. Four interviewees were returning participants, taking leadership roles in the class, while five were new participants in the class. Five were female and four were male. They came from a wide range of majors including Astronomy, Forestry, Fisheries, Computer Science, Engineering, and Biology—a representative cross-section of the variety of majors who enrolled in the course. I also attended a class session that focused on improvisation and embodied performance as a limited participant and observer. This research was exempted by the Human Subjects review board at the university where it took place. All of my study participants have been given pseudonyms to protect their anonymity.

Three Graduate Student Experiences

In this section, I discuss three key components of the course—public rhetoric of science, improvisation, and audience awareness—and highlight the experience of a graduate student with each of these three components. Findings provide a glimpse of graduate students from a variety of backgrounds negotiating the complexity of public communication. Ultimately, their accounts offer insider perspectives on the unique identity negotiations at work for graduate students as they move across scholarly and public audiences.

Teaching Public Rhetoric of Science

In order to help participants translate their research for public audiences, the group taught general principles for public rhetoric of science, such as the use of narrative form and avoidance of field-specific terms. One key guideline in the course was using the narrative arc to tell the story of one's research. Three participants discussed a storyboarding activity they did in the class as an important transition point in thinking about organization of the narrative. Returning instructor Ben explained:

> [Participants] have little sheets of paper like notecards where they quickly
> write down what they want to present and then…they can move the notecards

around and figure out how to put that into a form that would be easy for someone to follow.

The storyboarding activity encouraged participants to imagine themselves guiding audience members through a series of logical steps to help them arrive at the bigger stakes of their research. Given the emphasis on structure over content and context in their undergraduate learning, some participants described the narrative arc as just another formal constraint to be adopted without consideration of rhetorical aims. However, storyboarding pushed against this instinct and prompted students to think about logic and organization in relation to their audience.

Another course lesson in public rhetoric of science was the reduction of disciplinary specific jargon. Because its members represented a range of majors, the public communication class provided an opportunity for participants to get feedback on their language choices from those outside of their disciplines, which helped them to start recognizing insider knowledge more readily. Of course, with a class full of graduate student scientists, their understanding of a nonspecialist's prior knowledge of vocabulary was limited. For example, instructor Megan described one class period where the group struggled to discern whether the word "particle" was jargon: "It feels like everybody should know what a particle is but is that just because I'm a scientist? And all of us there, like nobody could really offer an unbiased opinion on that." This demonstrates how challenging it was for this group of students to distinguish between disciplinary jargon and common parlance.

Derek's Experience: PCS Lessons for Academic Writing

Derek was an Astronomy PhD student in the final year of his program and had been involved with the PCS course since its inception. As someone who intended to pursue a scientific research career, Derek was able to articulate how lessons from the PCS course were shaping his approach to academic writing, especially in thinking about the choices he made for his disciplinary audience. Like many of my participants, Derek received no training in scientific writing during his undergraduate career, and a discussion of writing came late even in his graduate work. He explained:

> I didn't start to get feedback on my writing until my third or fourth year of graduate school when I was writing my first scientific papers and my adviser had to go through those and iterate with me something that she felt like was acceptable to send to a journal.

In his final year of graduate school, however, he had begun working with a collaborator who was more heavy-handed with revisions. This was a common experience for my participants, who received thorough writing feedback from their advisors once they began to co-write articles. For Derek, his advisors' comments forced him to think more about things like paragraph structure and use of examples in his scientific writing. As he began to transition into professional communication in his field, Derek's perspective on scientific writing became more nuanced, and he recognized opportunities for rhetorical decision-making.

This also translated into Derek's understanding of how the PCS course has impacted his scientific writing. He saw the biggest impact on how he writes introductions to research articles, which he initially saw as "daunting." Derek noted:

> I think [the class] really helped me in writing introductions to papers, I actually put a lot of thought into what makes things fit together well, what makes things easy to read or at least easy to understand.

Derek describes a transition from simply listing all research on a topic to thinking carefully about the connections between different authors and ideas to tell a fluid story. He addresses organization specifically, and audience needs more broadly, as shaping the choices he makes in authoring an introduction. Thus, his discussion indicates how practice with public communication has the potential to help both undergraduate and graduate students recognize and value relationships among content, organization, and audience that exist in their scholarly writing as well.

Improvisation: Countering Dominant Scientific Identities

During the class session that I attended, a female guest speaker who had a background in both Astronomy and Theater led the group of graduate scientists through a series of improvisational games and talked about her experiences with public performance. In one game we all stood in a circle and pretended to pass a large orb to the person next to us, developing a unique and funny motion for passing it. The game was highly physical and required participants to think on their feet but without much risk; most passes elicited a group laugh. All these components were in line with the goals of improvisation for the course as class leader Derek articulated them:

> I call it getting comfortable with being uncomfortable. I think that the improv, you make a fool of yourself and you start to realize that it's not the end of the world if people laugh at you.

During interviews, four students referenced improvisation, citing either specific games or "the improv stuff" (Megan) more generally, as shaping their understanding of public communication. In their accounts, improvisation created an opportunity to imagine space for play and misstep within their scientific work, an activity which impacted not just their ability to communicate but also their feelings about their role in the scientific community. Students saw scientific writing as formulaic and scientific identities as rigid and serious. Improvisation activities, then, were influential in helping students to imagine a new kind of scientific identity.

Several participants described the PCS course as a productive space to play with new orientations to their research and themselves. Or as Kara explained, improvisation games "force you to be silly and not take yourself seriously and sort of loosen up." Similarly, the public speaker in the class I observed described her interest in the PCS as driven in part by a need to take on a different kind of scientific persona than the one she felt was available to her in the lab. She expressed her to desire to be feminine and "wear a dress" as a scientist, as well as to be able to leverage her love for theater and performance.

Megan's Experience: Incompatibility of PCS and a Research Career

Megan was a Fisheries student finishing her Master's thesis and interested in moving into a career in web design or public outreach for a scientific department or organization. Prior to graduate school, Megan had supported the online presence of both academic and research institutions, finding this to be an area with abundant opportunities because "most scientists are just very…anti-online anything." As one of the co-teachers for the PCS course in 2013, Megan positioned herself in opposition to scientific professionals, finding the world of scientific research to be stuffy and pretentious after her experiences with the course:

> I actually really hate hearing other science presentations now because I identify the jargon and I go 'Oh my god, you're just being an a**hole, you don't need to say that word.'

While her adviser was supportive of her public engagement activities, Megan still experienced what she described as a "cloak of shame" as a public communicator. This cloak was lifted when she ultimately decided to pursue a career outside of scientific research and began to publicize rather than hide her investment in public communication.

Megan saw the public communication career path as a natural outgrowth of her interest and motivation for becoming a scientist:

> The reason I got into science is because of feeling like science is under-represented in our country and the world and needs a voice [...] I realized that you can't really do research and communication as well as you could just do communication, so because I liked communication more, I've kind of moved my career trajectory from going on to a PhD to just doing science communication.

The incompatibility that Megan describes here between research and communication was a common theme in her responses. She often articulated an impression from the scientific community that she could not be both a communicator and a scientist. Her shift in career goals enabled her to respond to them: "that's why I'm not going to be a scientist and a communicator, I'm just going to be a communicator."

This notion of incompatibility appeared in other students' responses as well. Similar to Megan, Rebecca described her ideal career as based in public communication, as "director of some type of science foundation," and when asked how research might fit into those career goals, she reflected: "I mean it would be cool to be able to do both but I haven't really found out where I would fit in with that." Three of the other students who were focused on scientific research careers saw public communication as an addendum that they would participate in when possible—doing public talks on the side or including a communication certificate on their resumes—but did not have a clear vision for how the two would be integrated in their careers. Kara, who was nearing the end of her PhD in Environmental and Forest Sciences and preparing to go on the academic job market, recognized that demands on her time early in her career would likely mean that her main involvement in public communication initially might be "inspir[ing] more people to go out and communicate their science." However, post-tenure she saw the potential for recommitting to public communication efforts of her own.

Audience Awareness: Imagining a Listening Public

Just as public communication activities ask students to envision new identities for themselves as scientists, they also demand imagining an audience that is not necessarily familiar or accessible: the public. The graduate science students in this study had varying levels of engagement with publics outside the university depending on prior experiences—from Sue's participation in the Peace Corps to Derek's volunteer role with the local science museum. Thus, instructors focused on helping participants try to estimate their audience's interests and to adjust their talks accordingly. The challenge for both participants and instructors, however, was that they did not have access to feedback from the town hall audience prior to delivering their presentations. The primary source of public feedback in the PCS course was other course participants and instructors—all graduate science students.

One activity was a "cocktail party," in which participants assumed the role of guests. Instructor Megan explained that for homework students were asked to brainstorm possible attendees at the party for whom a presenter would need to tailor their delivery: "say you've got like a politician and an elementary school student and a retired engineer and a fisherman and…you actually think in detail about what that kind of person values and what their daily, day to day life is like." Within class, half of the students were scientists and the other half wore name-tags representing different kinds of audience members. Thus, the scientists had to consider how to explain their research to someone from this unique and specific background. This provided participants practice with the rhetorical flexibility needed to explain their research to a variety of listeners. Still, even while participants were able to recognize the importance of valuing an audience member's prior knowledge, this knowledge remained imagined.

Sue's Experience: Navigating Audience Assumptions

To envision her audience, Sue, a third-year PhD student studying prairie growth, drew on her experiences with public communication during her undergraduate studies and her time with the Peace Corps in Senegal. Working with a largely non-English speaking group with limited formal education, Sue had practiced translating her research into accessible terms:

> That was kind of the beginning of thinking like, "Okay how can I use simple words and how can I use concepts that any person can understand to [communicate my research]."

She also drew on her prior experiences with a community engaged project during her undergraduate work and a current citizen science collaboration to inform her view of an audience and goals for communication. In the context of her town hall presentation, she articulated the necessity of making her research accessible yet challenging enough to keep her audience engaged:

> The ability to be tactful and not to talk down to anyone or to make people feel like they are part of the conversation rather than just being talked at, I think that's a universal thing.

Sue's emphasis on a conversation and valuing audience members' prior knowledge resonates with current scholarship arguing against a deficit model for public science communication (Perrault).

Still, the town hall presentation did not facilitate the kind of audience exchange that informed Sue's previous work with public outreach, so she had to make decisions about her presentation based on her approximation of audience experience. Overall, she worked from the assumption that "a lot of people don't even know that we have prairies in Western [State]." Building from that imagined audience knowledge, Sue decided to focus her town hall presentation "more broadly on what do prairies do for us and why are they important and why should we conserve them." While she planned to briefly mention the prairie species that she studies, the bulk of the presentation would focus on the big picture of prairie growth. In doing so, Sue still relied on generalizations about her audience's lack of familiarity with the topic garnered from lessons in the PCS course.

Meanwhile, Will, a PhD student in Astronomy who was finishing his dissertation, was more critical of the town hall presentation model for the class precisely because of its limited opportunities for exchange. Will had been involved with the PCS course from the beginning, and he noted how presenting in classrooms on campus had enabled a more authentic conversation with attendees. For him, the people who would attend a scientific town hall presentation or would go to a science museum were not his ideal audience because they were already convinced of the importance of science:

> Making more programs for under-served schools and targeting low-income, minority, and first-generation college or even high school graduates is kind of where I'd like to speak with the public.

Will sees engagement with these less accessible publics as precisely where we can "make the biggest difference" to promote larger societal change.

Conclusion

The range of student experiences shared here demonstrates both the strengths and potential pitfalls of a PCS course. While this was a graduate course, the analysis here may also apply to undergraduate pedagogical contexts. Students had the potential to transfer contextualized and audience-focused views of communication from the PCS course back to their scientific writing but could also carry rigid perspectives on writing from their scholarly work into their public communication. This points to the need for instructors to take a genre-based approach to teaching the formats of PCS—having students examine multiple presentations with different approaches to create a list of shared features and places for creativity and innovation (Devitt).

In addition, the PCS course offered students alternative visions of who a scientist could be that both extended the range of possible identities available to them but also potentially alienated them from norms of communication in their field, even to the point where they might decide to change fields altogether. Given that women have been over-represented in PCS and under-represented in scientific leadership (De Welde, Laursen, and Thiry), Megan's is a troubling perspective that needs to be addressed by instructors of PCS courses. PCS instructors might consider activities that allow students practice with shifting their self-presentations, such as preparing cover letters, resumes, and personal websites that target a range of career paths, and bringing in speakers that represent a variety of career trajectories and possibilities.

Finally, students drew on diverse experiences with public engagement to imagine the public, but their presentations remained constrained by limited access to the specific audience that attended their talks. An activity like the cocktail party, for example, might benefit from better grounding in qualitative research to include interviews and observations. This might take the form of textual research, like reading blog entries by a local politician, or fieldwork, like calling an uncle who is a lawyer to talk about what might interest him about astronomy. In addition, instructors and leaders need to devote class time to discussing Will's concerns—questions about equity of access to public science talks and strategies for speaking to out-of-reach audiences who do not necessarily prioritize or seek out science.

The success and longevity of this course points to the value of letting graduate student interest and enthusiasm for public communication serve as the driving force behind future curriculum. Still, this article demonstrates that both undergraduate and graduate-level educational programs in PCS should be viewed with a nuanced and critical eye towards their benefits and risks for students and the public, including alienation from field-specific norms of communication and limited views of what constitutes a public and how they might be swayed. Overall, PCS courses can serve as a fruitful site for collaboration between writing and science scholars as it continues to grow as an area of teaching and research. On the other hand, if we continue to train scientists whose primary objective is communicating with their own niche disciplines, we limit both their future career opportunities and more importantly, we limit public access to, comprehension of, and trust in scientific information.

Works Cited

Berkenkotter, Carol, Thomas N. Huckin, and John Ackerman. "Conventions, Conversations, and the Writer: Case Study of a Student in a Rhetoric Ph.D. Program." *Research in the Teaching of English*, vol. 22, no. 1, 1988, pp. 9-44.

Clarkson, Melissa D., Natalie R. Footen, Megan F. Gambs, Ivan F. Gonzalez, Juliana Houghton, Megan L. Smith. "Engage, A Model of Student-led Graduate Training in Communication for STEM Disciplines." *2014 IEEE International Professional Communication Conference (IPCC)*, 2014, pp. 1-2.

Colbeck, Carol L. "Professional Identity Development Theory and Doctoral Education." *New Directions for Teaching and Learning*, vol. 113, 2008, pp. 9-16.

Crone, Wendy C., Sharon L. Dunwoody, Raelyn K. Rediske, Steven A. Ackerman, Greta M. Zenner Petersen, and Ronald A. Yaros . "Informal Science Education: A Practicum for Graduate Students." *Innovative Higher Education,* vol. 36, no. 5, 2011, pp. 291-304.

De Welde, Kristine, Sandra Laursen, and Heather Thiry. (2007) "Women in Science, Technology, Engineering and Math (STEM)." *ADVANCE Library Collection.* Paper 567, 2007, https://digitalcommons.usu.edu/advance/567

Devitt, Amy J. *Writing Genres.* Southern Illinois University Press, 2004.

Druschke, Caroline Gottschalk, Nedra Reynolds, Jenna Morton-Aiken, Ingrid E. Lofgren, Nancy E. Karraker, and Scott R. McWilliams. "Better Science through Rhetoric: A New Model and Pilot Program for Training Graduate Student Science Writers." *Technical Communication Quarterly*, vol. 27, no. 2, 2018, pp. 175-190.

Florence, Marilyn K., and Larry D. Yore. "Learning to Write like a Scientist: Coauthoring as an Enculturation Task." *Journal of Research in Science Teaching: The Official Journal of the National Association for Research in Science Teaching*, vol. 41, no. 6, 2004, pp. 637-668.

Gardner, Susan K. "Contrasting the Socialization Experiences of Doctoral Students in High and Low-completing Departments: A Qualitative Analysis of Disciplinary Contexts at One Institution." *The Journal of Higher Education*, vol. 81, no. 1, 2010, pp. 61-81.

Halliday, Michael Alexander Kirkwood, and James R. Martin. *Writing Science: Literacy and Discursive Power.* Taylor & Francis, 2003.

Kamler, Barbara and Pat Thomson. "Putting Doctoral Writing Center Stage." *Helping Doctoral Students Write: Pedagogies for Supervision.* Routledge, 2014.

Kucan, Linda. "Approximating the Practice of Writing the Dissertation Literature Review." *Literacy Research and Instruction,* vol. 50, no. 3, 2011, pp. 229-240.

Moskovitz, Cary. "Volunteer Expert Readers for STEM Student Writers." *Across the Disciplines,* vol. 11, no. 2, 2014, pp. 1-45.

Perrault, Sarah. *Communicating Popular Science: From Deficit to Democracy.* Palgrave MacMillan, 2013.

Rakedzon, Tzipora, and Ayelet Baram-Tsabari. "To Make a Long Story Short: A Rubric for Assessing Graduate Students' Academic and Popular Science Writing Skills." *Assessing Writing,* vol. 32, 2017, pp. 28-34.

Simpson, Steve, et al. "Creating a Culture of Communication: A Graduate Level STEM Communication Fellows Program at a Science and Engineering University." *Across the Disciplines,* vol. 12, no. 3, 2017, pp. 1-16.

Sundstrom, Christine Jensen. "The Graduate Writing Program at the University of Kansas: An Inter-disciplinary, Rhetorical Genre-based Approach to Developing Professional Identities." *Composition Forum,* vol. 29, 2014.

CONNECTING

Reciprocal Engagement and Imperfect Pedagogy

Christy I. Wenger

It's almost blasé to say that the Covid-19 pandemic drastically transformed higher education. But while we might be long past diatribes on emergency remote teaching, we are all still grappling with the new reality and heightened challenges the pandemic catalyzed. Many of us are facing budget restrictions and shrinking departments with fewer faculty and office staff. Most of us are troubleshooting the pedagogical challenges of teaching in and training teachers for Hyflex classrooms. And almost all of us are grappling with persistent concerns regarding student engagement.

As we emerge from the pandemic, the importance of student engagement in higher education has become more evident than ever before. Student engagement is more than getting students to our classes every day and more than getting them to do their homework on time. It's bigger work than retention, though, of course, engagement is predicated on our retention efforts. Student retention has been well-studied over the years to attempt to figure out why students sometimes persist and why they sometimes stop out. Vincent Tinto's research on retention introduces a student integration model, which focuses on how well students integrate fully into the university community and bases that integration on their likelihood of being retained. Tinto's work helps us understand that students need to feel like they belong at their universities, that they can identify and integrate within the academic communities of their chosen fields, and that they are invited to engage within those communities in meaningful and resonant ways.

In the work I've been doing with faculty since the pandemic began to find new pedagogical methods to improve engagement, one thing has become increasingly clear to the faculty with whom I work: engagement is a reciprocal process. We cannot define engagement as only what students give to us, but also how we as educators and mentors and guides enrich and support them. That's a mind shift akin to creating student-ready programs instead of asking for college-ready students. Too often, the narratives surrounding engagement aren't transactional and reciprocal but are instead based on what students aren't giving to us. Those meaningful and resonant ways Tinto identified as key to student integration and, in turn, retention? Those are cultivated by all of us working together and not only dependent on what students bring to us.

The pair of reflective articles in this issue of "Connecting" approaches this question of reciprocal engagement in a manner that helps us ask new questions not only of pedagogical methods that might capture our students' attention to promote engagement but also how the rhetorical context of bridging specific discourse communities and communities in practice are central to unlocking student engagement. Here, integration isn't just what the student does to immerse themselves into the university community but also what we do as academics to connect the various academic and professional communities to which our students affiliate and identify as part of their belonging process. Our academic silos don't just stand in the way of faculty collaboration but can also challenge meaningful student engagement. Focused on the rhetorical context of science studies, this article pair helps to unpack what it would mean to engage student-scientists as writers who need and want to communicate to audiences both within and outside of specific academic scientific communities. Certainly, there are lessons for all of us to apply to our own disciplines as well.

As Julia Kiernan remarks in her introduction to this special issue, not engaging students in transdisciplinary work that prepares them to dialogue with many audiences is a "disservice to science students who will leave our classrooms and enter professions where they are required, but often ill-equipped, to engage with myriad public audiences." Not to mention that siloed instruction limits the ways students will engage with our courses and academic content. Melissa L. Carrion and Ed Nagelhout in "Part 1: Creating Science-Citizens through a Writing Minor" detail how our efforts as educators should be in creating students that understand how to communicate effectively across disciplines, not just in the discipline of their major. Our authors are particularly interested in creating scientist-citizens who practice citizen-science to help expand the application of science to public matters and to generate a greater understanding of science and the scientific process among a general, public audience. Not surprisingly, getting students to practice citizen science entails supporting the development of their writing and communication skills beyond a first-year writing course and throughout a vertical writing curriculum embedded within disciplinary studies of science, a practice detailed by David Gerstle, Sarah Seeley, and Marc Laflamme in "Part 2: Learning to Communicate About Science: Writing About (Science) Writing and the First-Year Writing Requirement."

Naomi Gades in her "English 101" picks up the same themes in her poem to remind readers of the importance of teaching students meaningful communication strategies that go beyond simply the "rules" of writing. If what "matters in the end are ideas," as Gades contends, then we need to devote our time to engaging students in them, teaching them how to write their way to them, and modeling how to get their audiences engaged in what engages them. Amber Moore offers us a phrase that pulls together the discussion threads in "Connecting" with her nod to "manicured pedagogy." Like freshly painted nails, manicured pedagogy cannot last. What can persist—and make students persist—is the raw, chipped, and often imperfect methods we use to engage students in more than participation in our classes—in the work of interdisciplinary learning and writing to foster strong connections between students' academic pursuits and career aspirations after graduation. By doing so, we not only engage our students, but we identify meaningful work for ourselves.

Works Cited

Tinto, Vincent. *Leaving College: Rethinking the Causes and Cures of Student Attrition*. 2nd ed., University of Chicago Press, 1993.

Part 1: Creating Scientist-Citizens through a Writing Minor

Melissa L. Carrion and Ed Nagelhout

Many contemporary scientific and medical "controversies"—from challenges regarding the role of humans in causing climate change to questions about the safety of vaccines or the efficacy of masks in preventing the spread of COVID-19—persist despite overwhelming scientific consensus to the contrary (Ceccarelli). Public skepticism surrounding these issues has very real and deleterious effects, from halting meaningful policy change to jeopardizing public health. While research suggests that increased scientific literacy among the public can alleviate some difficulties inherent in this phenomenon, citizen-science, defined broadly as "public participation in scientific projects" (Heigl et al. 8089), has been shown to supplement increased public scientific literacy, which positively impacts trust in science more broadly: lay citizens play a central role in this activity.

As such, attempts to help scientists engage effectively in this process are a crucial, yet often overlooked, component of the citizen-science effort. Since scientists are still primarily trained to communicate findings in lab reports or in professional publications to a specific and well-informed audience, there has been far less attention to date paid to the pedagogical development of what Pamela Pietrucci and Leah Ceccarelli call *scientist-citizens*—those who "take up a rhetorical ethos that not only displays technical expertise but also demonstrates virtue, goodwill, and good judgment to communicate their specialized knowledge with people who do not already share it" (102). Understandably, attempts to help expert scientists engage effectively in this process are an important component of this effort. As Pietrucci and Ceccarelli write, "There are times when a solution to the tragedy of the expert-lay divide lies not in democratizing science or scientizing the public but in bringing scientists out of their isolation in the technical sphere so that they can embrace their rhetorical duty as citizens" (106).

While existing research has examined and offered suggestions for scientists who choose to engage with the public and citizen-science efforts (e.g., DeVasto and Creighton; Fischhoff), there remains, as Pietrucci and Ceccarelli note, "alienation of scientists from their responsibilities as agents in a broader civic culture" (99). This means, to us, that in order to harness the potential of the citizen-science model, educators need to cultivate its corollary—scientific citizenship. However, while these are values that are increasingly embraced in the broader public and civic culture, there has been less concerted effort to embed these values early and consistently throughout science education efforts. Responding to this gap, we describe our interdisciplinary science writing minor as a replicable, programmatic model for fostering scientific citizenship among STEM students. We outline ways that the program design provides students with explicit training in rhetoric and scientific writing for public audiences, fosters collaboration among faculty, and provides the flexibility needed to preempt the logistical and bureaucratic challenges that can often thwart such efforts.

Indeed, from epidemiologists with blogs to social media groups moderated by credentialed experts to outreach efforts from governmental agencies, recent years have seen a proliferation of scientists and health professionals engaging directly with the public in an increasing variety of ways, both formal and informal. These include efforts to involve lay publics in citizen-science, which can take many forms from crowdfunding to citizens who help collect data to participatory models where community members play a central role in determining study designs, intervention, and evaluation (Wiggins and Wilbanks). Research suggests that citizen-science can help to expand the public's scientific knowledge and understanding, facilitate effective science communication and greater understanding of the scientific process, and increase faith in scientific institutions more generally (Bonney et al.). Academic-based efforts to promote citizen-science engagement offer, therefore, an important avenue to combat broader trends toward science skepticism and anti-science attitudes.

While scholars have a fairly well-developed idea of what citizen-science looks like, we don't have an equally deep or robust image of the effective *scientist-citizen*. We have even less research and guidance regarding how to foster effective scientific citizenship from a curricular perspective; specifically, how to integrate effective training in scientific citizenship for STEM students in higher education settings. Those efforts that do exist tend to focus on either direct integration into STEM courses (i.e., asking STEM faculty to include lessons on effective communication alongside disciplinary content) or stand-alone science communication programs, both of which can pose logistical challenges for students, faculty, and administrators. We argue that effective strategies for fostering scientific citizenship must necessarily involve both faculty in scientific disciplines as well as those who can offer substantive instruction in rhetoric and writing more generally. We offer our interdisciplinary science writing minor as one model for how to develop sustainable pedagogical and curricular interventions to ensure STEM students receive adequate training in not only the content of their disciplines, but also in strategies to engage effectively with lay publics as a means to understand and embrace their potential as *scientist-citizens*.

To meet the needs for educating *scientist-citizens*, we developed an interdisciplinary science writing minor as part of a larger multi-layered and multi-disciplinary program that included a technical writing minor and a professional writing minor in the English department at the University of Nevada, Las Vegas. Our goal was to design a replicable, programmatic model for fostering scientific citizenship among STEM students by providing explicit training in rhetoric and scientific writing for public audiences. We also sought to foster collaboration among writing faculty and science faculty, as well as build in flexibility needed to preempt the logistical challenges that can often obstruct such efforts, especially from an administrative perspective.

Our theoretical framework builds fundamentally from the acknowledgment that professional practices related to effective technical communication are a science unto themselves. That is, research suggests that one major contributor to science skepticism relates to the tendency toward the Dunning-Kruger effect, or what some scholars have termed the "beginner's bubble" (Sanchez and Dunning): the propensity of individuals with limited exposure to a new topic to feel they have gained expertise to rival actual experts. To expect STEM faculty—in isolation—to be able to teach and prepare students in effective rhetorical and writing practices is committing the same error. On the contrary, we should acknowledge that effective science communication practices—while they might be situated within disciplines and departments, like English, which are historically tethered to the Humanities—are nonetheless areas grounded in a kind of scientific expertise. These practices are likewise informed by education, research, and practice that is not replicated quickly or easily. Efforts toward fostering the kinds of communication necessary for scientific citizenship are thus best supported, in a university setting, by faculty trained in these disciplines. In line with this approach, our interdisciplinary minors provide STEM faculty with the expert support that supplements their own disciplinary training in essential ways.

This theoretical orientation is related to a broader pedagogical benefit. Best practices in learning sciences suggest that effective and sustained learning occurs through a process in which students are introduced to a new topic/skill, given an opportunity to connect it to their prior learning and experience, offered a clear explanation and space for discussion, and finally encouraged to apply it in a real life scenario with opportunities for reflection. This latter component can and should be integrated into STEM disciplinary courses, along with requisite reflection, where students can practice communicating the real research- and lab-based findings generated via their STEM coursework in modes authentic to the discourse practices expected in their majors and future professional fields. However, to enable STEM faculty and students to focus their energy and efforts in this direction, students must have the opportunity to develop foundational writing skills and practice—in areas like audience analysis and communication design—that can be transferred across disciplines.

To offer a more specific background, our efforts to create a science writing minor began in 2019 when the English department began a larger curriculum reform initiative. Since we had already failed six times over the previous decade to secure approval for a legitimate professional and/or technical writing concentration in the department, we altered our approach to building a robust program in science, technical, and professional writing by focusing on minors. Concentrating our efforts on creating writing minors offered numerous advantages. In particular, a minor at our university requires only 18 credits and, more importantly, UNLV policy allows students to "double-dip"—or count a single course toward multiple requirements—which meant that we could allow students to use up to two courses in their major to count toward the minor. This ensured that the pursuit of a minor would not impede a student's progress toward graduation, even in a major with few elective options.

Structurally, our science writing minor requires 18 credit hours. These include four courses, or 1 credits, from those offered in the English department, and two courses, or six credits, designated by the college, department, or program in the sciences. Writing courses foster effective expert/public communication by training STEM students in specific rhetorical strategies that attend to issues of audience, translation, persuasion, and disciplinary discourse practices necessary to support the effective rhetorical training of future scientists, as well as explicit training in specific rhetorical strategies for scientists (e.g., Luzón) and "trans-scientific genres" (Mehlenbacher 1). These courses include many already existing in English, like document design, electronic documents and publication, and advanced professional communication, as well as some new courses, like a dedicated science writing course, that we have recently developed. As previously discussed, this combination of practice in discipline-specific discourse strategies and more transferable rhetorical principles helps future scientists to understand the relationships between the expertise and skills they offer within a specific scientific community and the tensions and responsibilities that exist in translating that expertise to more general audiences.

The designated science courses include those with an emphasis in writing and/or disciplinary literacy (i.e., the "ways of knowing" that characterize a field), and offer discipline-specific, authentic writing tasks that help students to apply their rhetorical training to situations they are likely to encounter as professionals when communicating with both their peers and public audiences. These two approaches provide students a range of options for developing more fully as writers and *scientist-citizens*. All courses are offered regularly, ensuring that students will be able to complete the minor in any two-year period, and the courses approved to fulfill the requirements of each minor also dovetail with courses counting toward requirements or electives from the collaborating majors.

Our initial outreach for the science writing minor targeted the College of Science (2,500 majors), the School of Integrated Health Sciences (2,000 majors), the College of Nursing (1,600 majors), and the Psychology department, a major in our own college of Liberal Arts (1,500 majors). This outreach began by scheduling meetings with the Associate Dean of each college or school, as well as with the Chair of Psychology. To prepare for these meetings, we developed a unique set of talking points, a flexible script, a series of prompts, and a one-page FAQ handout. Interestingly, each administrator that we talked with recommended our first follow-up be with the director of their advising center; each advising center director was extremely enthusiastic about the potential for our science writing minor. We have since met with a few department chairs and faculty to further explore options and opportunities.

Our primary goals for each of these meetings were to discuss writing across the following contexts: the value of writing for their students, the ways faculty currently use writing in their courses, and the opportunities to collaborate on and support the incorporation of writing into the student experience more effectively and more efficiently. Since interdisciplinary collaboration among faculty was central to our program design, we wanted to foster "a shared social value of writing" (Arduser 20); we used stakeholder theory to pay particular attention to strategies for creating the reciprocal opportunities that would lead to sustainable partnerships among both individual faculty members and the majors/programs they represent (for more information on this process, see Carrion and Nagelhout).

As our cohort of interdisciplinary minors wends its way through the labyrinth of the academic approval process, we offer Introduction to Science Writing in the coming semester for the first time. Ultimately, our experience with all students in the minors, teaching the writing courses, and collaborating with our disciplinary colleagues will shape our program over time. Initially, we found that a focus on specific colleges allowed us to develop a curricular plan to adapt courses in our catalog and propose new courses, build on our core program principles, create assessment plans that drive interdisciplinary development, and meet the needs of specific science majors. These pragmatic considerations are an important reminder of the various stakeholders and responsibilities that must be balanced in this process: while developing *scientist-citizens* is the goal, we are not doing so in a vacuum, but rather within a network of complex institutional needs and requirements.

The call for this special issue asked authors to "rethink the work that novice scientists engage with inside the classroom" in order to facilitate effective scientific citizenship. While STEM disciplinary classes and coursework provide one natural platform for this endeavor, we argue that interdisciplinary approaches—and specifically those involving faculty with explicit training and focus in rhetoric, writing, and communication—are required in order to ensure the development of sound and sustainable efforts toward this goal. In line with this assertion, we believe that collaboration among faculty and departments across disciplines is not only beneficial, but necessary—from a theoretical, pedagogical, and pragmatic perspective—and position our interdisciplinary science writing minor as one model for how we can facilitate such collaboration in a manageable and sustainable manner. We suggest our interdisciplinary science writing minor offers a model for how rhetoric and writing faculty can provide this foundation to ensure that STEM faculty can build upon these core skills in discipline-specific ways while not detracting from the ability to cover important disciplinary content.

This logistic consideration relates to what we see as the final benefit of the model we propose, which is its ability to overcome bureaucratic hurdles that can often thwart such efforts, both from a short- and long-term perspective. In particular, our interdisciplinary science writing model was grounded first and foremost in pedagogical considerations of the skills and experiences necessary to help students develop as *scientist-citizens*. But it was also developed with attention to the pragmatic considerations—related to issues of credit hours, progression toward degree, and faculty workload/course coverage—that can prevent an otherwise sound model from moving forward, flourishing, or sustaining over time. In this way, the collaborative approach that our model represents can allow STEM departments and faculty to continue the important work of fostering disciplinary scientific expertise, while also ensuring that students develop the integrated communication skills that will help them to be not simply scientific experts, but also the scientific citizens who can help us to navigate the myriad challenges—scientific, social, and cultural—that we'll face moving forward.

Works Cited

Arduser, Lora. "Specialized Technical Writing Service Courses as a Program Sustainability Tool?" *Programmatic Perspectives*, vol. 10, no. 1, 2018, pp. 12-43.

Ceccarelli, Leah. "Manufactured Scientific Controversy: Science, Rhetoric, and Public Debate." *Rhetoric & Public Affairs*, vol. 14, no. 2, 2011, pp. 195- 228.

Carrion, Melissa, and Ed Nagelhout. "Empowering Stakeholders in a Cohort of Interdisciplinary Writing Minors: Flexibility, Agency, Reciprocity, and Accountability." *Programmatic Perspectives*, vol. 12, no. 2, 2022, pp. 52-75.

DeVasto, Danielle, and Jean Creighton. "Inspired by the Cosmos: Strategies for Public Engagement in Nonpolicy Contexts." *Science Communication*, vol. 40, no. 6, 2018, pp. 808-818.

Fischhoff, Baruch. "Evaluating Science Communication." *Proceedings of the National Academy of Sciences*, vol. 116, no. 16, 2019, pp. 7670-7675.

Heigl, Florian, Barbara Kieslinger, Kathering Paul, Julia Uhlik, Julia, and Daniel Dörler. "Opinion: Toward an International Definition of Citizen Science." *Proceedings of the National Academy of Sciences*, vol. 116, no. 17, 2019, pp. 8089-8092.

Luzón, Maria Jose. "Public Communication of Science in Blogs: Recontextualizing Scientific Discourse for a Diversified Audience." *Written Communication,* vol. 30, no. 4, 2013, pp. 428-457.

Mehlenbacher, Ashley. *Science Communication Online: Engaging Experts and Publics on the Internet.* The Ohio State University Press, 2019.

Pietrucci, Pamela, and Leah Ceccarelli. "Scientist Citizens: Rhetoric and Responsibility in L'Aquila." *Rhetoric and Public Affairs*, vol. 22, no. 1, 2019, pp. 95-128.

Sanchez, Carmen, and David Dunning. "Overconfidence Among Beginners: Is a Little Learning a Dangerous Thing?" *Journal of personality and Social Psychology*, vol. 114, no. 1, 2018, pp. 10-28.

Wiggins, Andrea, and John Wilbanks. "The Rise of Citizen Science in Health and Biomedical Research." *The American Journal of Bioethics*, vol. 19, no. 8, 2019, pp. 3-14.

Part 2: Learning to Communicate About Science: Writing About (Science) Writing and the First-Year Writing Requirement

David Gerstle, Sarah Seeley, and Marc Laflamme

Educating empowered, empathetic, and efficacious citizens involves centering contingent, constructivist, holistic understandings of scientific knowledge. Most importantly, this involves enabling young people to communicate *about* science with innovation and savvy. It enables them, as discussed in Part 1, to become *scientist-citizens*. This is particularly important because most science students do not pursue postgraduate study; rather, they opt to enter the workforce immediately following graduation.

Our research team has come to think about these responsibilities through the lens of a multidisciplinary collaboration that synthesizes our shared concerns about science education, writing program development, and information literacy. This collaboration has resulted in insights on the professionalization of science students in relation to their disciplines, the expectations for science literacy in higher education, and the challenges of revising and bolstering professional communication curriculum where few resources exist. Before offering further discussion of our collective observations, we first provide a brief description of two departmental contexts that shape our work: the Department of Chemical and Physical Sciences (CPS) and the Institute for the Study of University Pedagogy (ISUP), both at the University of Toronto Mississauga (UTM).

The Department of Chemical and Physical Sciences (CPS) is a multidisciplinary academic unit that includes approximately 800 students across the disciplines of Astronomy, Chemistry, Earth Sciences, and Physics. In addition, CPS has a vibrant graduate student research community with 25 full time faculty who mentor approximately 40 graduate students. Similarly, ISUP is a multidisciplinary academic unit consisting of faculty from an array of disciplines that administers foundational skills, numeracy, and first-year writing initiatives. Of particular interest to this discussion is the first-year writing initiative. Our course, Writing for University and Beyond, is the first of its kind in Canada: a required FYW course that is administered from the writing about writing approach (Downs and Wardle). At present, this FYW course is required for admission to approximately 50% of the undergraduate programs on the UTM campus. Within the next five years, the course will be required for admission to all degree programs, which will make it a shared feature of the undergraduate experience for all 15,000+ students at UTM. Accordingly, we are now reflecting on several questions, including:

1. How can we forge partnerships within individual departments that will help position the FYW experience as a meaningful springboard into disciplinary writing?

2. How can we mobilize the "and Beyond" portion of the course title as a curricular inroad for public-facing communication strategies that are meaningful to students in an array of disciplines?

While these inquiries do arise from local exigencies, they are also rooted in familiar administrative and curricular pursuits, making them of broader interest to any educator who is working to prepare future scientists to communicate meaningfully with an array of public stakeholder audiences.

As a part of our ongoing work examining both the effectiveness of the FYW program and its relationship to science communication, our research team invited all CPS faculty to sit for individual, dyadic semi-structured interviews; 18 of 25 faculty participated. We chose to interview faculty from a single multidisciplinary science department with the intention of analyzing science faculty expectations for science communication in relation to science student experiences of FYW. Juxtaposing faculty expectations and student experiences allows us to engage with the two research questions outlined above: how to position the FYW experience as a meaningful springboard into disciplinary writing and, accordingly, how to fully mobilize university writing tasks to support students in communicating effectively with the public.

We are still in the early stages of data analysis, but we mention the contours of our larger project to contextualize some observations and discussions. For example, in interviewing CPS faculty, we asked faculty to reflect on the types of writing assignments they currently offer in their courses as well as comment on the extent and type of writing instruction and assessment they provide. Other questions dealt directly with faculty perceptions of the importance of writing for both the successful completion of the degree program and for the eventual transition of these scientific citizens into post-graduate pursuits. CPS faculty consistently noted the demands of delivering discipline-specific instruction, explaining that experientially-oriented science curriculum dominates what they are able to accomplish within a given course. Faculty indicated that, within the span of a single term (which is 12 weeks at UTM), they typically include written assignments and/or seminar presentations as part of their assessments, but they struggle with offering instruction in writing and/or communication practices alongside their science curriculum. This time-based tension is a familiar problem, and it is an obstacle to effectively integrating science communication into science programs. Yet, both writing *and* science classrooms can be pivotal sites for mobilizing scientific literacies in terms of individual identities, agencies, and larger citizen-making projects.

Despite this clear potential, our work has revealed disconnects between science communication and its terse relationship with professionalization. On one hand, many science students do not necessarily need to be proficient writers to be successful in their degree program. On the other hand, they *do* need to be proficient writers to succeed in whatever type of professional role they may assume after completing their degree. While our colleagues in the sciences consistently display genuine care in offering their students a nuanced education, that attention does not necessarily extend to students' writing-related needs. In many cases, faculty reported that they felt ill-equipped to teach writing skills. This is similar to situations where faculty in the social sciences or humanities may feel unequipped to discuss the nuances of scientific phenomena. This foregrounds a presupposition that is observable in many disciplinary contexts: Faculty are committed to the continuation of their discipline, but not necessarily undergraduate education that leads degree holders to act on their knowledge as professionals or citizens. For graduates of science programs, this is particularly dangerous. The ability to communicate with public, stakeholder audiences is an essential precondition for naming, contextualizing, and responding to all manner of socioscientific phenomena.

Insofar as teaching science is regarded as a moral obligation and science literacy is regarded as a citizen making project, that work necessarily includes teaching and learning communication practices, infrastructures, and ideologies. The precise "look" of this work will, of course, differ, as all campus cultures have their own assumptions, histories, and curricular centers of gravity. Here at UTM we see faculty suggesting that they cannot carve out space in the science curriculum to make room for additional writing curriculum, which points to another, familiar problem: There appear to be fundamental misunderstandings about writing as a contextual, imperfectible technology. This is to say that our colleagues in the sciences often perceive professional writing, and communication broadly, as simply a technical skill which—once mastered—will transfer across disciplines and audiences (cf. Adler-Kassner and Wardle). While these misconceptions are certainly not exclusive to the sciences, they are, in this context, standing as obstacles to powerful curricular and socioscientific change because they maintain unproductive binaries between the public and the academy, between citizens and scientists, etc.

Accordingly, our research team is exploring some interventions for integrating scientific and communication principles. We draw on our own local campus culture to formulate these suggestions, but we respond to issues found in science programs across contexts. Because of this, we hope these ideas and challenges will resonate more broadly as faculty consider and reconsider how to meaningfully and authentically enable science communication across degree programs.

One option for integrating additional writing curricula in CPS programs would be to take a writing in the disciplines (WID) approach. Because CPS is a multidisciplinary department, this would involve designing a series of WID courses. Stephen Mang, Kate McKnelly, and Michael Morris have, for example, written about their re-design of the course "Writing for Chemists" at University of California, Irvine. A cluster of similar courses within multidisciplinary departments like CPS could create not only a bridge between first-year and disciplinary writing, it could have strong potential for teaching essential public-facing communication strategies through the lens of contemporary scientific issues. If students are not socialized to accept the importance of communicating with stakeholder audiences, they will be unlikely to prioritize that work in their future careers.

All this said, we face what is likely a familiar roadblock to initiating this type of curricular change on our own campus. Some of the CPS programs already require many more credit hours than most other undergraduate programs across the disciplines. This, using the Earth Sciences as an example, stems from accreditation requirements set up by Professional Geoscientists Ontario (PGO), a regulatory organization that governs the practice of professional geoscientists. PGO does offer seminars that teach geoscientists how to communicate scientific information to public audiences, but the organization does not consider communication course work as a part of its accreditation structure. As such, some CPS faculty remain vocally opposed to the addition of any mandatory upper-year, non-discipline courses in their undergraduate programs.

A second option would be to design a series of smaller-scale writing workshops and/ or course modules targeting specific genres. For example, faculty in many science programs teach strategies for field book notetaking or lab report writing; we would advocate expanding this to also teach strategies for communicating complex scientific information to public stakeholders. There has also been discussion of offering "just in time" workshops to support writing activities such as these. There has similarly been discussion of offering one to two week "short courses" in writing for more complex genres. Both types of programming could create opportunities for the use of transdisciplinary pedagogies to cultivate dialogue, offer in-depth formative feedback, and otherwise enact the holistic potential of science communication education.

A third option would be to build a "science writing community" within the department where undergraduate students, graduate students, and faculty could come together on a regular basis to discuss writing. These would take the format of weekly brown bag lunches where active sharing of writing, at various stages, was encouraged. CPS faculty have suggested that this approach would productively normalize the fact that writing—for any audience—is hard. Inviting students to witness the challenges faced by experienced science writers could normalize the fact that writing is a contextual process that allows scientists to respond to social needs.

Science education often takes place with the expectation that undergraduates will pursue postgraduate study. Yet, most students—at least at UTM—do not. Rather, they tend to find industry, non-profit, lab-based, or government work. This suggests that the primary purpose of science education is not the perpetuation of disciplines, and we are working to foreground the fact that disciplinary writing is a process of joining a community. It is a process of grasping its language, history, concerns, and knowledge production. It is a process of becoming an ambassador from that community: communicating with diverse public audiences in ways that account for their needs, values, experiences, and presuppositions.

Writing initiatives for science students must prepare them to communicate *about* science, to make their knowledge understood more broadly by non-expert audiences in a science-driven society. By understanding their disciplinary community, students build actionable tools for embracing the obligation to be strong communicators of science as part of their professional growth and citizenship in such a society.

Works Cited

Adler-Kassner, Linda and Elizabeth Wardle. "Naming What We Know. The Project of this Book" *Naming What We Know. Threshold Concepts of Writing Studies*, edited by Linda Adler-Kassner & Elizabeth Wardle, Utah State University Press, 2015, pp. 1-14.

Downs, Douglas, and Elizabeth Wardle. "Teaching About Writing, Righting Misconceptions: (Re)envisioning 'First-Year Composition' as 'Introduction to Writing Studies.'" *College Composition and Communication*, vol. 58, no. 4, 2007, pp. 552–84.

Mang, Stephen, Kate J. McKnelly, and Michael Morris. "Redesigning a "Writing for Chemists" Course Using Specifications Grading" *ChemRxiv*, 2020.

English 101

Naomi C. Gades

I get it:
you like complete sentences.
I do, too.
In fact, my favorites have that liturgical lilt,
handsomely balanced and perfectly parallel
to their periodic ends, saving and savoring
their own momentum, rolling
into a flashy finish.

I confess:
I like grammar,
probably more than you.
I like it so much I diagram sentences,
stretching bodices taut over a wire dressmaker's form
that reveals their shape
for trimming and arranging.

I even took up a language that boasts
not three tired articles, but
whole parquet matrices of them
to dance and trip across.

And I am very sorry your students
do not know what a sentence is
because they do not have the words
subjects and subordinates,
much less absolute and infinitive phrases
that masquerade as independent.
Parts of speech are not as popular as they were
for reasons practical, pedagogical, and maybe even political,
and that's fine. Civilization endures.

So while I wish I had the time to indulge
in comma splices and modifiers misplaced,
I don't. I only comment if, being so obscure,
error distracts or confuses.
Instead we practice pacifying the whims of
disciplinary professors like you:
each audience has its own demands,
so we name them and paint by their numbers.

What matters in the end are ideas:
the scaffolding of evidence supporting claims,
the responsibility of citation and its consequences,
the story of an argument.

And if they manage not to assert but to prove,
not to collapse before apparently arbitrary expectations
but to notice and honor them,
and to have encountered at least a few beautiful sentences,
then for a semester, that is enough,
a plenty of progress.

Sessional spa time

Amber Moore

My nails creep
  p
u
from under a silver lining.
The polish is called
"Unfrost my Heart."

It's time to wipe them clean,
layer another color.
Maybe
"On Pinks and Needles"?

I like it when the job is fresh and untarnished -
that brief period
before digging through your purse
for a credit card,
keys.

Or before
washing two-day old dishes and
scuffing them up,
leaving remnants of red curry
On sore palms, peanut butter under
square cut flesh-spades.
(that's borrowed from Shakespeare;
I like how his description is both hard
and soft,
with fluctuating nutrition).

So renew my teaching contract and
fill my cap.
I have manicured
pedagogy
to offer.

AEPL Members Respond to Lynn Z. Bloom's *Recipe*[1]

Lynn Z. Bloom, Bruce Novak, Geri DeLuca, Libby Falk Jones, Jeffrey Seizer, and Elizabeth Vickers

Introduction

Geri DeLuca

Lynn Z. Bloom's recently published book, Recipe (2022), is an elegant work in the Bloomsbury's Object Lesson series. It offers a wide range of reflections and information on recipes. Lynn is a scholar, teacher, prolific writer, and joyous cook. She calls our attention to recipes as cultural artifacts, as conversation, as ritual, as celebration, and as comfort that holds us close in hard times. She discusses how recipes are created, improvised, and adapted at home and worldwide. She also reminds us of the moral dilemma of some of us creating beautiful, abundant meals in a world filled with starving people. Both level-headed and extravagant, her book is a perfect text for a class centered on the economy and cultures of food. It is also a gift for cooks, would-be cooks, and those who benefit from the culinary labors of others.

Inspired by her book, AEPL held several Friday afternoon sessions on Zoom in the fall of 2022 to share our own recipes and to think about what they evoked in us: why we value them, the labor they involve, the pleasure we share with each of them.

The first recipe here is Lynn's, "handed down" as they almost always are, from someone older and from a different place.

I. Fifi's Luscious Lentil Soup

Lynn Bloom

This soup nourishes body and soul. I got this recipe fifty years ago from my Greek friend Fifi, short for Euphrosina, one of the Three Graces, and have served it with pleasure ever since. The name, meaning *gracious* and *friendly*, suits the soup as well as the source of this delectable dish, whose fragrance fills the house while it's cooking. It's a succulent centerpiece for family gatherings, such as lunch the day before Thanksgiving, or the day after Christmas, a filling but not fattening dish that people of all ages will enjoy, served with crusty bread and a green salad. The recipe aspires to be fat- and salt-free and thus heart healthy, but there will inevitably be salt in the chicken broth and the canned tomatoes.

When my children were in elementary school, they didn't like conventional breakfast food, but they loved lunch food, especially Hearty Breakfast Soup, thick enough to

---

1. Bloomsbury, 2022, 160 pp.

stand a spoon in. They lapped it up, but ssssh—we warned them not to tell the teacher, whose taste ran to Wheaties and Pop Tarts.

1) In a Dutch oven sauté:

> 2 Tbsp. oil, canola or any bland kind
> 2 (or more, ad lib) large chopped onions, until translucent
> 3 cloves chopped garlic
> celery tops and the heart section with lots of leaves
> 6-8 oz mushrooms

2) Add to the pot:

> 6 cups chicken broth, preferably made from scratch
> 1 # (lb.) dry lentils (washed first)
> ¾ pound carrots, cut into chunks or rounds
> 2 28-oz.-cans crushed or stewed tomatoes
> dribble of olive oil
> dried or fresh basil (ad lib); a few rosemary sprigs are also nice
> slug of dry red wine

3) Bring to a boil; turn down heat and simmer until lentils and carrots are tender (c. ½ hour).

> Add water during the cooking as the lentils expand. How much depends on how thick you want the soup to be.

4) Add dashes of red wine vinegar to taste, in each bowl. The thick version may also be topped with nonfat yogurt and parsley.

My Mother Makes Leftover Turkey Gumbo, Late 1960s[2]

Libby Falk Jones

> First you rope the okra, that's an "o" not an "a" in "rope" (remember Miz Sybil got in trouble on that tv cook show in Florida when the emcee misunderstood?). Stir the okra, it'll rope around the side of your big gumbo pot, then the strings'll begin to dry (you don't want goo in your gumbo!). Use a little Wesson oil with the okra, then add your celery (tops too) and onions and garlic (what Louisiana dish could live without them?) When that gets mushy (you'll know when), add the broth you cooked the giblets in (you saved it, right?) and the broth from when you boiled the turkey bones, add onion and celery there too (in this gumbo you get every bit of good out of that turkey). Add the leftover gravy and little neck meat bits if you didn't use them in your Friday morning turkey hash, yes, it's worth it to cook a big bird (you always loved the leftovers more than Thanksgiving dinner). With your hash be sure to make your biscuits

2. Previously published in the author's book, *Yakety Yak (Don't Talk Back): Poems* (Workhorse, 2022).

(best thing you got from your eighth grade home-ec class). Then make your roux (gumbo has to have roux), stir the flour and oil forever, go slow, if it burns it's ruined but it has to get dark, dark (get Roger to help you). Use that cast iron skillet you got for your wedding (doesn't it work well since I cured it for you?) Add a little water—watch out! it'll steam—then stir it into the pot, you can add tomatoes, tomato sauce, that makes it rich. Taste it (you could cool a little spoon for Catlet), add some salt and pepper, you and your father always wanted cayenne, maybe Tony Chachere's seasoning, but go light. Let it cook awhile. It's better the next day, like I always told you when I tucked you in each night, remember? ("Tomorrow is a *new* day.")

II. UNBAKED POEMS: A Poem as Recipe

Elizabeth Vickers

Here is a poem about writing as recipe, which she was willing to share with me, as she has shared her wonderful dishes:

It's unwise to reveal poems until they're fully baked
unless put back in the oven for a second time
—like biscotti, nicely crisped up—but sometimes
poems have been long in the mind's oven
without awareness, and, yeasty, suddenly rise,
can be slid out done well enough for the hungry.

In my pre-dinner kitchen, along with a glass of red
a not yet grilled steak, raw green beans
poems elbow into my menu almost cooked
at least the mental recipe started with intention,
—a couple of ingredients missing—and this is one
of those poems still a bit wobbly in the middle
a poem for right now, half-baked, underdone
perhaps to be reconsidered over dessert.

III. Rose DeLuca's (Nanny's) Labor-Intensive Eggplant Parmegiano

Geri DeLuca

(I, her daughter, know this recipe because I watched her make it over and over. The first time I actually made it was for this piece!)

Two really big eggplants peeled and sliced into quarter-inch slices.

In a colander (aka a "scala pasta"), lay out the pieces of eggplant, on top of one another.

Sprinkle each piece with a little salt, not too much!

When done, put a plate on top of the pile of eggplant pieces. Weigh it down with a heavy weight, preferably a large can of Luigi Vitelli whole tomatoes.

Leave the colander in the sink so that the bitter water can drip out of the eggplant: several hours.

Rinse the eggplant so that the water and the salt run off. Pat the eggplant dry.

Beat three or four eggs into a bowl. Dip the eggplant pieces in the beaten eggs

Then dip the eggplant in white flour.

Fry the eggplant slices in olive oil until the pieces are a light, even golden brown. If you walk away from the stove, you will burn them. So stay where you are. Listen to music. This process takes forever. Pay attention. If you get hungry, eat a piece or two just as they are! They are delicious.

Use your own homemade tomato sauce, which took you three hours to cook: OR, you can use a good jar sauce. Rao's Marinara is my favorite.

Slice three fat balls of good quality mozzarella cheese which melts easily.

In a 9 x 12-inch baking pan, spread a thin coating of tomato sauce over the bottom. Alternate layers of eggplant with layers of mozzarella cheese and layers of sauce. Spread a little fresh basil around as you go.

Repeat until you are done with all the ingredients. I had three layers.

Bake in a 350-degree oven until the sauce is hot and the mozzarella cheese is melted and oozy: there will be tiny bits of sauce bubbling at the top. Make sure the center is hot. About 35 – 40 minutes.

Serve with an Italian wine, a green salad, and some crusty Italian bread. If this is for a holiday, there will need to be antipasto and pasta and a roast chicken as well—or maybe a pork roast. And then Italian pastries and espresso. Then lie down and try not to think about the dishes.

IV. If Food Be the Music of Love, Cook On: A Gastronomic Romance

Bruce Novak

"Ask me to marry you!"
"What??"
"I said, 'Ask me to marry you!'"
I stammered.
"Please. You won't be sorry. I promise."
"OK. (Pause.) (Big pause.) Will you marry me, Amy?" "No. But thanks for asking!"
We had just had another one of our memorable dinners, and she had pulled to the side of the street—Michigan Avenue and Washington Street in downtown Chicago, to be exact—so I could catch my bus back to the southside. This was life with Amy. Dramatic and hilarious. And looking back, I'm pretty sure my life on the whole, maybe hers

too, would have been much happier than it has so far turned out if we had both been serious that night.

Instead I fell in love with someone who helped me sort myself out and rise in life—which was good for a while, until I had risen so far it began to scare her. *She* had asked *me* to marry *her* when my life was pretty low, but just as I was really starting to make my way up in the world, she got out, not wanting to play second fiddle, or even share first chair, in any way in anything, at least with me.

Soon afterward, I called Amy, for the first time in a decade. And then I cooked her her first birthday dinner. Her tears that night spoke to how the many meals we had shared over many years had bonded—and in some ways married—us. Every year after our first meeting, about fifteen in counting, she took me out, on my birthday in August, on her meager waitress's income, to one of the nicest places in town, and we lived for a few hours high on the proverbial hog. And almost to the day six months later I would cook her—and sometimes her boyfriend at the time—an elaborate dinner. Now we live in different cities, but we still religiously call one another twice a year, returning in memory to the scene of the feasts.

The dish that Amy remembered most clearly at our reunion was Chicken Marengo. Named after a victory of Napoleon in Northern Italy, it is a kitchen sink kind of dish, supposedly concocted to show Napoleon the bounty of everything Marengo would have to offer its new conqueror. Throw everything in and see how it melds together in exquisite and unexpected panache.

You MUST have a large circular platter, preferably glass. In the center, of course, is a huge mountain of sautéed chicken parts. Surrounding the chicken is a circle of the largest shrimp you can find, and around the edge of the platter are circular toast points topped with fried eggs. The circles upon circles are hypnotizing. Then everything is bound together with a rich pink sauce made with reduced chicken stock, pureed tomato, and just enough cream to make the platter glisten.

The first time I made Chicken Marengo was as the centerpiece of a major party I had for high school friends. The recipe book, which I found as a teenager, was written by the Italian count Francesco Ghedini, from recipes left by servants who had cooked for his family for generations. He compiled it as a gift to his American wife shortly before she died of cancer. And then he, out of grief, took his own life. Like Amy's and my story, this tale of love and sadness redeemed by rich and delicious food is painful but also ultimately consoling, bringing tears of both sorrow and joy to all who love eating as one of the greatest expressions of tender love that there is. I outgrew other loves. But Amy and Chicken Marengo are loves savorable for life, and eternal sweeteners of its sadness.

V. Ham, Asparagus and Cheddar Quiche

Jeffrey Seizer

"Chef Jeff" is Nanny Rose DeLuca's grandson, Geri's son (which goes to show you that sometimes the passion skips a generation.) Jeff started watching cooking shows, and cooking from them (a round perfect omelet), when he was 10 years old. He has been making beautiful food ever since.

You will need either a Pyrex baking pan or a tart mold with a removable bottom.

For the short dough:

> 580 grams all-purpose flour
> 2 teaspoons salt
> 1 lb cold butter cubed into ½ inch cubes
> 11 grams ice water
> 1 whole egg

For the filling:

> 12 whole eggs
> ½ bunch asparagus, chopped
> ½ lb ham
> ½ lb cheddar cheese

To make the short dough, add flour into a mixer or bowl, add the cold cubed butter and salt. Mix or pulse until the butter is in small pieces but can still be seen. Add 1 egg and the salt. Add the ice water slowly until the dough comes into a ball. I like to finish mixing the dough on the counter by hand until it holds together but is still flaky. Wrap in plastic and chill. Once the dough is cold, roll it out to about ¼ inch thickness and place it into your desired backing pan.

Once dough is in the pan, chill again for at least an hour. When ready to bake, pre-heat oven to 350 degrees. Use a fork to poke holes in the bottom of the dough. Blind bake with dry beans and wax paper until the crust sets. Remove the beans and wax paper and set aside. Bake for another 10 minutes until the bottom is just turning golden.

Mix the eggs with the diced ham, asparagus, and cheddar and about a tablespoon of salt. Pour mixture into the baked tart shell. At this point turn your oven down to 275 degrees and put the quiche back into the oven. Bake until firm, around 45 minutes. Cool for at least 30 minutes, remove from baking pan, cut quiche into even pieces, and serve!

And there you have it, dear readers, all sorts of foods and culture, memories and language, and nourishment and pleasure.

Contributors to *JAEPL*, Vol. 28

Zoya Adeel graduated from McMaster University with a Bachelor of Science. Currently, she is completing her Masters in Biochemistry at McMaster, studying the effects of small molecules on cancer immunotherapy. Her interests lie in advancing formal science communication education, seeking to identify pedagogical approaches that empower students to effectively convey complex scientific ideas to diverse audiences. zoya.adeel99@gmail.com

Stacey Stanfield Anderson is Associate Professor, English Department Chair, and Composition Director at California State University Channel Islands. This is her third collaboration with Kiki Patsch. In fall of 2020, Anderson, Patsch, and Raquel Baker contributed to a special issue of enculturation centered on Rhetorics and Literacies of Climate Change. stacey.anderson@csuci.edu

Sarah E. Austin (she/her) is the Director of Student Affairs and Registrar at the U.S. Air Force Academy Preparatory School in Colorado Springs, CO. She also serves on the English faculty and as an academic advisor. Sarah earned her PhD in Technical Communication at Texas Tech University and is the co-editor of *Academic Labor: Research & Artistry* and book review editor for the *Journal of Veterans Studies.* Sarah.Austin@afacademy.af.edu

Lynn Z Bloom is the author of *Recipe*, some 20 other books, and 200 articles/ creative nonfiction on auto/biography, composition studies, ethics, travel, and food writing. She is Aetna Chair of Writing Emerita and Distinguished Professor of English, University of Connecticut, Storrs. Lynn.Bloom@uconn.edu

Lillian Campbell is Associate Professor of English at Marquette University. Her research focuses on rhetorics of health and medicine, feminist rhetorics, and technical and professional communication. She is working on a book that examines how newcomers learn rhetorical body work in the fields of nursing, physical therapy, and tele-observation. lillian.campbell@marquette.edu

Melissa Carrion is an Assistant Professor and the Undergraduate Program Coordinator in the English Department at the University of Nevada, Las Vegas. Her research focuses on the rhetoric of health and medicine, especially in the context of scientific controversy, and she regularly teaches courses in technical and scientific writing. melissa.carrion@unlv.edu

Geraldine DeLuca is a professor emerita of English, Brooklyn College, CUNY. She directed Freshman English and WAC programs at Brooklyn for many years, and in 2018, she published *Teaching Toward Freedom: Supporting Voices and Silence in the English Classroom,* Routledge. She is finishing a collection of Buddhist-inflected essays and stories called *Notes from Snow White's Stepmother.* gerideluca228@gmail.com

Erica Duran is tenured faculty at MiraCosta College in Oceanside, CA. She earned her Master's degree in Literature and Writing from California State University San Marcos and has published and presented on multiple intersections of STEM and the Humanities since 2019. eduran@miracosta.edu

Alix Dowling Fink is a professor of biology at Longwood University. For more than two decades, she has partnered with faculty and staff across campus to facilitate interdisciplinary, place-based courses that immerse students in meaningful civic engagement, particularly related to the stewardship of public lands. finkad@longwood.edu

Naomi C. Gades is an assistant professor of English at Frostburg State University, where she teaches composition. Her research interests include the intersection of modernist poetry and science and college pedagogy. She has contributed to The Robert Frost Review, JMMLA, The Imaginative Conservative, and JAEPL. When she has spare time, she enjoys engaging in outdoor activities, playing video games, and composing questionable poetry. ncgades@frostburg.edu

Jeff Gagnon is an Assistant Teaching Professor and the Director of the Warren College Writing Program at UC San Diego. He designs courses and curriculum that explores the intersections of science, engineering, and communication in the field of writing studies and composition. He has a Ph.D. in Literature from UC San Diego and an MEd from Harvard University. jgagnon@ucsd.edu

David S. Gerstle is Science Liaison Librarian at the University of Toronto Mississauga Library, covering information fluency instruction, reference and collections for the Life Sciences, Chemical and Physical Sciences, and Health Sciences. His student instruction and research concentrate on the rhetoric and communication of scientific information to non-expert audiences. david.gerstle@utoronto.ca

Alexander Hall is an Assistant Professor in Science Communication at McMaster University in Ontario, Canada. Dr Hall is a historian of science whose work combines mixed-methods research and science communication practice to better understand the development of popular science media and the public understanding of science in society. halla45@mcmaster.ca

Amy J. Hawkins is an Assistant Professor at the University of Utah School of Medicine, where she directs a Graduate Certificate in Personalized Medicine. Previously, she was a postdoctoral fellow at The Genetic Science Learning Center, authors of Learn. Genetics, most widely-used life science website in the world: https://learn.genetics.utah. edu. amy.j.hawkins@utah.edu

Libby Falk Jones is the author or co-author of four books of poetry, most recently *For Your Good Health, Drink Flowers* (Bass Clef Books, 2023). Professor Emerita of English at Berea College, she leads writing workshops locally and nationally and co-directs Coming of Age, a program for Kentucky women writers over sixty. libbyfalkjones@gmail.com

Julia E. Kiernan is Assistant Professor of Communication and Director of Technical and Professional Communication at Lawrence Technological University. Her research and teaching are intimately linked, and regularly examine the shifting impacts of pedagogical and curricular design in science communication, digital humanities, and environmental humanities. Julia's favoured research methodology is action, design-based research, which focuses on the impacts of listening, reflection, and feedback throughout learning processes. She has published several edited collections in these areas over the past several years; additionally, her work has appeared in a number of peer-reviewed journals: *Composition Forum, Interdisciplinary Humanities, Communication and Language at Work, Journal of Global Literacies, Technologies, and Emerging Pedagogies*, and *Composition Studies*. jkiernan@ltu.edu

Edward Kinman is a professor emeritus of geography at Longwood University and a long-time leader in the Virginia Geographic Alliance. A creative and experimental pedagogue, he contributed to three of the Brock Experience programs as well as Longwood's integrative environmental sciences and elementary education majors. kinmanedward74@gmail.com

Stephen Lafer is one time professor of English education, advocate for progressive education in the tradition of James Moffett, Vygotsky, Piaget, and Paulo Freire. I am co-author with Stephen Tchudi of *The Interdisciplinary Teachers' Handbook* and, recently, on my own, *Progressive Education for Democratic Society: Smitty, Not g, Mr. Spearman*. lafer@unr.edu

Marc Laflamme is a Professor in the Department of Chemical and Physical Sciences at the University of Toronto Mississauga. His research interests concern the fossilization of the oldest animals on Earth by combining laboratory decay experiments with extensive field-based studies in Newfoundland, South Australia, and Namibia. His pedagogical interests look to improve undergraduate communication and to develop strong teamwork skills in multidisciplinary research groups. marc.laflamme@utoronto.ca

Heather Lettner-Rust, professor of English, currently serves as the director of Civitae, a four-year general education program at Longwood University focused on developing students as civic leaders. Her interest in science communication is based in teaching general education courses in Virginia, the Colorado River, and YNP. lettnerrusthg@longwood.edu

Tim Li is a research program coordinator at the University of Toronto. He has a Master of Science Communication from Laurentian University and a Bachelor of Science from McMaster University. litky@mcmaster.ca

Jonathan M. Marine is a writing teacher and PhD student in the Writing and Rhetoric program at George Mason University. His research interests include writing engagement, content analysis, longitudinal writing development, graffiti rhetorics, and the pedagogy and theory of James Moffett. He can be reached at jmarine@gmu.edu.

Katie Moisse is an Assistant Professor at McMaster University in Ontario, Canada, teaching science communication. She is also the Associate Director (Curriculum & Pedagogy) of the School of Interdisciplinary Science at McMaster University, and a science journalist with bylines in *Scientific American*, *Spectrum* and *The Atlantic*. moissek@ mcmaster.ca

Amber Moore is an Assistant Professor of Teaching at The University of British Columbia. Her research interests include adolescent literacies, feminist pedagogies, teacher and teacher librarian education, arts-based research, rape culture, and trauma literature, particularly YA sexual assault narratives. Her work can be found in journals such as Cultural Studies ⌷ Critical Methodologies, Feminist Media Studies, Journal of Adolescent and Adult Literacy, and Qualitative Inquiry, among others. amberjanellemoore@ gmail.com

Daniel Aureliano Newman is Assistant Professor of English (teaching stream) and Director of Graduate Writing Support, Faculty of Arts & Science, at the University of Toronto. His research appears in journals including *Configurations*, *Journal of Narrative Theory*, *Partial Answers*, and *Oikos*, and in *Modernist Life Histories* (Edinburgh UP 2019). daniel.newman@utoronto.ca

Bruce Novak served AEPL in a number of capacities from 1998-2008 and 2013-2023, including 4 1/2 terms as Co-Chair. Co-author of *Teaching Literacy for Love and Wisdom: Being the Book and Being the Change* (2011) and co-editor of *The Routledge International Handbook of Holistic Education* (2019), he is working long-term on *The Opening of the American Heart: The Great Educational Awakening on the Horizon of Democratic Life* and, more immediately, on projects encouraging the greatness of soul inherent in *bona fide* democracy, to counter the authoritarian psychology that undermines and corrupts the soul at all levels of life, and lies at the root of our current political corruption. brucejnovak@gmail.com

Kiki Patsch is Associate Professor of Environmental Science and Resource Management (ESRM) at California State University Channel Islands, where she teaches courses related to the beach, ocean, and Geographic Information Systems (GIS). Patsch aims to bridge the gap between policy makers, scientists, engineers, and the community on coastal issues. kiki.patsch@csuci.edu

JoEllen Pederson is an associate professor of sociology at Longwood University. A campus leader in integrating service-learning and quantitative methods into a variety of course contexts, she has been part of the faculty team for LU@YNP since 2014 and has co-taught LU@Alaska since 2017. pedersonjg@longwood.edu

Phillip Poplin is a Professor of mathematics at Longwood University, where he teaches mathematics and statistics. He has been part of the faculty team for LU@YNP since 2011 and he has co-taught the LU@Alaska course since 2017. poplinpl@longwood.edu

Melissa Rowland-Goldsmith is a professor of Biological Sciences and Biochemistry and Molecular Biology at Chapman University. She is dedicated to pedagogy and training others in novel teaching methods. Melissa serves on the Scientific Outreach and

Communication Committee of ASBMB and is the Chair of the Science Communication Subcommittee. rowlandg@chapman.edu

Sarah Seeley is an Assistant Professor in the teaching stream and the Associate Director, Curriculum at the Institute for the Study of University Pedagogy at University of Toronto Mississauga. Her current research explores topics such as confidence and knowledge transfer among Canadian first-year writers; faculty perceptions of online teaching and learning; and the affective dimensions of generative AI technologies. sarah.seeley@utoronto.ca

Abeer Siddiqui is the Science Librarian at McMaster University and Adjunct Lecturer in the School of Interdisciplinary Science. She provides course-embedded science literacy instruction across the Faculty of Science and teaches a 4th year science communication seminar titled Science & Storytelling. Her instructional practice enables students to take risks and embrace failure, while her research focuses on community-engaged teaching and dialogue-based science communication. siddia33@mcmaster.ca

Adina Silver is a McMaster University graduate with a Bachelor of Science in Honours Life Sciences. With a focus on improving undergraduate science communication training, she is passionate about bridging the gap between complex scientific research and public understanding through effective and accessible communication strategies. silvery@mcmaster.ca

Lauren M. Mecucci Springer is an English Professor at Mt. San Jacinto Community College in Southern California. She is also one of the college's Professional Develop and Distance Education coordinators. Her research centers on feedback practices, STEM-themed composition courses, and linguistic justice for writing classrooms and across the curriculum. lspringer@msjc.edu

Erica M. Stone (she/her) is a content designer and researcher with experience in both academia and industry. Erica's writing can be found in journals, including *Journal of Technical Writing & Communication; Technical Communication; Writing Program Administration; Kairos: A Journal of Rhetoric, Technology, and Pedagogy; Spark: A 4C4Equality Journal; Community Literacy Journal;* and various edited collections. erica.m.stone@gmail.com

Sarah Symons is a Full Professor in the School of Interdisciplinary Science, McMaster University in Hamilton, Ontario. She is the Coordinator of the award-winning Honours Integrated Science Program at McMaster University, teaching primarily in science literacy/communication and history of science. symonss@mcmaster.ca

Elizabeth Vickers is a graduate of Bennington College and has an MFA from The Art Institute of Chicago. Her past career was creating print media and websites for educational programs, with an emphasis on study abroad. She has been writing poetry seriously and devotedly since 1995 and co-leads a yearly poetry writing course for OSHER at Dartmouth. vickersetal@gmail.com

Nicole C. Woitowich is a Research Assistant Professor and Administrator at Northwestern University's Feinberg School of Medicine. Formally trained as a biochemist, her work now explores the "science of biomedical science" from multiple perspectives including science policy, workforce development, public engagement, and communication. Nicole.woitowich@northwestern.edu

Now with Parlor Press!

Studies in Rhetorics and Feminism
   Series Editors: Cheryl Glenn and Shirley Wilson Logan

Emerging Conversations in the Global Humanities
   Series Editor: Victor E. Taylor

The X-Series
   Series Editor: Jordan Frith

New Releases

In the Classroom with Kenneth Burke by Ann George and
M. Elizabeth Weiser

*Design for Composition: Inspiration for Creative Visual and
Multimodal Projects* by Sohui Lee and Russell Carpenter

*Writing to Learn in Teams: A Collaborative Writing Playbook for
Students Across the Curriculum* by Joe Moses and Jason Tham

Writing Spaces 5: Readings for Writers edited by Trace Daniels-
Lerberg, Dana Driscoll, Mary K. Stewart, and Matthew Vetter

Rhetorical Listening in Action: A Concept-Tacticc Approach
by Krista Ratcliffe and Kyle Jensen

MLA Mina Shaughnessy Prize and CCCC Best Book Award 2021!

*Creole Composition: Academic Writing and Rhetoric in the
Anglophone Caribbean,* edited by Vivette Milson-Whyte,
Raymond Oenbring, and Brianne Jaquette

Check Out Our Website!

*Discounts, blog, open access titles, instant
downloads, and more.*

www.parlorpress.com

Printed in the USA
CPSIA information can be obtained
at www.ICGtesting.com
LVHW041010071023
760468LV00037B/647